T. G. Moore

About the Author

CAROL ADRIENNE, PH.D., has assisted thousands of people through the process of making life changes. She is the author of the bestselling *The Purpose of Your Life* and its sequel *Find Your Purpose, Change Your Life*. She is the coauthor with James Redfield of the *New York Times* bestseller *The Celestine Prophecy: An Experiential Guide* and *The Tenth Insight: An Experiential Guide*. Her books have been translated into more than fifteen languages. An intuitive counselor and teacher since 1980, Adrienne has appeared on *Oprah* and conducts lectures and workshops internationally. She lives in El Cerrito, California. Visit the author's website at www.spiralpath.com.

ALSO BY CAROL ADRIENNE

The Purpose of Your Life:
Finding Your Place in the World Using Synchronicity,
Intuition, and Uncommon Sense

Find Your Purpose, Change Your Life

The Numerology Kit

Your Child's Destiny

WITH JAMES REDFIELD

The Celestine Prophecy: An Experiential Guide

The Tenth Insight: An Experiential Guide

WHEN LIFE CHANGES
OR
YOU WISH IT WOULD

A Guide to Finding Your Next Step Despite Fear, Obstacles, or Confusion

Carol Adrienne, Ph.D.

Quill

An Imprint of HarperCollinsPublishers

Excerpts from *Always We Begin Again,* copyright © 1996, 2001 John McQuiston II. Reprinted by permission of Morehouse Publishing.

Excerpts from *The Essential Rumi,* copyright © 1995 Coleman Barks with John Moyne, A. J. Arberry, and Reynold Nicholson, HarperSanFrancisco. Originally published by Threshold Books.

Excerpt from *Awareness Beyond Mind: Verses in Haiku and Senryu Style,* copyright © 1996 Kenneth Verity, Element Books, Inc., Rockport, MA.

A hardcover edition of this book was published in 2002 by William Morrow, an imprint of HarperCollins Publishers.

WHEN LIFE CHANGES OR YOU WISH IT WOULD. Copyright © 2002 by Carol Adrienne. All rights reserved. Printed in the United States of America. No part of this book may be used or reproduced in any manner whatsoever without written permission except in the case of brief quotations embodied in critical articles and reviews. For information address HarperCollins Publishers Inc., 10 East 53rd Street, New York, NY 10022.

HarperCollins books may be purchased for educational, business, or sales promotional use. For information please write: Special Markets Department, HarperCollins Publishers Inc., 10 East 53rd Street, New York, NY 10022.

First Quill edition published 2003.

Designed by Jo Anne Metsch

The Library of Congress has catalogued the hardcover edition as follows:

Adrienne, Carol.
    When life changes or you wish it would / Carol Adrienne.
        p. cm.
    Includes bibliographical references and index.
    ISBN 0-06-018896-0
    1. Change (Psychology). 2. Life change events. I. Title.

BF637.C4 A37 2002
158—dc21   2001051913

ISBN 0-06-093456-5 (pbk.)

03   04   05   06   07   ❖/RRD   10   9   8   7   6   5   4   3   2   1

Contents

Acknowledgments

I OWE a debt of gratitude to all those people who responded to my questionnaire about making life changes and to all those who freely offered their time for individual interviews. I deeply appreciate all the people (you know who you are!) with whom I have worked in seminars and who have shared their stories and insights with so much passion and laughter.

I could not have written this book without the ongoing support of special friends, such as Zenobia Barlow, Elizabeth Jenkins, Ellen Duenow, Bonnie Coleen, Larry Leigon, Donna Hale, Penney Peirce, Patrick Tribble, Selma Lewis, Georgia Rogers, Giorgio Cerquetti, Jaye Oliver, Justine Toms, Joyce Petschek, and Lindsay Gibson. Special thanks go to my daughter, Sigrid, and her husband, Jim Matthews (for quality-control feedback and emotional support), and to my son, Gunther Rohrer, and his wife, Eliza Ramirez (for humor and technical support). Thanks to Rosemarie Ramos for assisting me in the myriad administrative details, which ensured I could meet my deadlines.

I am very grateful to William Morrow and Company, Inc., for their work in publishing so that so many of us can learn and grow in ways that we hope contribute to the planet.

Once again I want to thank my wonderful agent, Candice Fuhrman, for her ever-ready inspiration and guidance, and Linda Michaels for her superb and caring work in finding an international audience for the book. Also I count among my personal blessings that I have been able to work with Joann Davis, whose editorship and friendship have meant so much over the past six years.

A published book passes through many hands. I would especially like to thank Susan Brown for her careful copyediting of every word, and lastly, my editor, Toni Sciarra, whose gift for organization and thoughtful precision has helped bring it to its best possible form.

Preface

LIFE IS not quite the same as it was. But then, it never really is. The pace of change does seem to be picking up. Like it or not, our lives are externally affected by technology, innovations, political decisions, the weather, and millions of daily events that take place in the world without our knowledge. The effort to control our lives in the face of unrelenting change and increasing uncertainty is often overwhelming. We run but can we keep up? We want to adapt and thrive, but don't always know what is expected of us. We want to do more than survive, we want to thrive. We want to fulfill the purpose we know (or hope) lives within us. We want to discover that purpose so that we can make a contribution. We want to be happy.

Living in the twenty-first century requires that we be masters of change.

When Life Changes or You Wish It Would is a handbook that shows both how to *handle* change and how to *create* change, so that you can become who you are meant to be—even though the journey must take you into uncharted territory. The premise of the book is that your unfolding life purpose is a *navigating force that is always taking you where you need to go.* Your job is to pay attention to the message in the changes that occur to you and to respond from your true self. In mythic terms this is the hero's (and heroine's) journey.

As a human being, you are unique because your life *evolves*—through daily change and daily choices. You grow because of how you handle these various and often profoundly challenging experiences. Your inborn talents and desires, which strive to be expressed as your life purpose, continually create new conditions for growth.

However, if this movement forward is based on intentions, motivations, or choices made from your false and ego-centered self, you will create change for the wrong reasons. If we have not taken the time to examine ourselves and *what is right for us,* we find that we are still living according to beliefs that may not hold much interest to us anymore. These beliefs tell us that the only way to be a good person—the only way to receive love and respect—is to please others rather than to become who we were meant to be.

Everyone wants to be loved and recognized for his or her uniqueness. Everyone wants to make a contribution to life. On the one hand, we want new life but, on the other hand, we often resist going into uncharted territory. Instead of being happy and excited about change, all too often we face the unknown with fear, trepidation, and resistance. *When Life Changes* expresses the view that by expanding our spiritual connection, developing a stronger sense of self, and staying awake to the purposeful movement of change in our lives, we will be more able to handle whatever we face.

To live successfully on our growing edge, we must be willing to do four things: (1) commit to being true to our inner integrity; (2) shed our need to overcontrol; (3) act on what has heart and meaning; and (4) trust that there are no accidents. By reclaiming our inner guidance and taking action on what we value, we begin to bloom in our own right. Experiences of success and increased self-esteem allow us to face the unknown with more trust and resourcefulness.

As you read on, you will be reminded of some of the most enduring and supportive spiritual teachings of the ages. You will be offered practical methods for changing your life for the better, and you will be introduced to others just like yourself who are enjoying traveling into the unknown.

Please note that most names in the stories have been changed to ensure privacy.

To capture insights and track your own life changes, you might find it useful to start a life changes journal, where you can allow thoughts to flow freely and keep a record of your intentions, intuitions, and directional signals.

Introduction

THE CALL

WHILE I was working on the outline for this book, my friend Jaye Oliver, who lives in Santa Fe, New Mexico, suggested we swap houses for a couple of weeks. At first I said no, thinking that this would be too much of a disruption to my writing. She persisted, though, and I realized that getting away from my daily routine might be a good idea. I agreed but immediately felt a mixture of guilt, pleasant anticipation, and apprehension that I might get lonely by myself for two weeks. I called another friend, Zenobia Barlow, who agreed with delight to accompany me, along with her partner, James Tyler. As it turned out, the retreat from routine was exactly what I needed to catalyze my thinking about this book.

After several days of visiting places of beauty and serenity, and playing and photographing in the beautiful landscape of New Mexico, Zenobia and I found ourselves on the sunny back porch of our temporary home avidly discussing life change. Working collaboratively has always been inspirational for me, and suddenly ideas, which had been germinating in the dark—in my procrastinating void—began to take a more coherent form. Out of our dialogue grew the Map of Change (page 12) and a new format for my stories.

GERMINATION TIME

A FEW months earlier I had visited the Metropolitan Museum of Art in New York to see the portrait paintings of Jean-Auguste-Dominique Ingres, the French painter who lived and worked around the time of Napoleon. I remember being struck by the description of one of his most famous portraits of an aristocratic beauty. The description mentioned that the *germination time* for this piece had been twelve years. The idea of a necessary germination time on a creative project struck me anew. I have come to trust that, when a piece of information stands out like that, it is somehow important to my own work and life.

I have always been the type of person who moves ahead with a project fairly quickly. However, this book seemed to resist my normal speed. Of course, I thought, this must be *my* fault. I should get more disciplined. I should just sit down and start writing. Those internal voices of duty, criticism, and urgency began to get louder. Yet I could not do more than rewrite a few of my interviews. The idea that there is a germination time for things let me off my own hook. I had not been honoring the process that was unfolding within me. Evidently the unknown of the finished book was not yet ready to be known.

TIMING

AS SOON as Zenobia and I roughed out the map of changes, I could see clearly the path for the rest of the book. But this was not to be the end of what needed to happen in Santa Fe.

The day after Zenobia and James left, I had another visitor, a mutual friend of Jaye's and mine, Justine Toms. Justine had left her car at Jaye's house a few days before and came by to retrieve it. Many of you may know Justine's name from the radio program *New Dimensions,* which she cofounded and produces with her husband, Michael Toms, the show's host. Justine's arrival and our discussion now seem like divine serendipity. Her unexpected visit showed me once again that our projects are always nourished by the larger ground of synchronicity and purposeful timing. At the time I merely thought of her arrival as a pleasant opportunity to chat over a cup of tea.

The reason Justine had left her car in Santa Fe was a sad one. She had just settled into a friend's home in Taos, an hour's drive north of Santa Fe, for a much-needed time alone. Then she got word that her best friend, Sedonia Cahill, had been killed in a car accident in Morocco while on holiday with her family. Justine immediately drove to Santa Fe to travel to California for Sedonia's funeral, leaving her car at Jaye's house. Now she was back to return to the hills north of Taos. As we sat together having breakfast in the warm, colorful dining room of Jaye's house, Justine told me this story.

"I had arrived in New Mexico from California only three weeks before I got the news of her death," she began. "The odd thing is that it was Sedonia who originally suggested that it would be a good time for me to go on retreat for a while. The minute she said this, I knew it was the right thing to do. All my life I have been in relationships, always living with a man, a husband, children, and running a business. At fifty-seven I'm not sure I know who I am outside of my roles and duties!"

LEARNING AS WE SIT IN CIRCLES AND LISTEN TO STORIES

"I HAD known Sedonia for many years," Justine went on. "Her life's work was to be a kind of spiritual guide for people. She led hundreds of people on vision quests and wrote books on ceremonial circles. She wanted to show people the importance of sitting together and working with each other. That was her whole mission in life. She died on the precipice of her sixty-fourth birthday.

"A few months before her death, Sedonia told me, 'I feel complete in my soul's assignment. I feel I have accomplished what I have come here to do. If I'm going to stick around, I feel I need a new assignment.'" Life changes.

THE AGELESS STORY OF THE CYCLE OF CHANGE

AS I listened to Justine, I could feel a rising energy. I realized that she had come to tell me something I needed to include in this book.

Suddenly Justine remembered a myth that perfectly reflects the psychological process of death and rebirth we experience through the cycles of change. The story is a five-thousand-year-old Sumerian myth about Inanna, the Queen of Heaven, who, upon hearing that her sister Queen Ereshkigal is in pain and calling out for her, sets out on a journey to the Underworld to visit her. While Inanna rules the Upper World, Ereshkigal is Queen of the Underworld. (Again I was struck by the synchronicity! The night before I had rented two videos from the Mythos series by Joseph Campbell, in which he had lectured on exactly this theme.)

Queen Inanna is told that in order to reach her goal of visiting her sister, she must pass through seven gates. At each gate she must pay a price, stripping away her crown, her garments, everything she has relied on so far. At the last gate she is totally naked. Inanna finally stands in front of Ereshkigal, who is angry and wrathful. The Queen of the Underworld takes one look at Inanna, now bowed and humbled, and strikes her dead. Inanna's body is hung on a hook and after three days begins to rot. She is dead and in the void. Tiny helpers travel down into the Underworld and find Inanna's body. Through their ministrations she is returned to life. How does this myth speak to us across time about our own life changes?

Pain and suffering are often the great initiators of change in our lives. Major life changes, such as the loss of a job, financial setback, serious illness, divorce, or the death of a child all signal the beginning of a descent into the underworld. We are being called to heal a part of ourselves that is suffering and in pain. Life changes, and it is time for a change.

The theme of the Inanna-Ereshkigal myth recurs in worldviews as diverse as Anglo-Saxon pagan traditions, the Classical Greek and Roman pantheon, the Christian resurrection story, and modern-day psychoanalysis. This archetypal story of death and rebirth is central to the human experience. Seasons, for example, reflect the yearly death experience of winter and the renewal experience of spring. On a mundane level, movies, biographies, and novels present stories in which characters go into pain and conflict, only to emerge in a new (and positive) way—making what is called in screenwriter parlance a character arc.

The Inanna story reminds us that there comes a time when we must face certain pain or self-concepts that we have pushed down in our psyches. When we have suffered defeats, setbacks, and other losses, we, like Inanna, feel vulnerable. We are called to deal with painful unresolved personal issues. We are forced to confront our fears about ourselves. There are times when we simply cannot escape the descent into the underworld.

Queen Inanna is the part of ourselves that we show to the world—our authority and social mask. She represents the ego, who thinks it knows who we are and what we are about. But when we suffer setbacks, we may be stripped of everything familiar. Like Inanna, we are forced to pay a price that leaves us naked and vulnerable. We do not know what is happening. We are in the dark, and we are lost. Our old roles and relationships don't work anymore.

During the journey into the darkness of our repressed area, we start to fall apart. We are "dismembered," shorn of status, cut off from help, and lost to clarity. This dismemberment forces us to reform ourselves for the next stage of the journey.

Ereshkigal stands for any parts of ourselves that have been ignored; she represents the parts we have rejected. Far from weak, she (our shame or pain) has the power to call us *down*. Our former identities as orchestrated by our egos have little value in our broken state, because it's time for a change. It does not matter who we think we are.

Of course, we don't take this lying down! When everything around us is altered or taken away or not working for us anymore, we tend to move through rage, anger, disappointment, depression, and disorientation. In chaos our egos die (hang on the meat hook until they begin to rot). The rotting, however, is symbolic of the relentless transformative process that will take us to a new level if we work with it. Transformation requires that we find new meaning in our lives, new sources of spiritual energy.

Ereshkigal also represents the values that we have dropped or compromised but that rise up to be reexamined and honored. Our childhood dreams and the holy quest for a meaningful life are reexamined, and we gradually return to pursuits that engage our hearts and minds.

The requirement for initiation into new life is sometimes nothing less than the death of the old personality. The fulfillment of Inanna's life purpose in the story, and our life purpose in our own stories, necessitates the inclusion of what has been excluded. We must bring to awareness what we have been denying. We must become authentic. This is the work of individuation, aligning ourselves to our true selves and making ourselves whole.

Justine summarized the journey of Inanna by saying, "The only way we get the gift of our new selves is by going down into the unknown and meeting whatever tasks and challenges are given to us. We journey into the unknown with intact egos, with all the authority of our identities, but everything is called into question. We have to give up what we know about ourselves as the only reality. Only then can we learn and experience something new about ourselves, and return to a new balance, radically changed, with a far bigger picture of what life is about. This transformation allows us to be more compassionate and resilient, and to have the confidence of our hard-won experience.

"On a daily basis, our egos' clothing is invisible to us. We get up every morning, and our egos automatically jump on us without our really questioning them—until life changes or we pay attention to that voice that begins to ask for something new. We have to strip away all of this to break open to a much larger landscape. The only way to break open is to face this negative side, which will destroy our positive side unless we are willing to recognize that we have both.

"It's interesting that this story has come up today, since I am going back into my retreat now that Sedonia's funeral is over." Justine smiled. "Like Inanna, I am shedding the identities of my work life and my married life—at least for a while. I will have no relationships to deal with for a while. I will be nobody's mother here. I am nobody, doing nothing."

SEDONIA'S QUESTION

JUSTINE TOLD me that, before her death, Sedonia presented her vision quest group with this question: *What is it that you most deeply fear is true about yourself?*

You may want to ask yourself this question now. Do you fear that you will be proven inadequate? Do you fear being unclear about what is being asked of you? Do you fear that you are not up to the task of finding your life purpose?

Rest assured that this question and its answer will come up as you go through all of your life's transitions. All our emotional reactions to life changes—in relationships, health, work, and loss or confusion—may stem from this single question. As long as we avoid this fear of finding out some unbearable truth about ourselves, we will act unconsciously out of that fear, not out of our true selves. We accumulated these inner fears early in life. They may be both our gifts and our burdens, depending on how we work with them or deny them. These unrecognized judgments and fears drive us forward, and we avoid them as much as possible by choosing to overeat, take drugs, drink alcohol excessively, throw ourselves on unsuitable partners, and work compulsively or without joy. But the call to the underworld will come. Life changes and breaks us apart, and these times are the opportunities for facing ourselves and making new choices that bring us back to dynamic balance.

GOING DEEP ENOUGH

BEFORE JUSTINE left she told me, "What is so important is not to try to leave that time of the void prematurely, not to run away from the challenges too soon. If we merely try to patch up our lives to make them tolerable, we abort the cycle of change. We'll keep coming around to the same question again and again because we haven't taken it deep enough.

"I remember a story I read about the Po River Valley in Italy, which had been dammed. It was raining and raining, and they were concerned there would be a landslide that would burst the dam. They drilled down into the earth to see if the land was shifting, and they detected no movement. But they didn't pay attention to the fact that all the cows and other animals had moved off the mountain. The animals knew something was going to shift. It turned out that the *whole mountain* moved, and its mass displaced so much water it was like a tidal wave downstream. Hundreds were killed. Sometimes we think we have gone deep enough in our understanding of how we feel or what we want to do next, but we usually can't do it alone. We need reflection from our peers and mentors who know us well."

A CIRCLE OF PEERS, MENTORS, AND ELDERS

SO I invite you now to sit in circle around the fire with me and the people who bring us their stories—your peers, neighbors, mentors, elders, and guides—as we explore together the vagaries and virtues, the shocks and tsunamis, the insights and wisdom of life changes. Let these stories lead you. Let these stories heal you. Let these stories move you forward into the unknown.

1

⸙

Embrace the Cycles of Change
How, What, When, and Where Are You Changing?

The right-hand path is fixed. We live in expected ways. The left-hand path is where there is incongruity, and we think, "This doesn't go with me." [It is also] the way you follow your own bliss. It's the realm of no rules. It's uncertain, and you don't know where you are going. There is danger, adventure, things you've never beheld before.

Whenever ego becomes uncertain of its moral position, everything in the psyche starts to move. . . . What has been pushed down is going to come up.

JOSEPH CAMPBELL,
The Power of Myth

Where Are You in the Cycle of Change?

LIFE CHANGES propel us into the unknown—the place that mythologists refer to as the left-hand path of new beginnings, hope, growth, and further development of the purpose that brought us to Earth. From the comfort of the familiar and known world, we often imagine the unknown as chaotic or unpredictable. We resist going into the unknown, fearing perhaps that more will be asked of us than we can summon. We mistakenly believe that to make any change of real value we must make changes on a grand scale.

We tend to hold on to what we have, even when it's a problem. We assume out of fear that there is no pattern to the changes that toss us about. If there are any rules to remember as you move into the unknown, they are these:

Change is inevitable. There are no accidents. Everything happens for a reason. The unknown is already being shaped by your beliefs, life perspective, emotional ties, and life purpose. You are always receiving life energy in the form of people, opportunities, timely assistance, and guidance through the Law of Attraction. This universal law states that each of us is always in a flow of energy that brings to us what we want or need. At a spiritual level of understanding, we could say that we attract people and opportunities that match our vibrational state of being. Our state of being is how we feel about ourselves unconsciously and consciously. Therefore, changes in the material world reflect inner shifts in our spiritual purpose and development, which bring us new trials, challenges, and revelations.

If you are wondering where you are in the cycle of change, take a minute to look at the Map of Change: The Portals. Each portal on the circle represents a life condition, a point in the cycle of change. A portal is defined as an entrance or door, perhaps to a palace, tunnel, or mine—all appropriate metaphors for the times when we experience success, when we are searching for the next step, or when we are grappling with stagnation or loss.

A palace, of course, is the edifice that demonstrates our accomplishments and status. The palace—no matter whether it is grand or humble—bespeaks of who we are and what we have become in material terms. Our career résumé, bank account, family reputation, creative projects, material possessions, as well as our social contacts and relationships are all part of our palace. The palace is the place where we live, perhaps which we have outgrown, or which is taken away in misfortune.

The tunnel (or cave) is the place we go when we are confused or trying to burrow through obstacles. It symbolizes our attempt to find our way in the dark.

A mine is also a dark place, but it is associated with treasures and resources, which are waiting for us. Going into the mine symbolizes making a shift in our normal, everyday perspective to what we have repressed, denied, buried, or overlooked. Going within always holds the promise of finding gold. In medieval times, for example, the science of alchemy was undertaken not so much to make dross into gold as to gain the inner powers of the realized soul.

Locate Yourself on the Map of Change

THE FOUR portals, or life conditions, could be roughly described this way:

The Break—time of big changes, disruptions; you experience feelings of insecurity or excitement.

The Void—a period of stagnation or loss of purpose; you experience feelings of low energy or confusion.

The Return—you can see a light at the end of the tunnel; however, you need to keep moving forward.

Dynamic Balance—a period of relative stability in which life is generally good and you have enough challenge to feel worthy and productive; you are looking ahead to what's next with curiosity and enthusiasm, but your goals are still somewhat unclear.

Let's look at some typical statements that may help you identify where you are in this cycle. Which of the following questions comes closest to what you are asking yourself these days? You might even want to jot down a few words or comments as you read through them.

THE BREAK

SOMEONE EXPERIENCING the break may say something like "I've just lost my job. I have no idea what I'm going to do next." She might also say, "I feel a shift happening." "I'm in the middle of big changes." "I'm at a crossroads right now." "I'm definitely in transition!" "I feel like I'm having a breakdown." "I just had the rug pulled out from under me." "I got the shock of my life." There is a *break* from what has gone before. Options are shifting. You're being challenged to come up with something new.

- Has a recent change rocked your sense of identity, living situation, or support system?
- Is there an intolerable gap between what you want or need and what you have?

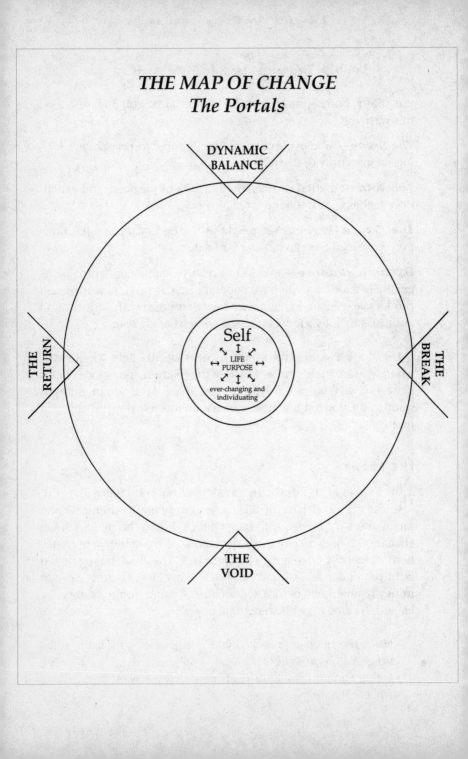

- Have you lost a sense of direction or meaning?
- Key question: Regardless of fear and self-doubt, what do you really want at this stage?

Answering yes to any of these questions indicates that you are in the midst of change, and that it is time for a change. How do you think you are handling these changes? What do you think would help you handle this time more easily? These are useful questions to write about in your life changes journal.

THE BREAK

There's a shock factor that I'm still in the middle of. You're hit with everything feeling gone. . . . God is a weird thing to talk about. When you feel such an onslaught of loss, change . . . I always assumed I would become a cynic, would shut my heart down. Instead, it may be the moment where you go, "*Whoa*, Dude, You *so* have a plan here. What a fool I was, thinking that I had any control. Whatever You say, Dude of all Dudes!" I may believe in love more than ever.

Laura Dern, in *Talk* magazine, after finding out that her live-in boyfriend, the actor Billy Bob Thornton, had suddenly married the actress Angelina Jolie, while she was out of town working on a movie

THE VOID

THE VOID, in contrast, is a kind of nonchange time, when we feel stuck. You may be saying, "I've really been a hermit lately." "Nothing is happening." "I don't know how to get past these blocks." "I feel stuck." "I'm depressed." "Nothing is going right for me." "I've tried to move forward, but nothing is changing." "I can't see my way out of this situation." "It's the pits!"

- Do you feel helpless or hopeless?
- Does life seem out of control? Are you unable to see a clear path or direction?

• Does life feel meaningless? Do you have no sense of purpose?
• Key question: What can I do to relax today?

The void usually makes us feel anxious, disconnected, and unmotivated. Therefore, if you think you are in the void, it might be very helpful for you to do two things: (1) write out your feelings; (2) seek someone you trust to share your feelings with.

Isolation is a big pitfall in the void. You need not suffer alone. Visiting a good professional counselor or talking with a supportive friend can provide wonderfully helpful feedback and validation for your feelings. This book is designed to be a support for you. If all you do is open it at random and find something that makes sense to you, the void will inevitably shift. It's important to let the void run its course; trying to control it or fix it usually isn't the real answer.

Here are the key points to consider when you feel you're in the void: Am I staying in a bad situation rather than admitting something is not working? Am I making a change just to relieve tension? Do I have the courage to ask for what I really want, or am I just accepting what I think I can get? Am I suffering alone because of pride?

THE RETURN

AFTER A period of loss or stagnation, the return has the quality of rescue as good things start to happen. Perhaps you've been having a hard time and suddenly something wonderful happens. You call a friend and say, "You won't believe what just happened!" "I found the right job!" "I'm in love." "I've just had a story accepted for publication." "I've had a breakthrough." "I've finally let go of my ex-husband and all that negativity!" The return is the part of the cycle of change that holds new promise. The change in your life now feels positive, gives you fresh energy, and opens new doors.

In myth and storytelling the key component of the return is coming home with a boon or prize. The prize may be the overcoming of an obstacle, a feeling of relief, a tool that achieves the goal, or the promise of a happy future. It could be a new insight that helps you reconnect to your true self. The return is characterized by recognizing new strengths in yourself, as well as accomplishing something that makes you feel good. In the deepest sense you are connected again to love, purpose, and meaning. Hope returns and faith is strengthened.

- Can you now see the light at the end of the tunnel?
- Are you taking care of yourself again?
- Do you feel grateful, motivated, and generally more optimistic about life?
- Have you forgiven someone or resolved a past issue?
- Do you have a better sense of what lessons you have been learning?
- Key questions: Are you able to listen to your intuition and trust that synchronicity will help you get where you want to go? Are you feeling energized by new options and challenges?

If you answered yes to most of these questions, then you are either in the return or already moving into dynamic balance. Or you may be experiencing a break but coping (most of the time) with enthusiasm rather than anxiety.

DYNAMIC BALANCE

ONCE THE return has begun, a new direction starts to take hold and build. We eventually establish some form of dynamic balance. Our lives begin to feel normal again. We talk about being past the rough part. We say, "Everything's good, can't complain." "I finally feel I know what my purpose is." "I'm so glad I got my degree." "This career is perfect for me." "My family is doing so well, and I have time for myself again."

For those who thrive on chaos, dynamic balance could even be described in these ways: "Everything is crazy right now." "I'm up to my eyeballs in projects." "I need to slow down, but I love what I'm doing." Some people have a higher need for a fast pace and stimulation, and for them a feeling of balance includes lots of calculated risk, multitasking, challenges, and options. Whatever your description of dynamic balance is, it means that life has returned you, like Dorothy in *The Wizard of Oz*, to Kansas.

- Do you look forward to getting up in the morning?
- Do you enjoy what you're doing most of the time?

- Do you feel you have options and good prospects for the future?
- Do you believe that you are making a contribution in one or several areas, even though you may not be able to define your life purpose?
- Key questions: What new interests do I want to develop? What can I do to give back?

If you answered yes to most of the preceding questions, you are probably in dynamic balance. Congratulations.

Misperceptions That Tend to Paralyze Us

THE RETURN starts a new direction, but we still may not know where we are headed. If you don't have a clear sense of direction, you are probably looking too far ahead. Step back and take care of business in the moment; keep your vision on the kind of life experience that would make you the happiest. Every decision you make will lead you to a better place *if you keep choosing things that make you feel good.* When we feel generally good most of the time—when we look forward to the future and keep a sense of humor and perspective—we naturally tend to handle problems or setbacks better. When we have an optimistic and open attitude to life, we may get stuck here and there, but we still feel as if we are in the flow of life. However, when we have a long period when it feels as if the flow is just not happening, a feeling of depression or anxiety sets in that tends to paralyze our ability to make a decision or take any action. We see no opportunities or possibilities. This paralysis is generally an outgrowth of limited thinking, old and unconscious conditioning, and destructive self-criticism.

Here are five misperceptions that tend to paralyze us:

1. *Assuming that you must have 100 percent clarity about your direction before you take any action.* Instead of looking for a *guarantee* of success, simply move in the direction where you feel a spark of interest. Make a tentative goal and see how life answers it. Keep taking small steps in the best direction you can see or feel in the moment. Let the best outcome emerge.

2. *Being afraid to make a mistake and look dumb.* Remember that we learn and grow by exploring the world. We stand and fall many times before we learn to walk. See life as an adventure rather than an obstacle course. If you expect any change to be perfect from the start, you're guaranteeing disappointment. A certain amount of failure is part of the natural process of change. Failure is a part of learning, and change is learning.

3. *Assuming that you have to be different from who you are to be successful.* You were born with all the talent you are going to need. Do what you naturally do well, and learn new skills because it's fun to learn.

4. *Thinking that only big steps will get you where you want to go.* Again, it's wise to take small steps in the best direction until you are ready to take bigger ones. Taking small steps gives you (a) time to check things out; (b) flexibility; (c) room to learn; and (d) the chance to make mistakes on a smaller stage. Honor your internal sense of timing and readiness. When you are *ready,* changes happen naturally.

5. *Forgetting that you always have a choice, and you can always make another decision.* Be willing to start again.

DON'T PANIC TOO SOON

Shifts occur in cycles, and cycles have different lengths. In the wine business, for example, it took eighteen months before consumers would become aware of a new label or price change. However, after only three or six months, our managers would be in meetings, panicking and trying to change directions because they thought it wasn't working. But the fact is, the cycle for a price change is eighteen months. You have to set your expectations in line with the built-in, natural rate of change in whatever you are doing. One of the biggest mistakes I see in business is that people panic too soon after they make a change, thinking it's not working.

Even a personal change has some kind of natural cycle, because you are part of a natural system. Within any system there is a certain amount of normal fluctuation. Be aware of the cycle, and set your expectations in line with that natural system.

Larry Leigon, business consultant

2

❧

Trust That Change
Is Purposeful

The wholeness and freedom we seek is
our own *true nature,* who we really are.

JACK KORNFIELD,
A Path with Heart

Imagine Yourself as a Circle of Energy

CHANGE OCCURS first in the deep level of our psyche, symbolically
at the center of self. We may not be aware of the shift until we see it
manifested in our physical world. Before that we may have experienced vague feelings of restlessness, anxiety, or yearning for new
opportunities. All those feelings spring from the motivation to
express our life purpose. The Map of Change: The Flow uses the
circle to symbolize our field of energy as it shifts through the four
general conditions (portals) of change.

The circle, said the psychologist Carl Jung, is a primordial image
for humankind and a symbol of the self. The circle is the vessel of
our dreams, our psyches, our souls, and our songs. Using the symbol of a circle allows us to explore the concept of a central radiating
core of life purpose and how change affects us as we flow from one
state of activity to another.

THE MAGIC CIRCLE

When a magician wants to work magic, he puts a circle around himself, and it is within this bounded circle, this hermetically sealed-off area, that powers can be brought into play that are lost outside the circle.

Joseph Campbell, *The Power of Myth*

Your Unfolding Life Purpose Brings Meaningful Change

YOUR UNIQUE life purpose—even if you are not able to define it right now—is like an energy field with a goal. Your energy is focused on something that you came into this life to create, to learn, or to be. During each day you naturally pay attention to certain things. They catch your interest for a reason. They are somehow in line with your deep life purpose, but this doesn't necessarily mean that you could define that purpose. For example, let's say that you always collect information and like to talk about what you learn to others. You may not work in a school, but one day you realize that you are always teaching someone something. When you look back over the changes in your life, they seem to have been moving you in the direction of learning and sharing what you learn. Your energy field is motivating your choices and actions at a subconscious level, to keep you on the path of your purpose.

Your energy field contains all your character traits and your beliefs about yourself and the world, as well as memories of past experiences (some of which hold locked-up energy because you haven't dealt with them completely). Your field contains your goals, values, hopes, fears, and hang-ups.

To help you fulfill your purpose, your energy field attracts people, places, and events into your life. In response to your radiating purpose, and with laserlike precision, the universe brings you exactly the change you need to become who you were meant to be.

As we will see in the stories of people in this book, life changes

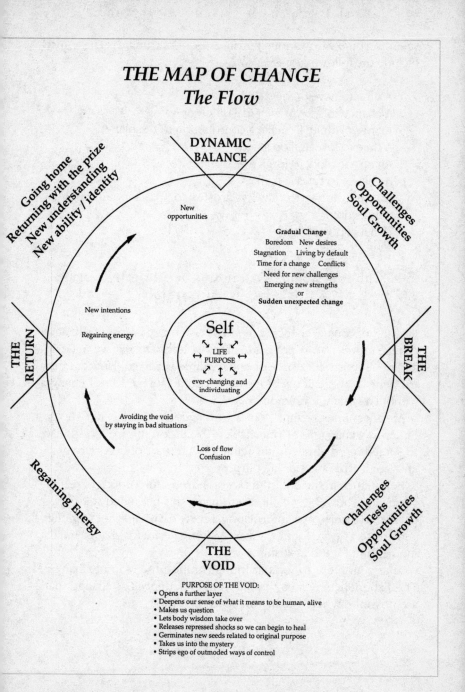

THE MAP OF CHANGE
The Flow

DYNAMIC BALANCE

Going home
Returning with the prize
New understanding
New ability / identity

New opportunities

Challenges
Opportunities
Soul Growth

Gradual Change
Boredom   New desires
Stagnation   Living by default
Time for a change   Conflicts
Need for new challenges
Emerging new strengths
or
Sudden unexpected change

New intentions

Regaining energy

Self
LIFE PURPOSE
ever-changing and individuating

THE RETURN

THE BREAK

Avoiding the void
by staying in bad situations

Loss of flow
Confusion

Regaining Energy

Challenges
Tests
Opportunities
Soul Growth

THE VOID

PURPOSE OF THE VOID:
• Opens a further layer
• Deepens our sense of what it means to be human, alive
• Makes us question
• Lets body wisdom take over
• Releases repressed shocks so we can begin to heal
• Germinates new seeds related to original purpose
• Takes us into the mystery
• Strips ego of outmoded ways of control

seem to come with various purposes or opportunities. These may include the following:

1. A time to develop new skills
2. A chance to see yourself in a different way
3. An opportunity to make a contribution to the planet
4. A time to love and be loved
5. An opportunity to forgive
6. A chance to release pain
7. An opportunity to develop greater compassion and spiritual connection
8. (Fill in a possibility)

Change Comes Gradually or Abruptly but It Is Always Purposeful

WE ARE, of course, changing moment by moment. Most of the time change moves us forward gradually as we age. One day we wake up and we are forty, fifty, sixty, or one hundred years old! How did that happen? Daily small decisions have a cumulative effect of change without any significant moments.

At other times change comes as a sudden, unexpected shock. Either way change is (1) inevitable; (2) purposeful; (3) a response to something that needs changing; (4) and part of our journey to know ourselves and our life purpose.

Being stuck in the doldrums is also purposeful. Periods of rest or stagnation (however we choose to name this becalmed state) give us time to receive new information, reflect on what is not working, and create a desire for new vistas. A strong desire for change builds momentum for the next shift.

Take a moment to look at the illustration the Map of Change: The Experience. Notice the different experiences of change that are possible. Where might you be in the flow?

DISMEMBERED AND RE-FORMED

Put your face in the mouth of the lion. Have an experience of life. We shut ourselves down by naming and categorizing, and we don't look for the meaning [of what's happening]. You must be dismembered and re-formed.

Joseph Campbell, *The Power of Myth*

Gateways to Something New

EITHER SUDDENLY or gradually, a break in our routine opens a *gate* to something new. Typically we experience change through five major gateways: work and career, relationships, health, money, and loss. Sigmund Freud made a now-famous statement that only two things matter in life: work and love.

Selma Lewis, a psychotherapist in California, works extensively with people undergoing major life changes—such as surgery, catastrophic illness, death or divorce of a mate, parenting and stepparenting. I asked Dr. Lewis what she recommends during transition in the five major areas.

CAREER CHANGE

Leave Time for Nurturing Relationships

"CHANGING CAREERS usually means a very big learning curve," says Lewis. "This protracted time of learning, during which your self-esteem and income are at stake, creates a lot of anxiety. It's a time when self-doubt and criticism are especially high. The natural inclination, of course, is to gear up and spend all your time at the business. It's easy to cover up the anxiety in the excitement of getting going. Because so much is at stake in terms of self-worth, identity, and security, it's a very tender period when you *really* need to leave time for nurturing relationships. We Americans place so much value on being productive, we tend to fill up every moment with work-related activities."

THE MAP OF CHANGE
The Experience

DYNAMIC BALANCE

Going home
Returning with the prize
New understanding
New ability / identity

Challenges
Opportunities
Soul Growth

- Sense of purpose
- Curiosity and optimism about options
- Coping with daily challenges
- Ability to laugh
- Stress is motivating

Gradual Change

Boredom   New desires
Stagnation   Living by default
Time for a change   Conflicts
Need for new challenges
Emerging new strengths
or
Sudden unexpected change

Renewed Sense of Purpose
New insights   Gratitude
Ability to meet most new challenges
New opportunities
New sense of self/Individuation

THE RETURN

Vital Energy Is Re-formed

A Door Opens

Gateways of Change
- Relationships
- Work • Money
- Health • Loss

THE BREAK

Self
LIFE PURPOSE
ever-changing and individuating

Response Continuum
Regaining energy
Following intuition
(Acceptance   Surrender)
Taking small steps
Trust   Patience
Getting support/therapy

Response Continuum
Happiness
Optimism   Well-being
Sense of adventure   Faith   Trust
Confidence   Fruitful action
Profiting from change
New strengths/identity
Shock   Anger   Denial
Lack of confidence
Feeling overwhelmed
Depression

Avoiding the void
by staying in bad situations

FEELS LIKE:

Anger   Blame
Resentment
Halfhearted action
Resistance

Loss of flow   Chaos
Apathy   Feel lost
No energy   Confusion
Doubt one's ability
Negative comparisons to others
No sense of purpose
Addiction   Feeling forced to the edge

Regaining Energy

Challenges
Tests
Opportunities
Soul Growth

THE VOID

PURPOSE OF THE VOID:
- Opens a further layer
- Deepens our sense of what it means to be human, alive
- Makes us question
- Lets body wisdom take over
- Releases repressed shocks so we can begin to heal
- Germinates new seeds related to original purpose
- Takes us into the mystery
- Strips ego of outmoded ways of control

JOB SEARCH

Create Your Own Structure

THE WORST and most frightening transition for most of us is looking for work. The sudden lack of structure and not knowing the path, because there is no one path, leaves us feeling overwhelmed and scattered. Lewis recommends, "Create a structure for yourself. Set your alarm clock and rise early. Look through the want ads, then take a walk or get out and do something physical. Look on the Internet for jobs, but be sure not to spend all day inside by yourself. Lack of structure gives you too much time to think."

Make Looking for Work Your New Job

LEWIS SUGGESTS that you have a few versions of your résumé ready to send out for different types of work. Ask your friends or a professional to look over your résumé if you aren't getting the responses and interviews you want."

Lewis also recommends that you reward yourself for the actions you've taken. Go to the gym and do your workout as a reward, but don't use the gym as a place to hide out. Have lunch with working people as often as possible. Don't get lost in household errands or shopping, which can expand into the whole day.

Keep Up Social Contacts

LEWIS SAYS, "Your worst negative judgments about yourself come up and seem to be fed when you've temporarily lost your sense of identity. It's very important to make sure you have enough social contacts so that you don't get too inward-focused and depressed."

WHY NOW?

Look for the Spiritual Purpose Behind the Obstacle

ALONG WITH the practical adaptations we make to changes in our work lives, it's important to consider the spiritual implications of what has happened to us. What has *needed* to change? What else has to be developed in our lives? What is the deeper call of this moment?

Arielle Ford, who heads a public relations firm for prestigious clients such as the authors Deepak Chopra, Louise Hay, Joan Borysenko, and Wayne Dyer, says, "Having a devastating downturn in my previous career in marketing was ultimately the most important thing that ever happened to me in business. Through losing everything I found my true purpose. Otherwise, I would still be hating my work."

FAMILY LEAVE

Create Relationships with People Who Also Work at Home

WHEN SOMEONE leaves work to stay at home with a new child, everything that previously gave him or her identity and status—work friends and colleagues, daily structure, going to parties and identifying himself or herself as a lawyer, analyst, teacher, or designer—falls away. A new mom is under tremendous physical, emotional, and financial stresses, and loss of familiar and supportive relationships can be devastating to self-esteem. Lewis strongly encourages stay-at-home mothers or fathers to create a network of friendships with people who are not working full-time. "Start engaging people who work at home for lunch, walks, and outings," she says. "A lot of women go from being very busy at work with opportunities for daily chitchat to being home alone with a baby and nobody to talk to. They can hardly wait for their spouses to come home because the loneliness builds up! Mothers' groups have been a wonderful new development."

DIET

Fill the Space with Something Meaningful

RELATIONSHIPS ARE often structured around common interests and social rituals, like going out for dinner and drinks. What happens when you stop drinking or go on a regimented diet? Any life change can cut away something you previously used to bind you to your identity. For example, if your doctor has given you strict instructions on food and you were used to going out with friends to eat, your social life may drop away drastically. This could be the time when it's important to look at what else feeds your soul. What hobbies or interests could you develop to fill the space that social dining and drinking took up? Again, finding solid and meaningful support with others is crucial to regaining a sense of identity and well-being, and to balancing what has been dropped.

RETIREMENT

Start Developing New Interests a Year Ahead

SOME PEOPLE have a passion that they can't wait to get to once they retire. However, for many of us the idea of what to do with our retirement years can be hazy or rather daunting. Dr. Lewis advises doing some thinking ahead before the gold watch is strapped onto your wrist. "I suggest that people begin to find activities that are meaningful to them about a year before they expect to retire. Start with volunteer work, or try your hand at something you're good at, like informal sports coaching, or begin to take different kinds of classes. Become active at a hobby *before* you have too much time on your hands."

Create Groups of Friends with Diverse Interests

MOST PEOPLE don't realize how much social life initiates at work, and the degree to which work relationships support our identities. Therefore, you need to create different groups of friends and acquaintances to pick up the deficit of work encounters that you took for granted. It's as shocking to retire as it is to move to a new town. Without familiar work relationships, retirement can feel like exile. We are social creatures. Regular social interactions contribute a large part to helping us maintain our identities. Lewis recommends that people find diverse interest groups to see who and what really appeals to them in this new period and that they schedule activities for at least four days a week.

Become Involved Wherever You Are

IF YOU start feeling like a shut-in, you are becoming stroke-starved. The term *strokes* is used by some psychologists to mean those brief but necessary encounters with neighbors, friends, and family that give us a sense of place and connection. They are the common daily hellos and chitchat that provide us a sense of being heard, recognized, and generally *okay*. Studies have shown that we need a certain number of these strokes every day to maintain health and well-being.

MOVING

Make Moving an Adventure

MOVING TO a new town can be extremely stressful. You have to recreate everything in your life—find a new grocery store, haircutter, doctors, dentist, dry cleaner, friends, and school for children. Research shows that it takes two years to feel somewhat settled in a new place. Again, it's important to begin to widen your circle of acquaintances as soon as possible. Ask your neighbors where they shop or obtain services. People love to give advice, and this is a good time to be open and let people know what you're looking for!

ILLNESS

Listen to the Message in Your Symptoms

HOW MANY of us have gone through a big change of outlook by way of illness and recovery? Illness is one of the major gateways leading to increased spiritual awareness. Many of us, not finding true healing in conventional medicine, have been forced to look at how our lifestyles might need changing. To broaden our search for healing, we are guided to read certain books or investigate certain healers. We experience the mysterious movement of Spirit. We are impelled to go within and listen for what our illness is telling us about the balance in our lives. Illness, therefore, may also be the catalyst for an expression of life purpose.

GOOD NEWS

Be Prepared for Changes in Relationships

WHEN A positive change finally occurs—for example, you marry a wonderful mate, win the lottery, lose those forty pounds, or finally leave the job you always complained about—you may have to change your whole way of relating to others. Having a sudden or visible success, such as publishing a book, becoming famous, inheriting a lot of money, or being promoted to a high position could potentially create a barrier in friendships or family relationships that were not strongly supportive in the first place. Even though success seems like a good thing, the imbalance in perceived status by the person who didn't have the success may cause jealousies that eventually create a rift that cannot be easily repaired. Sometimes friendships drop away because they were based on a particular problem—such as two single moms who support each other through the hard times. If one of them marries and moves into another lifestyle, their mutual bond or theme of struggle is changed. Each relationship has appeared for a reason and will last for as long as that purpose is still operating.

The Pace of Change Seems to Be Increasing

AS HARD as we try to plan and control our futures by storing up resources against the storms of life, life has cycles of joy and despair that seem inexplicable and random. Unexpected changes force us into unknown territory, where our greatest resource is the ability to adapt spontaneously. The first lesson we learn is that the only control we have over change is how we handle it.

As we know, technology increasingly dominates both our economy and our society. Futurists claim that all the technological knowledge we have today will represent only one percent of the knowledge that will be available by 2050. Demands on our work life continue to grow. For example, the cycle from idea, invention, or innovation to imitation is shrinking steadily. Up until about 1940 product cycles could stretch thirty to forty years. Today some cycles last only thirty to forty weeks. Medical knowledge is doubling every eight years. New ethical questions arise as new choices in medicine become available. For example, via surrogate motherhood or selective fertilization, parents will be able to choose genes for skin color, height, or intelligence for a prospective fetus. At the other end of the life spectrum, we now must consider what constitutes extraordinary life support or when to terminate life support.

The rapid growth of technology fits in with the recent shift to the Aquarian astrological age, whose dominant influence is the energy of unexpected change. The author and spiritual teacher Joyce Petschek notes, "The influence of Aquarian energy, for both the individual and the collective, now brings not only the innovative and expansive into our lives, but also the erratic and unexpected. This means that all of us must be expected to receive and handle change at a pace that was unimaginable a few decades ago. For many of us, life now tends to feel chaotic. The chaos comes from not being able to see clearly what direction to take. The best way to adapt to this fast pace of change," says Petschek, "is to trust that change will shift us into the right place." She believes we should be able to proceed without needing to know the outcome beforehand, trusting the solution that will come to be. "I think it's important— *especially* when you have no idea what you are doing—to say, 'Okay, I don't know what to do here,' and ask life to show you the best way to accomplish what you want to do. At a crossroad you need to believe that the best way to accomplish what you want will shape itself. I try to recognize and respect that obstacles signal I am going in the wrong direction. Obstacles usually indicate that an unknown direction is before me, and that I need to trust, remain still and centered, and wait until this new energy unravels itself." Petschek advocates watching "left field," the place of the unexpected. She believes that one must ask the universe for what one wants or needs, then wait to see if it will appear, rather than try to force the issue prematurely.

Petschek tells of how she met a potential candidate for her new business. "I started a needlework business following the publication of my book *Beautiful Bargello*. We manufacture needlework kits for worldwide distribution. After three years, and many requests, it seemed clear that it was time to produce retail items. My vision was also to help bring creative opportunities back to the community level, so I began to employ women in third-world countries to stitch the needlework for finished retail product. The rapidly expanding business now needed a general manager. My vision was for a retired executive who knew about growing a business and who would find this project as inspiring as I do.

"One evening I hired a car to take a colleague and myself home from a dinner meeting. To make a long story short, the driver of the car turned out to be exactly the person I was looking for. At the time I met him, he was working with the car company as a business consultant and was driving the car as part of his investigation of their business. This kind of event reflects the unexpected answers which indicate and confirm a new direction in our lives."

In trusting that change is bringing us what we need and is the means by which we become more of who we were meant to be, we must become more adept at reading the signs of what life is trying to tell us. When we feel confused it's a good idea not to react but to wait until things clear, then take action from our intuition. Often a clear dream, an unexpected encounter, or an intuitive feeling leads us to a new direction that enriches our lives with surprise.

The Ego Resists Change

AS MUCH as we long for positive changes, our egos want us to feel safe and on familiar ground. They crave stability because stable things are easier to manage. The ego's first concern is control. Our day-to-day mind-set, which is firmly entrenched in our egoistic concerns, blinds us to the need for change. The ego refuses to leave our comfort zone. This is the part of ourselves that chooses to live under the illusion that life is rational. Its credo is: Work harder. Be careful. Who do you think you are?

Lindsay Gibson, a therapist and author of *Who You Were Meant to Be: A Guide to Finding or Recovering Your Life's Purpose,* writes, "The ego is that part of yourself that is rooted in fear, guilt, and grandiosity, and is directly at odds with your true self. The ego believes that your greatest safety lies in becoming whatever others need you to be. It exists to preserve the status quo and to prevent you from leaving the fold." Does this help explain why you procrastinate? Why you would rather have a root canal than go out and look for a new job?

SIGNS OF EGO

REMEMBER IT'S the primary goal of the ego to keep us small, safe, and approved by others. In her book Dr. Gibson mentions these key signs of the ego's negative influence:

- You dread change.
- You wallow in indecisiveness.
- You worry about everything without resolving anything.
- You fill your time with meaningless tasks.
- You procrastinate.
- You make things complicated.
- You feel you have to do everything perfectly, so you do nothing.
- You blame others.
- You revert to sarcasm or cynicism to justify lack of effort.
- You are always waiting for the other shoe to drop.
- You constantly worry about lack of time and money.
- You are envious of what others have.
- You want to save the world but never act on anything.
- You rationalize, using statistics to support the view that nothing can be changed.
- You sound like your mother.
- You sound like your father.

EGO OR INTUITION?

HOW DO we know whether our egos or our intuition is talking to us? For starters, if you are not in the habit of listening to that quiet inner voice we call intuition, you may not hear much guidance. In seeking to appease others and gain approval, you may have given up even knowing what your own needs and desires are, for fear they might conflict with those of important people in your life. Making life changes seems overwhelming because you are out of touch with your inner guidance. Genuine guidance is recognized in the following ways:

1. The intuitive voice is quiet but persistent. Thoughts keep coming back, but they are not marked by urgency. The ego's voice demands that you make a choice *now* out of fear that something will disappear.

2. Intuitive messages point you in a direction of self-development and a feeling of being more fully expressed. The ego, by contrast, says, "Why bother?" "It's too much trouble." "It costs too much." The ego rationalizes away action and defends the status quo.

3. The intuitive voice uses simple declarative sentences, such as "It's time to go back to school." "You need to write." "Move on." These statements are specific and useful. The ego keeps rehashing the same old ground and relies heavily on justifying statements.

4. Intuition comes directly and clearly into your mind. The ego voice is indecisive and anxious. It's concerned with trying to figure out the best way to minimize or control events.

5. The intuitive voice moves you out of your comfort zone, but you know in your heart that it is guiding you to the right thing to do. The ego voice loves to tell you horror stories.

6. The intuitive voice gives you one step or goal at a time. The ego sets up contradictory goals or creates a no-win situation.

7. Intuition tells you what to do to be true to yourself. The ego tells you what to do to make things good for others.

Once we become attuned to some of the beliefs and behaviors that keep us stuck, we can begin to walk through our gateways with a greater sense of adventure, trust, and enjoyment. To regain a zest for life and motivation, Dr. Gibson offers the following insights and suggestions:

1. Feed your fascination.
2. Don't be afraid of selfishness.
3. Remember, helplessness may be just inexperience.
4. Expect setbacks.
5. Use persistence as necessary.

Change Asks Us to Release Something

ONE OF the purposes of change is to shake off the complacency our egos have carefully developed. Complacency is a mask that covers up fear, self-doubt, and unexamined issues. We can't grow well if we get too complacent and don't make necessary changes.

In his book *Transitions: Making Sense of Life's Changes,* William Bridges reminds us that "transition[s] reactivate our old identity crises." Life changes are the times when we clean house, sweep the porch, and reorganize the basement. Before we can begin something new, we must complete our unfinished business. Otherwise we take that unfinished business into the new direction. For example, we may be bitter about the way someone left us. Our bitterness—although it's not a healthy connection—may keep us connected to those people who play an outdated but important role in how we define ourselves. ("My ex-husband was a big CEO in the movie industry." "My wife was a beauty queen in South Carolina.")

When we don't attract the changes we want, it may be because we need to release an outmoded definition of ourselves or rethink a dream that has become old. For example, Janice, a fifty-five-year-old professional woman, had been single for fifteen years. After going into therapy to look at why she was not finding someone to love, she realized she was stuck on an old vision of marrying an "age-appropriate CEO-type." By opening her mind to other types of men, she developed a wonderful relationship with a nurturing blue-collar guy ten years younger than she. Janice had to let go of a dream that was part of an earlier vision of herself. Being open to someone who did not fit her picture of the perfect man allowed life's intelligence to bring her what she really needed for this stage in life.

Change Brings a New Playing Field

AN E-MAIL from an Australian I shall call Phil illustrates how illness forced an ending to an old way of life and identity, and allowed a new beginning to emerge. Phil writes that he had suffered a heart attack followed by months of severe depression. "My story begins not as a child but as an adult aged forty-two. My previous life was a combination of good times, dinner parties, alcohol with friends, drugs with friends, poor diet, and heavy stress from my job as general manager. All of these factors led to a physical and mental meltdown. Plagued with feelings of lost immortality and loss of future direction, I have stumbled through with no perceived goal. I have had this feeling of permanent bad luck, that nothing was ever going to change."

Here we see Phil's *ending* of the old life, and the dark confusion as he muddled through the void, finally confronting his feelings of loss of identity. Gradually he came to understand that, in order to have new life, he had to let go of the way he had been living—because it wasn't viable. With that realization he began the return to health and well-being. He writes, "Recently I have begun to feel that maybe I *do* exist for a purpose. I used to think the hype about the power of positive thinking was just that—hype. But lately I have opened my mind to the idea of karma, which has given me a feeling of peace. I believe that even though we die in the physical body, we move on to another plane of existence. The idea that we have a purpose and that we get clues about that purpose has opened my eyes.

"I've always done some form of teaching. I've coached sports for thirty years, and I've managed people in various business projects. I also assisted people with disabilities, so they could participate in mainstream sports. I look forward now to pursuing the next phase of teaching in whatever field I feel guided toward. I am able to feel that my journey once again has purpose and is moving forward. I know that I have one last vice to rid myself of—cigar smoking—but I am positive this will occur shortly."

Phil's statement "I feel that my journey once again has purpose" is the essence of the stage of return. He doesn't know where the journey is taking him, but a sense of purpose is enough to indicate that positive movement is happening. Knowing the specifics of what he will *do* with his life is less important to him than feeling connected to something that matters, something larger than himself.

Living with Uncertainty Helps Us Stay Flexible

THE ABILITY to live with uncertainty is one of our greatest gifts. Trusting that somehow everything will make sense someday is a milestone on the spiritual path. Trust, self-love, and compassion are the fruits of living through the dark night of the soul. Phil, for example, is able to acknowledge the ending of his former more superficial and less awake life and to look forward to moving to a deeper level. It took a dose of fear of death, loss of ego strength, and temporary confusion to detach him from his previous modes of staying unconscious (drinking, drugs, and a casual attitude about health). Crisis necessitated the building of a stronger and ultimately healthier foundation. It's not often one hears a sports coach talk openly about karma!

Everywhere, wherever you may find yourself, you can set up an altar to God in your mind by means of a prayer.

The Way of a Pilgrim

3

Find the Spirit of Adventure

The first rule is simply this:
live this life
and do whatever is done,
in a spirit of Thanksgiving.
Abandon attempts to achieve security,
they are futile,
give up the search for wealth,
it is demeaning,
quit the search for salvation,
it is selfish,
and come to comfortable rest
in the certainty that those who participate in this life
with an attitude of Thanksgiving
will receive its full promise.

JOHN MCQUISTON II,
Always We Begin Again

Leaping

THE UNKNOWN is our chance, perhaps, to sing another song, to find another way to express ourselves. In approaching the future, we have the best chance of success when we release some of the old story lines that don't serve us anymore. We can begin to cast ourselves in larger roles—the adventurer, the pioneer, the role model, the happy partner, the artist, or the one who serves with joy.

Robert Scheurer e-mailed me an interesting tale of following his passion and leaping into the unknown. He writes, "I started conducting research on the Knights Templar, and their treasure trove of hidden holy objects, which were excavated from the subterranean vault of King Solomon's Temple in Jerusalem. I was being led to archives, museums, monasteries, and cloisters. This new path was miraculously just unfolding. It was in the dimly lit chapel of a secluded cloister that I found a Templar tomb effigy map of Jean d'Alluye, from the Loire Valley in France, dated A.D. 1248. A map was etched on the knight's shield, and being a cartographer, I photographed this marvelous find, which I eventually mapped. The secrets of this map concern Jesus Christ, the Templar treasure trove, and the missing holy objects from Solomon's Temple! My research became an obsession and my new passion in life. I couldn't believe that I was writing my first book, called *The Circle of Light*.

"When I went back to my office in the corporation that had employed me for the past thirty years, I had another epiphany. The first day back, I started my normal work routine, and then for some strange reason . . . it dawned on me. I couldn't force myself to be isolated in front of a computer doing noncreative work for the rest of my life. At 11:30 in the morning, I calmly walked into my manager's office and informed her that I would be retiring in half an hour, at 12:00 that day! I then informed her that I would forward her my resignation, and would return within several days to clean out my cubicle! That was the happiest moment of my life. . . . I had taken a leap of faith and started moving forward in my life!

"Since then, I have almost finished my book. Part of my research has been accepted by the History Channel for an upcoming documentary called *America's Stonehenge*. All I can say is, believe in yourself . . . whatever you focus on will come true, and never give up on yourself. You can really do it, whatever it is!"

It Was a Very Hot Summer Day

WHEN OUR lives change dramatically, we are all but forced to open to something new. On the threshold of a new beginning, the unknown can look pretty scary and insecure compared with what we have already accomplished—even if what we have accomplished is not where we want to be anymore. There is no one right way to make life changes. We must do what feels right for us in our own time.

PAY ATTENTION TO WHAT HAS *YOUR* NAME ON IT

SOMETIMES WE ask, How do I get through the roadblocks I see between me and what I want? Can anyone achieve success, or do only special people with a special destiny make the grade in life? If we are wise, we start paying attention and just do what comes naturally. When we follow what captures our interest, doors open. One of our biggest mistakes is in thinking that we have to figure out all the steps to get where we want to go. In reality, the steps are more or less revealed to us, if we pay attention to where the energy feels strongest.

Renay Jackson, a janitor in Oakland, California, for twenty-two years, had his share of seemingly ruinous life changes during a rough patch. Like Robert Scheurer, Renay found that he opened a door to his own talent, seemingly by accident, and he has recently become an author. However, unlike Robert, Renay maintains his day job as a custodian for the Oakland Police Department. His story illustrates how, despite the press of ordinary life pressures, dramatic reverses, and unexpected loss, the creative spirit is always working within us to redirect our feet onto the path of our life purpose. Our job is to be patient and take action on what has heart and meaning.

Renay lost his wife, career, and financial balance in 1982. He had been on his way to major success in the newborn rap music industry when his marriage ended, leaving him with three small daughters. Shortly thereafter he took in his niece as well. Within just a few months his whole life—and his future prospects—had changed completely. He had lost his wife, his home, his car, and his music career, and was in debt to the IRS.

"My rap career was over because I didn't have money for studio time or promotion," says Renay. "Suddenly, my heart wasn't in it anymore. The industry had changed by that time. When I started, rap was clean, but it was beginning to have too much profanity and violence," he said. "Life changes? Yeah. I grew up in the projects of

North Richmond, one of the poorest communities in California. My mother had eight kids, and we lived on welfare. So after I got married, here I was, a rapper, a happily married man—a guy whose life was going great. It all collapsed."

DO WHAT IS FUN

RENAY RECALLS the time his youngest daughter came home from her first day at seventh grade and showed him what she had written for an assignment. It was only two lines: "This summer I went swimming. I had a great time." Renay remembers telling her, " 'Baby, you aren't in the sixth grade anymore. You have to describe things in more detail. Write about what it was like to jump in the water.' " He sat down at the computer to show her how to write a more detailed description. The Muse had struck. He says, "I started writing the words 'It was a very hot summer day, at least ninety-five degrees' to describe washing my car on a hot day. It turned out to be the first page of my first mystery novel, *Oaktown Devil*."

Once Renay started, sheer curiosity about what would emerge next kept him at his computer. "It was so much fun to come home after work, cook dinner, sit down at my computer, and go into my own world that I realized, Hey, I'm onto something here. I'm just as happy as I can be now that this new career has opened up. My books deal with murder, double-crossing, cheating, life in the ghetto, sex, and drugs. I write in black-speak, or Ebonics, just like the people who live in the neighborhoods speak."

Renay has now finished two novels. Publishing and marketing is his next step into the unknown, a process he appears to relish.

AVOID PRESSURING YOUR MUSE WITH SPECIFIC OUTCOMES

WITH ANY creative process or life change—which is always a walk into the unknown—it is important to let things emerge without too much pressure about having them be a certain way. If, for example, we squeeze and pressure our Muses with the goal to gain fame or a huge amount of money, we can easily shut down the creative flow that naturally opens doors to new dimensions that are *right for us.* When our motivations spring from ego needs, our decisions are tainted by the need to control confusion, which opens the door to self-doubt and second-guessing. When we try to bend ourselves to the ego's need for approval and safety, we make choices for the wrong reasons. If, however, we proceed out of an inherent love for and interest in something, that creative energy is more likely to produce the best outcome.

New ideas for self-development, such as going back to school or finding a mentor, arise intuitively as we get closer to fulfilling our purpose. "I believe that I will be successful because I'm hand-selling my own books. I'm not selling them through the normal route," Renay says. "I've sold five thousand copies of my two books in eleven months, and my name is getting out there. I also have started back to college, and I know my daughters are proud of me and what I'm doing."

Renay Jackson's story shows one way of stepping into the unknown—simply paying attention to the moment and noticing how much fun it was to write. Without conscious planning, each step became clear, and what was utterly unknown before—the emergence of a talent and a career path—was made known without worry or undue risk. The message is to show up in our lives, be present for what is happening, and let ourselves move in the direction that makes us feel more alive.

NOTHING TO LOSE

Nothing can truly be taken from us. There is nothing to lose. Inner peace begins when we stop saying of things, "I have lost it," and instead say, "It has been returned to where it came from."

Epictetus, circa A.D. 60–120

Jumping Off

THE CATALYST

THE PREPARATION needed to embark on the road less traveled may begin years before we set foot on the path. Our lives may be shaped and nurtured through events whose meaning is hidden until the right moment. The desire to quit our jobs, to simplify our lives, and to have time for creative explorations is a fantasy for most of us, although typically we file those ideas in the "someday" category. Anne C. Scott of Louisville, Kentucky, however, came to a point when she did quit her job, pare down her possessions, and set out to travel the open road with no agenda. Anne had spent thirty-five years in various aspects of the helping professions—from social work, adoption placement, and addiction treatment to fund-raising for United Way. In addition she worked for eight years as a stockbroker. About the time that she was beginning to feel she wanted to do something more meaningful, she ran into an old acquaintance. The friend told her about a nonprofit organization in need of an executive director. The opportunity to work with people with mental retardation would turn out to be a profound catalyst that would not only deeply connect Anne with a new level of values but also free her to explore the unknown with a sense of adventure and trust.

"The work was a leap of faith for me," says Anne, "but it turned out to be the most remarkable nine years of my life. It's what I feel most passionately about. I feel so honored to have worked with all the people I served and their families. These are extraordinary people who illuminated for me the importance of relationships, and the significant difference between what I want and what I need. They helped me see what is really important in life beyond the materialism, money and possessions, and speed, that run our culture. They exemplify each day the importance of joy and openness, unconditional love, mutual respect, and sincerity. They taught me how to be vulnerable and open. I probably never would have been able to let go of my old life and do my trip without the friendship of these individuals."

MOTIVATED BY A DESIRE FOR SIMPLICITY

When Anne turned fifty in 1996, she made the decision to live a simpler life. She realized that in order to make changes after a lifetime of heavy responsibilities—which included having been a single mother of two children, spending years caring for parents through their end days, and working tirelessly in her careers—she was going to have to make a *dramatic* change. She began to sell or give away half of her possessions. "I had always lived under great pressure (often self-imposed) to take care of everybody. Every day of my adult life I had awakened with at least six appointments on my calendar. As executive director, my job was to bring in one and a half million dollars every year to fund our program. I was involved in conflict resolution all day long. My new goals were to never attend another meeting and to never again wear panty hose!"

FOLLOWING THE INTUITIVE DESIRE FOR COLOR

IN MYTHICAL terms, this is the point when the hero's or heroine's journey begins to take shape. As Joseph Campbell says, we are *dismembered* through our desire for new growth. We must leave the membership of who and what is familiar in order to be transformed into our new selves. Anne began to feel the call. She says, "I wanted to take a trip where I had no agenda. I just wanted to be open to whatever was out there. In the beginning people would ask me, What are you looking for? and What will you do when you come back? I'd say, I don't know and I don't want to know. The only thing I knew for sure was that I wanted to be in the Northeast in the fall to see the fall colors." This desire to see the fall colors in the East is a simple but excellent example of the subtle ways our intuitions begin to set the course toward whatever will bring us into balance and wholeness.

We also get a glimpse of Anne's unconscious at work in how she responded to the curiosity of friends who pressed her for her motivations and plans. Without conscious intention she remarked a couple of times, "Maybe I'll work at L. L. Bean [a clothing manufacturer in Maine]. Two people told me that they knew someone at L. L. Bean, so when I arrived in Brunswick, [Maine], I called this person and left a message. We met for lunch at a deli bakery. I never did work for him, but the deli bakery turned out to be one of the first places I went to work. I was only going to stay a couple of weeks, but I wound up staying six months. In retrospect, I think I was exhausted and I needed a place to get used to this new lifestyle."

A TIME OF HEALING

ANNE SOLD bagels and espresso drinks. Since the café was a community gathering place, she met everyone in town. "By the time I left I knew a lot of people on a first-name basis. I still keep in touch with friends there." In this first sojourn in Maine, Anne was already living the simple and satisfying life she had dreamed of. Her desire to be open to life and to make natural personal relationships a bigger part of her daily life was being achieved. No longer were her relationships with others based on her need to take care of them or resolve their conflicts. This is a wonderful example of how *moving in the direction of positive energy* (fall colors, simplicity, or the freedom to sit and chat in a café) can take us where we want to go. In contrast, trying to *figure out logically solutions to problems or figure out what's wrong with us* usually keeps us spinning in the problem.

Maine became a place of deep healing for Anne as she enjoyed being by the ocean, working in a compatible environment, and making friends. She says, "I rented a room from a woman, and all it contained was a bed, a dresser, and a chair. I have never been happier than in that stark little room. I just kept feeling so incredibly happy. I could clean the room in five minutes and then go down to the ocean and play the rest of the day. It confirmed for me what it was that I had been looking for."

PUTTING TOGETHER A JIGSAW PUZZLE THAT WORKS

OVER THE next few months Anne continued traveling. She lived for a couple of weeks on Ocracoke Island, twenty-three miles out in the Atlantic Ocean and part of the Outer Banks, North Carolina. Typically she would decide to stay for a while in a place that felt good and would find two or three odd jobs, such as housekeeping in motels, busing tables, or cashiering, that would provide enough income for meals and lodging. Living and working in a community easily created opportunities for new friendships, as well as time to explore nature, read, and just be.

ANOTHER LEVEL OF LETTING GO

THE HERO'S journey typically requires some kind of ritual release or surrender in the face of a challenge to return to the past. When her son got married, Anne went home to Kentucky for a couple of months. In Louisville she came to the decision to sell the beautiful one-hundred-year-old home that she had lived in for twenty years. Maintaining a large old home—even though it contained so many precious memories—did not fit her picture of living a simple life. Following the sale of her home, she was back in her GMC van traveling on back roads that would take her all over the United States. In one stop, at Star Lake, Wisconsin, a hamlet of seventy-three people, she found work at a family-owned resort. "I had three jobs in the area, and I stayed for a month. Two or three days a week I would commute seven miles through a deep forest where every day I saw all kinds of wildlife. I loved it! In addition to cleaning cabins for the resort, I worked in a little retail shop, where I did inventory, worked on their mailing list, and stocked the shop."

TRUSTING WHAT BECKONS

WHEN WE live life from the intuitive level, and trust that our needs are being provided for, we tend to be less anxious or concerned about controlling everything. We know that we will be guided to outcomes that are better than anything we had imagined. Anne's journey continued to unfold as she listened to her intuition about when it was time to move on and followed leads. For example, one Wisconsin man told her he was sure his brother in Whitefish, Montana, thousands of miles away, would have work for her. As it turned out the brother did not have work, but since she was in Whitefish she decided to visit Glacier National Park. Intrigued by a sign that read, "Going to the Sun Road," Anne signed up for a tour of the park. While waiting for the tour bus at Lake McDonald Lodge, one of the historic lodges of the West, surrounded by majestic trees and mountains, she decided to ask if they needed help. Within twenty minutes she was signing papers with the human resources department. She worked for three weeks in housekeeping and cashiered in the restaurant. "I really enjoyed my stay at the park. For $7.50 a day I was given three meals and a wonderful room in an old stone house facing the lake. I'd sit on the porch with some of the other staff, drinking beer and watching the sunset. Working and traveling is a great way to see the country. I got paid $5.15 an hour, and I could work as many hours as I wanted. I always tried to live on what I earned, and I dipped into my savings only once in a while for birthday presents or special dinners. In over two and a half years, I only paid for a motel room twice. Usually, when I was on the road, I would sleep in my van in Wal-Mart parking lots, or in campgrounds and national parks. There were only a couple of times traveling when I felt even a little bit uncomfortable, otherwise I always felt safe and protected. I had no car trouble, and only had one flat tire in two years. When it happened there was a couple behind me who helped me change it."

THE ADVENTURE OF FINDING COMMUNITY

"I NEVER had any problem finding work or a room to rent—even though I explained to people that I would not be staying long. I'd look for community bulletin boards and read the local newspapers, or just look for help wanted signs—they're everywhere."

Anne's journey is a wonderful model of recognizing and honoring the innate sense that something has to change, and of trusting that this change is healthy and purposeful. When I met her in Sedona, Arizona, where she was working at the front desk of the motel where I was staying, she was planning to return to Kentucky in time for the birth of her first grandchild. "I'm going home for a while, although I don't think this is the end of the journey. There's no way to put into words what this period in life means to me. I met a German man named Thomas one day while I was traveling. He was riding a bike from Alaska to Argentina. We were talking about being on the road alone, and how you cannot convey what the experience is like. I said to him that I was amazed that people didn't ask me more questions about my trip. Thomas said it beautifully when he replied, 'It's not on their horizon.'

"The adventure for me," says Anne, "is coming into a small community for the first time. It's like a puzzle. Where am I going to live? Where am I going to work? Where's the grocery store? Where's the library? Every day is a little adventure. You find the most marvelous and unique people. And our country is so incredibly beautiful and so diverse. I am stunned by the majesty of the landscape and the seascape. My main response to every single day is to be open to what I am meant to receive. I trust now that I will know what to do when I need to do it. And I truly believe it is my friends with mental retardation who set me free."

LIFE CHANGES IN GRAND CENTRAL STATION

In 1956 I walked into Grand Central station in New York City with two friends. We were all going to summer camp together. I looked down the rows of waiting passengers and saw a man. I said to myself, "I'm going to marry that man." I didn't tell my friends or even believe it myself. When we got to our camp in Massachusetts, he was in charge of the group. He was smitten at the time with a beautiful blonde, and I was going steady with someone else.

Before the camp was over, I told him he was doing this [relationship] all wrong. We went to dinner to talk about it, and we talked about our lives and our families. We both knew when we got up from the table that we'd be married. We married a year later and had a son and a daughter. We were married for nine years.

Lisa, project manager

There Are No Accidents

THE MOST powerful tool with which to move into the unknown is the right attitude. There are two very useful attitudes that many spiritual teachings highlight, albeit in different terms: (1) *Every event has a purpose.* (2) *Any event could be either good or bad.* The first attitude automatically shifts our attention to what Divine intelligence might be trying to present through that event. It directs our thinking to what is to be learned and to what is to be harvested from the experience. The attitude that we can gain or learn from everything helps prevent us from feeling that life is unfair or that we are being singled out for failure. With this perspective we avoid the victim mentality. When we feel helpless or hopeless, we not only tend to attract further confusion, pain, and suffering but also tend to overlook anything positive that may be available in the experience.

With the second attitude—that any event could be either good or bad—we avoid the trap of judging an event too quickly on limited information. We learn to wait and see, taking stock of the lesson and listening even more deeply for our inner guidance to suggest another step.

I interviewed hundreds of people about how they handle change and the unknown. I asked questions such as these:

What changes are you facing right now?
How have you moved toward your goals?
What difficult life changes have you had?
What helps you with fears and doubts?
How did you become successful?

I began to see patterns in people's responses. For example, the top response from career changers was "I knew there was a reason why I was fired." "If it hadn't been for my awful boss, I would never have opened my own business." These responses exemplify the attitude of looking for the purpose behind the event, *as if it were bringing a gift.* Similarly, people who have survived catastrophic illnesses often said that illness brought them insight. More often than not, women who survive breast cancer will say, "When I got cancer, I began to wake up to my spiritual side."

In beginning this book I instinctively turned to the timeless spiritual teachings that continue to inspire us. One book on the history of the ancient Mediterranean left me with the feeling that life over the last ten thousand years has followed a cycle of development—from the entrance of new ideas and technology to the maturation, failure, or completion of a system or philosophy. New civilizations spring up and thrive until the invasion of a ravaging horde (the evolutionary thrust of new culture and divisive ideas). It began to seem to me as if the legacy of most ancient cultures could be described as the "remains of the broad-skulled, flat-faced people." The humbling thought occurred to me that, after all our struggles and ambitious striving, each of us may simply end up being lumped together as one of the broad-skulled, square-faced people. It helped put everything into a broader and more humorous perspective! Each civilization has a purpose in giving individuals a life stage to live upon, and each culture contributes a piece to the larger evolutionary picture, even though they have fallen into obscurity.

Ten Basic Principles for Moving Forward

IF YOU are restless for change but at an impasse, read over the following basic principles of how to handle change or attract positive change. As you read, notice which one gives you a *slight charge of energy*. Let that principle be uppermost in your mind for the next few days.

1. *Start by loving yourself.* Appreciate the unique, stubborn, quirky, boring, fascinating, dumb, clever, wonderful, and nutty person that you are.

2. *Tell the truth.* What do you *really* need and want? Don't be shy. *What really matters to you?*

3. *Ask for a clear answer to your current question.* Give the universe an assignment, such as "Show me what I need to do to find a new job." Or "Show me what I need to see in myself in order to attract the best partner."

4. *Pay attention.* Once you ask your question, stay alert. Listen to what your intuition tells you. What signs and signals do you see that indicate options or directions?

5. *Listen for answers everywhere.* Notice what kinds of answers show up through people, chance comments, books, events, dreams, or intuition.

6. *Take right action.* Contemplate where you are in life and the cycle of change. Are you *beginning* a phase that requires you to explore an unknown path or a new identity? Are you *ending* something that requires you to forgive, let go, or move on? Are you *in the middle* of something that requires perseverance?

7. *Assume whatever happened, happened for a good reason.* Reframe whatever is happening right now as if it were a *positive* development—even if it looks like a catastrophe (this

may take weeks, months, or years in the case of severe loss, but it's an invaluable exercise in helping to regain balance and a feeling of resourcefulness). Besides, this assumption is true at the highest spiritual level.

8. *Use honesty, humor, patience, and forgiveness in all your dealings.* Give up trying to be clever and competitive. Just be your down-home self.

9. *Be open to what happens.* Assume the universe has your best interests at heart and is working at this moment to help you achieve your vision. Why not?

10. *Stay still until you can see what to do next.* One of my favorite quotations from Carl Jung is this: "When you are up against a wall, be still and put down roots like a tree, until clarity comes from deeper sources to see over that wall."

LIFE STAGES

0–25 **Development:** Dependency, submission, authority, competency, performance, failure
Virtues: Comeliness of appearance, good conduct, obedience, sense of ethics

25–45 **Mid-life time of transition:** A person of knowledge
Virtues: Temperance, love, courage, courtesy

45–70 **Years to spend in the forest**
Virtues: Wisdom, justice, generosity, cheerfulness

70– **Old age**
Virtues: Looking back with gratitude, looking forward to a return home

Joseph Campbell, *The Power of Myth*

4

※

Follow Positive Energy

They had much in common. They were curious, artistically gifted, and sexually vigorous. Despite their dark sides, they laughed, and many of them danced, too; they were drawn to "gentle sunlight, bright and buoyant air, southerly vegetation, the breath of the sea, [and] fleeting meals of flesh, fruit, and eggs." Several of them had gallows humor close to Nietzsche's own—a joyful, wicked laughter arising from pessimistic hinterlands. They had explored their possibilities, they possessed what Nietzsche called "life," which suggested courage, ambition, dignity, strength of character, humor, and independence (and a parallel absence of sanctimoniousness, conformity, resentment, and prissiness).

ALAIN DE BOTTON,
The Consolations of Philosophy

A Page from Personal Experience

IN MY book *The Purpose of Your Life,* I shared some of the experiences of my own life that led me to write the book and connect with many others, just like yourself, on this path of constant change. At the moment of this writing, I seem to be in a fairly stable period—living near San Francisco, in a home that expresses my artistic tastes and love of color. I am fortunate to have a close relationship with my married grown children, and I have many deep friendships with people here and far away. I have work that I love, which takes me all around the world. My health is good. I have time to pursue a yoga practice, read mystery novels, cook recipes I find in the newspaper for small dinners with friends, and go to the movies. This is a very different life from the one I was living only twelve years ago.

From 1970 to about 1982 my life was dominated by being a working single mother. My main struggle was to continue my painting career (nights and weekends) and study metaphysics (usually doing intuitive readings for clients after work and on Saturdays) while working full-time and keeping our household functioning. Jobs—catering manager, lunch chef, and a variety of administrative jobs in mostly nonprofit organizations—came and went. Life was uncertain, rather hectic, but fun and interesting. I managed to put some time every week into my painting and study of metaphysics. These interests and activities nurtured and sustained me, as did watching the emerging personalities of my children and spending time with good friends.

Between 1988 and 1990, however, I experienced a traumatic level of change—one that my therapist told me was off the scale. The precipitating event was a diagnosis of stage three breast cancer involving eight lymph glands (after nine months of being told by two doctors that there was nothing serious about the growing lump in my breast).

The weekend I began a massive dose of chemotherapy was also the weekend I moved from my house of ten years out in the country, into San Francisco. From that moment on my physical being went through major transformations. Maintaining self-esteem in the face of surgery and the debilitating and aging process of chemotherapy—complicated by the onset of early menopause— was, needless to say, difficult. A badly compromised immune system twice threw me into the hospital.

On the heels of my mastectomy, my second husband of five years moved out. My children were already in college and pretty much on their own. Continuing with a year-long radiation treatment and more chemotherapy, I could no longer keep my job as an office manager. My finances were in ruin. I took in two successive roommates to help with the rent. My father died. My mother died twelve months later. Circumstances forced me to leave the house in San Francisco and relocate to a small room in the basement of a good friend's house in Berkeley.

During this time I came to many realizations, one of which was that the illness was waking me up in order for me to decide what was worth living for. Was I going to settle for the old routine or really get serious about what I loved to do? Although I will always be an artist in my core, I decided that I was a better intuitive counselor. I got more satisfaction out of my interactions with people than I did out of trying to sell art, so I made the choice to put my attention on developing a full-time intuitive counseling practice.

The challenge was to find a way to support myself without going back to a day job. I knew I had to develop a livelihood that truly expresses who I am, because the life changes resulting from the cancer had forced me to look at the deeper issues of what's worth living for.

Like two wheels on a bicycle, there were two movements within me. The first was the idea that my real purpose was working with people using metaphysical principles. The second was the wheel of necessity—how to make more money and stay on the chosen path. I have come to believe that Necessity, with a capital *N,* is a friendly Muse that helps us get very creative very fast.

Even though I loved living with my friend Lorraine in Berkeley and was quite happy with my simple lifestyle, I felt an urge to move on to my own apartment or house. A move, however, meant I had to create more income. One morning I woke up with the question of how I could supplement my counseling income in a way that would be interesting, and that used my talents. What my intuition whispered to me was "Maybe you could help someone with their writing." To this day I have no idea why this idea popped into my mind. I had never, at that time, written professionally, nor had I studied writing.

How could I move forward on this idea? I pondered. My first thought went to the one friend I knew who worked in writing, Candice Fuhrman, who had started her literary agency a couple of years before. I called Candice and asked her to keep an eye out for anybody who needed help with writing. Later that day, she called me with a lead. She told me of a medical doctor who wanted help with a book he was writing. Without any résumé or past experience to accredit me, I took the leap and called him. As it turned out, he hired me without even asking for a sample of my writing. I worked with him for six months to bring his book to fruition. After that another ghostwriting opportunity materialized, and I gained further experience with this curious process of writing books. Writing had never been on my list of things to do with my life, but I was following my intuition, and the universe was responding. What had been a complete unknown to me became familiar, successful, and joyful territory. I've been writing ever since.

Today I can see how each change of circumstance was forcing me to grow—even when all I wanted to do was stay safe.

I look back on two old life scripts that I inherited from my parents. These ingrained comments had become a backdrop against which I measured my attempts to change my life. Instilled in grammar school, they ran my life until I finally recognized the extent to which they were shaping how I saw myself. The two statements that went deep into my psyche were *Who do you think you are?* and *You want too much.*

Own What Has Happened

I INCLUDE some of my own life changes here because I believe that we cannot heal without owning our circumstances. It's important that we not fall into feeling we have special problems no one else has. Telling our life stories over and over from the perspective of "the wound" not only focuses our attention on the negative in our lives, but is a crutch that too-often *rationalizes* inaction and keeps us stuck. It does not serve us to think that we can't change our lives because our problems are special or insolvable. Many of us do have severe handicaps—be they mental, physical, or emotional. We *all* have challenges to face, and that fact gives us the unique opportunity to become who we were meant to be. For example, as a youth, the great psychologist Dr. Milton Erickson was paralyzed by polio. He spent years in an iron lung. During that time the only thing he could do was move his eyeballs. He spent countless hours observing people who came into his room. Years later this observational ability allowed him to become an innovative master of human nature and motivation, leading him to develop a unique and effective method of therapy.

THE FORM BENDS TO ACCOMMODATE

The accident that blinded James Thurber in one eye and eventually the other (his brother shot him with an arrow) while he was still a small boy neither set his life course nor blew him off it. The form bends to accommodate and finds purpose, like his early writing skills, like the "amateurish quality" of Thurber's outsized cartoons, drawn with odd scale and perspective.

James Hillman, *The Soul's Code*

I believe that it is through these *specific* (and maybe even necessary) challenges that our life purposes and our characters are developed. We all have justifications for feeling "Why me?" What then do we do?

Your life is inevitably changing in a particular direction. Why? *Because at some level you already know what you want and where you want to go.* That inner directive alone will attract insights and ideas of what to do, as well as opportunities and the right people to achieve the goal. Your inner state of being is always working to fulfill your destiny, and you have the best chance to receive new ideas and a broader perspective when you are relaxed, open, and empowered by the belief that your life can and will change for the better.

Some Values Never Change— We Have an Essential Core

ONE OF my best friends, Larry Leigon, fifty-two, recently visited his parents in Texas. I was struck by his story of going home and what it says about the power of homeostasis.

"My mother wanted me to get rid of my stuff in the attic," Larry told me. "I hadn't been up there since I was twenty-two. It was the classic dark attic with an overhanging lightbulb; there must have been over a hundred boxes of my belongings, preserved untouched for thirty years, like an archaeological site. I started to go through the boxes of household items from my first marriage in

Houston. Office stuff from my first job. Notebooks from college.

"What was so startling was that my old notes look just like my notes today. Thirty years ago I bought the same kinds of tablets and pens I use today. The diagrams of how to start a company I made at twenty look just like the diagrams I make today. I read my old poems, and they use the same kind of language I write today. As a twenty-two-year-old writing poetry, I had the same concerns I have at fifty-two. My dream journals were the same. My hopes and dreams about my future life were the same. If I had taken the dates off and put today's date on, I'm not sure I would have noticed.

"There was both a comfort and a sadness in this realization. The things I ached for then, I still ache for. The things I cared about are still the things I care about. I think there is a cord there that doesn't change. I still try to live near water. I still have way too many books. I still have the same kind of stuff around me. It was a really spooky feeling to step back thirty years with my fifty-two-year-old mind. I saw that I knew the same things then that I know now. I might learn how to use some new gadget like a PalmPilot, but in the things that really matter to me, like poetry and language, I always knew what I needed to know.

"I guess what I feel after that experience is that the time to act is now. Don't wait until you're richer. Don't wait until you're smarter. Don't wait until you know the right people, or have taken the next class. Do it now.

"Three years ago I attended a friend's art exhibit. She had taken photographs and blown them up, and attached her poetry to them. I thought, What a wonderful thing to see the poems together with the photographs. It struck something in me, and I wanted to do something like that. When I was in the attic, I pulled out this old photo album that I had completely forgotten about, and I saw that I had done that when I was twenty-five! I had put my poems under the photos. I had completely forgotten about this. This book had no earthly use. I had done it just because I loved doing it. It was exactly what she had done. I had already done it twenty-seven years ago. It was so personal I had never shown it to anybody. If someone said to me, Choose one thing that will show somebody a thousand years from now exactly who you are, I'd give them this book. It's the part of me that does not change. It's an expression of my soul. Maybe not precisely, or entirely, but it's a piece. The part that is unchanging."

What brings *you* joy? How are you expressing that?

WHAT DOESN'T CHANGE

To me the most important part of a book on changes is the part of us that doesn't change.

Larry Leigon

Change Requires a Leap of Faith

STEPHEN J. HOPSON, deaf since birth, became a stockbroker in 1992, after leaving a long and secure career in banking. Starting from zero income, within three years he had developed a client list of over three hundred and was earning $300,000 a year. He won awards and was at the top of his game. Even so, with many friends and a great life in New York City, Stephen said he didn't feel fulfilled. On one of his semiannual vacations to Miami, to escape the rigors of his fast-paced life, he was lying on the beach reading Marianne Williamson's book *Return to Love.* "Suddenly, as I was reading," he told me, "I was both laughing and crying. I was overcome with a feeling that I can only describe as a revelation of major proportion. I suddenly had a clear message that, although I was born deaf, God had given me the gift of speech. I knew, without a doubt, in that moment that I had been born to be an author and an inspirational speaker. I was floored by this idea, but I absolutely *knew* that this was the purpose of my life. At that time I had not spoken to a live audience for fifteen years, although I had spoken quite a bit during college, and I had no writing credentials. Even so, I felt like I had won the lottery. I couldn't wait to get back to New York."

A NUMINOUS EVENT CONCENTRATES ENERGY

When a numinous event occurs . . . it draws a large concentration of psychic energy around it.

Ira Progoff, *Jung, Synchronicity, and Human Destiny*

Go with the Flow—*and* Keep the Vision

AN ENTIRE year went by before Stephen said good-bye to Wall Street. He had no clue as to how he would develop this new career of speaking and writing. During his confusion he began to rethink his decision to give up his six-figure income, retirement plan, and benefits for . . . what? In a moment of panic, he sent out some résumés. No one would hire him. "It didn't take long," he says, "before I had to acknowledge that God did not want me to go back to that old life. I had done that, and I had to move on."

Stephen spent the next year laying the groundwork for change. He lived on unemployment benefits and savings, and surrounded himself with supportive people. "When money got really tight," he says, "I would look for things to be grateful for. I kept a journal as a place to examine my feelings and define my goals. I learned to ask for what I want and let God provide."

After about a year of wondering how his destiny was going to unfold, Stephen got an opportunity to work on a book project. However, the project required him to leave the known world of New York City for the unknown world of Michigan. Taking another leap of faith, Stephen packed all his belongings into a ten-foot truck, had a farewell party, and drove himself to Michigan. "I remember that I had a little rock inscribed with the word *faith,* and whenever I'd get scared, I'd reach into my pocket and feel the surface of that little rock. This kept me feeling that I was on the right track and that things would work out."

After one year he and the man for whom he was working had a falling out, and the project, along with all his hard work, evaporated. Was this a failure?

"It quickly became clear to me that when I first came to Michigan, my ego was in the driver's seat," he says. "I was thinking, Oh, good. Now I will become a best-selling author, everybody will know me, and I'll make even more money than when I was a stockbroker. But I was putting all my faith in my relationship with this other man and his ability to make the fame and money happen. When we had a parting of the ways, I was forced to look at what I had expected out of him. I had put him on a pedestal. Ending the project did for me what I could not do for myself at that moment. I was forced to move on, and forced to acknowledge that I was not in charge. It was very humbling."

Stephen's new ending seems to signify the conclusion of a maturation process. Like Queen Inanna (in the introduction), who was forced to leave her accoutrements of authority at the gates to the Underworld, Stephen left his known way of life. He put behind him all his success and authority as a stockbroker to pursue his dream. In that pursuit what he had to face in the underworld—his inappropriate and less evolved desire to be dependent on the success of another—came galloping in in the form of the author-collaborator. In order to pursue the next phase of his life purpose, he had to learn to stand on his own talent and walk his own path. Upon realizing the purpose of this seeming failure, he gained the prize of insight and took back his own power. This lesson brought clarity rather than confusion. Once his block in perception was shifted, amazing opportunities followed within a week.

"I had written two stories and sent them out to editors," Stephen says. "Right after the end of the book project, I received a letter saying that one of my stories had been accepted, out of eight thousand entries, for *Chicken Soup for the College Soul.* I didn't even remember having submitted that piece. My dream of becoming a published author had begun to manifest. Shortly after that I secured a lucrative speaking engagement, and that money got me through the rest of the summer. A month later I found out that the second story had been accepted in another book, called *Heart Warmers.* During this same time I also qualified for my pilot's license! My dreams are manifesting faster and faster."

Following Positive Energy Deepens Trust

GREGG BROWN from Vancouver, British Columbia, writes about his experience of following synchronistic signals from the universe. Staying connected to what really matters to him has given him a new level of trust and effortless accomplishment. Trust is one of our greatest allies as we approach the unknown of our unfolding path.

"I got involved in prison work eight years ago," says Gregg, "after reading an article in the newspaper about inmates being denied access to health care. I had no experience with the criminal justice system, but I just knew that I wanted to help. So I began volunteering, which started me on my training and consultation career.

"The work at the prison is mostly about teaching these guys how to take better care of their health, and how to relate to each other in nonviolent ways. Some of them have taken up Buddhist meditation, and others have begun providing care to other elderly or sick inmates. They take classes in first aid and CPR, and even study complementary therapies such as aromatherapy. It's fascinating work, and also kind of funny to watch these big, tattooed guys sniffing different fragrances and doing foot massages! They love it. I'll bet that if we could track these guys over a period of time, we would find that they reoffend to a lesser degree than others. When these guys hug each other, instead of slug and hit each other, I feel they are learning to live in new ways and, when they do get out of prison, will be able to contribute positively to the community. It is truly meaningful work."

When Gregg's organizational consulting contract was renegotiated recently, he felt resistance to the change. Then, he says, "My intuition told me that it is all part of letting go of the sense of 'security' and stepping off the cliff to trust even more in the infinite power. Time to practice, with greater faith, what I have been reading and preaching! The one thing I did realize was that I would miss the work in prisons. No one else does this work at the organization, and the program would probably be discontinued. Although this is only a very, very small portion of my consulting practice, it is a very, very meaningful portion. I spoke to the people at the organization, and they were open to my working fewer hours for them and just doing the prison work one or two days a month. The other neat possibility is that there may be an opportunity to do some organizational development training with them, which synchronistically ties into the work I'm doing on my master's degree.

"What I have realized over the past year is that when things seemingly 'end,' there are always reasons. These reasons usually mean that better opportunities more in line with my life purpose are just around the corner. Once I'd worked through this in my mind, I got two more training contracts, and another work project on a topic that is exactly in line with my school work. The phone just rang again from another organization wanting to hire me to review their workshops and facilitation manuals! Abundance, or what!

"Needless to say, the insights I have had have been *huge*! Once the blocks are removed, energy flows into me, I become aware of my intuition, which in turn makes me aware of the synchronicities. . . . Sounds simple! I have known and practiced this for the last year; however, my level of trust is now deepening. I have found the deeper the trust, the more the energy flows. Life becomes almost effortless. I feel I am definitely on purpose. I reread my notes from last year about what I wanted to accomplish. Today I have everything that I wrote down. I just love this process."

Handling Confusion

EVEN THOUGH you may be in chaos, on the edge, in the middle, over the top, spaced out, freaked out, or in the void, there are things you can do to take advantage of the circumstances.

• *Get into it.* Admit you are totally confused. Write your feelings in your life changes journal, or speak privately into a tape recorder. Talk about how awful you feel. Tell God you're upset. Tell Her what your problem is. Get it out. Throw a fit. Cry. Get mad. Write down on a sheet of paper all the things that are bugging you, ball it up, and throw it into the trash or burn it in your fireplace. Stay with this process until you quiet down.

• *Notice where the tension is in your body.* If possible lie face-down on a quiet, clean, grassy spot. A large, smooth boulder is even better. If you have to stay inside, lie on the floor. The point is to put your belly onto the earth. Visualize all the heavy feelings you are carrying in your body draining down into the earth. According to Peruvian traditions, the earth is our mother, and she loves all that heavy energy, so let it drain away. Then once you've emptied out, find something beautiful, inspiring, and calming to look at. Draw in that "refined," beautiful energy and fill yourself up.

You can also imagine sending some peaceful, clear, white light into that spot. If you are auditory by nature, try talking peacefully and lovingly to any places of tension as if you were talking to a small upset child. Or you might try turning on your favorite soothing and uplifting music and imagine the music bathing that area.

Running, walking, or working out will work wonders when you're feeling confused. Yoga stretches are perhaps the best of all for calming the mind. Your goal is to disconnect from the swirling thoughts and recenter in your *physical* body to establish a calm, grounded feeling.

• *Assume there is a purpose to your present state of chaos.* Something in you is changing. You are shedding an old skin. Unexpected change can bring a delicious new day, new possibilities, no matter where we are on our journeys. Anything is possible.

• *If you need to make immediate decisions, write out all your concerns, options, fears, and hesitancies.* Create a visual map of the ideas, feelings, and questions that are going through your mind. Let's say you are getting divorced and you don't know if you should move out of town, quit your job that you've been unhappy with, go back to live with your parents, or just take a long trip to Mexico. There is a kind of natural organizing process that happens as you put things on paper. Start with your most urgent questions and feelings of confusion on the left side. List what you want or how you want to feel on the right side. Allow ideas to group into natural categories such as problems, people to call, letters to write, variables about which you need more information, and so on.

• *Draw a circle and write inside the circle all the things you want.* Go for it. Don't even think about whether you have enough money, whether you deserve these things, or whether they are possible. Just write. Review your list in six months or a year. You will be amazed at how your life has changed in the direction of those things you wrote down. Don't take my word for it. Try it.

• *Make a collage of magazine pictures reflecting scenes, words, and people that uplift you.* Spend a happy evening with yourself or a couple of friends. You'll need a good pile of old magazines, scissors, a glue stick, and a few pieces of poster board or colored construction paper. Put on some nice music and begin to leaf quickly through the magazines to see whatever attracts you—words, sentences, pictures of items that you want, scenes that evoke great enthusiasm in you. Tape together a couple of big pieces of the poster board or construction paper to use as a background on to which to paste your cutouts. You will begin to see a kind of flow or natural organization happening as you put together your collage.

Keep your collage where you can see it for a while as it begins to stimulate new things coming into your life. If it no longer has the initial excitement for you, put it away where you cannot see it. Pull it out in a year and see what has come into your life that matches something on the collage!

• *Do something simple that's been nagging at you.* If we are confused, our natural tendency is to feel overwhelmed by *everything*. Our usual mode of coping is to revert to our favorite habits of releasing tension, such as eating, drinking alcohol, taking a pill, or watching television. We also procrastinate. Doing even one little thing, like cleaning off your desk or cleaning out a single drawer, can give you a lift. Whenever we feel better about ourselves, our energy naturally rises, and we relax. When we're relaxed we are much more likely to feel we can handle things.

• *Stop telling everyone you're confused.* You've already talked with yourself about how confused you are. Continuing to build a case for your confusion will not produce the result you want. This habit of hashing over the current problem is hard to break. Of course, genuinely speaking from your heart with a trusted friend who can truly listen is a gift from heaven. However, too often we launch into our current story of woe, and it really does nothing to uplift us or the person listening. Just notice how your own energy starts to drop when you hear other people's sad tales.

• *Don't wait for clarity to take action.* Trust your feelings. I have often heard people in my workshops talk about how once they achieve clarity *then* they will move forward on a plan. I have found that I rarely have clarity going into the unknown, be it a new job, a new project, or a new love affair. I may have it in a few days, months, or even years later and think, Yeah, that was a good thing I did. I'm sure glad I did that. But going into it? Usually not.

What we are asking for when we ask for clarity is a guarantee that, if we do this thing, we will have success. We confuse clarity with guarantee. We want clarity in order to make sure that we never make a mistake and that everything will turn out all right *forever.* However, not waiting for complete clarity does not mean you have to jump into something impulsively and hope that it will take you where you want to go. *You can set an intention to stay in your flow as you move in a certain direction.*

• *Focus on the results you desire, the feelings of success and happiness you want.* Instead of waiting for the phantom clarity to emerge, begin to imagine yourself feeling good. We create change from within, although we usually forget this. You will move ahead further and more quickly if you think about how good you are going to feel when you have the new results. If you act from a place of confusion and upset, things do not usually turn out well.

• *Make a simple but authentic statement that inspires you.* Think back to a time when you felt really great and on purpose. For example, a woman in one of my classes remembered a time she felt a lot of pleasure when she redecorated her apartment— painted the walls vivid colors, put up curtains, framed some pictures, and placed some plants in her kitchen. As she thought about her pleasant memory, she wrote down some of the feelings. Out of that memory, it occurred to her how important beauty and simplicity were to her. Her statement was "I am a being who lives in joy, beauty, and simplicity." This simple statement is a good mantra or affirmation of how she wants to feel. Life will always move us in the direction of our strongest intention.

Handling Endings

WHEN CHANGE brings the end of something—a relationship, a lifestyle, a career or job, a way of identifying ourselves, or financial security—we often do everything in our power to stop or forestall that end. For example, when we divorce, instead of feeling our loneliness and learning to be comfortable alone, we may move too quickly to install a new relationship. In the same way, when we are laid off from a job, we may simply reach blindly for any available job in order to pay the mortgage without taking the time to find something that really makes us happy. If, over many years, we build up a pile of badly handled endings, we usually wind up feeling resentful and angry without realizing the real foundation of the dis-ease. This emotional residue of many unresolved feelings is often referred to informally as "baggage." The primary way we tend to manage the unconscious tension caused by this emotional junk is to deny our own responsibility in the choices we made. It's easier on the ego to blame circumstances or other people.

Endings are a natural part of life. We are programmed to learn, mature, and grow. If we procrastinate in ending something with which we are truly finished, life has a way of ending it for us.

• *Feel the pain.* Endings are most often painful, and they usually don't come about in the most graceful way. We may have a lot of regrets after an ending and wish we had done things differently. Life is messy, and there is no one right way to do anything. Perhaps the best thing is to let this time teach you something by feeling the pain, sadness, disappointment, anger, fear, or letdown.

Grieve for as long as you need to. This is a stage that is all too often leaped over, glossed over, denied, or shrugged off. We naturally don't want to feel hurt, or that we have failed, or that someone doesn't want us anymore. But endings are an opportunity to disengage from something that apparently wants to leave our life. We are growing, and someone is pinching off our dead leaves.

• *Take your time.* Allow yourself some downtime. Pamper yourself a little bit or a lot.

• *Notice what else the ending feels like.* Does leaving your marriage bring up memories of loss from childhood or old internal tapes about how you never finish anything? If you feel overwhelmed with grief or depressed over something that seems on the surface not terribly significant, you may want to seek professional help from someone who can assist you in seeing the larger pattern. Use the context of the ending to learn more about who you are and what's important to you.

• *Honor what has left.* Be grateful for the lessons that came through your experience. Describe your situation in your life changes journal and talk about your feelings. Insights naturally emerge when we are quiet and genuinely desire to integrate our experiences. Write down everything you are grateful for, now and in the past situation.

• *Write notes to friends.* If you've just ended a job in a company, are there people who were kind to you? Can you imagine how they would feel if you wrote them short notes of thanks? Doing so will feel good to you, too, and perhaps make the completion more meaningful, especially if the leaving is not of your choosing. Write these notes only if you truly feel gratitude for people's friendship or for their having made life a little easier for you.

Handling Beginnings

ONE OF the most distressing feelings in life is moving out of one's relatively safe comfort zone to begin a new project or look for a new opportunity. However, *not* moving in the direction of something that is calling us is almost more draining because we know we should move forward, but instead we are using our creative energy to resist rather than to create. That takes a lot of energy! One of the best things to tell yourself when initiating a new direction is that it's okay if you aren't perfect at something right away—unless, of course, you are flying a jetliner for the first time or performing brain surgery! Many of us suffer from having unrealistic expectations about what is going to be expected of us, or from the idea that we have to know with certainty that a new direction is the "right" one before we can even investigate its potential. In order to handle a beginning skillfully, be prepared to increase alertness and receptivity to intuition. Remind yourself that you will learn what you need to know, and that you will handle whatever comes up. Keep affirming that you will always be in the right place at the right time.

• *Go for it.* Make a list of reasons you thought this new beginning was such a good idea, and keep it where it will energize you in times of doubt.

• *Make sure it feels like fun.* Life changes present us with many options. We don't know if they are right for us, but the best guidance are your own internal systems. Does this thing or person make you feel good about yourself? Are you looking forward with enthusiasm, even if things are a little scary? Keep checking in with yourself and ask, What does my instinct tell me? Is this interesting and fun? Am I learning something new?

• *Ask for help.* Beginnings are strange and new. You won't have all the answers, but other people might have. If you don't know something, now is a great opportunity to give someone else the pleasure of telling you, provided you make your own decisions! Ask the universe to provide you with exactly what you need. I have heard countless stories of people who have asked for information on something as obscure as the sex drive of camels in ancient Abyssinia, and found an expert by asking two or three friends who "knew somebody who knew somebody." We've all experienced that fascinating form of synchronicity called six degrees of separation—the idea that we are separated by only six other people from whomever we want to meet. If you wanted to make a new beginning with a career in television, who would you ask who might know someone who knows someone who is first cousin of the producer of *The Tonight Show*? Remember, we are all connected, and the universe is doing everything in its power to help you succeed.

> Love it the way it is.
>
> Thaddeus Golas, *The Lazy Man's Guide to Enlightenment*

5

❧

Hold the Vision

A craftsman pulled a reed from the reedbed,
cut holes in it, and called it a human being.

Since then, it's been wailing a tender agony
of parting, never mentioning the skill
that gave it life as a flute.

RUMI

Hold the Vision of What You Want

WHEN YOU keep your vision on what really turns you on—even if
it's on the back burner of your mind—the universe will send opportunities your way. Fifty-year-old Paul Sladkus of New York grew up in
the shoe business, which he liked well enough, but he really
dreamed of going into show business. He worked for a while at CBS
television on the production side and eventually created a successful business marketing for ethnic radio stations.

Paul is enthusiastic about all the facets of his business. Even as his
work took a variety of turns, he maintained a strong vision of someday producing a news program that would feature only positive and
uplifting news. He says, "Most of my life changes have happened by
going with the flow. About four years ago I was working with one of
my managers, and I was telling him that I'd love to do positive-
minded programs on television—but I couldn't afford to buy a television station! He said to me, 'Why don't you do it on the Internet?'

I thought it was an interesting idea, and even though I didn't pursue it at that time, the seed was planted. Two years ago I sublet some of my office space to a dot-com business. As a result of being around these young, energetic, and experienced Internet gurus, I started to think more about my idea for the program. The father of one of the guys said to me, 'Why don't you just start it?' So I did! I started my Internet program on July Fourth in 1998. It's called *The Good News Broadcast* (www.goodnewsbroadcast.com).

"I've had some really good people on the show, and it's growing," Paul says. "Our goal is to find, receive, or produce nonviolent, life-affirming, thought-provoking educational good news. If people would like to share their good news, they can call me at (212) 647-1212 or e-mail me at goodnews@goodnewsbroadcast.com."

> What a splendid day!
> No one in all
> The village
> Doing anything!
>
> Shiki

Desire Brings New Life and Change

DESIRE IS a driving creative force within us. Far from being the root of suffering, as Buddhist ideology posits, desire is needed for us to change and create, *as long as we don't get attached to a particular outcome.* Life, of course, brings suffering. Suffering is what we feel when there is a big contrast between what we have and what we want. However, within that very contrast lies the opportunity for creating and learning. Desire is a marshaling of energy directed to the universe that will attract new life and change.

You Create with Every Thought

EVERY TIME we think about something, we direct our attention. For example, let's look at three intentions:

I want to find my life purpose.
I need this [particular] client to call and order another [x,y,z].
I want to write, but I don't have the time.

Sometimes we don't get what we want because our intentions are not very clear or pure. As you read the preceding statements, what do you see as the core *motivation* of each? In the first one, "I want to find my life purpose," the intention is pretty straightforward and definite. The motivation is centered on connecting to something that feels fulfilling and in alignment with what you love to do. It is a declarative statement that will serve you. It reminds you that you are exploring situations to find those that feel right for you.

In contrast, the statement "I need this [particular] client to call and order another [x, y, z]" implies that your abundance can come only from one person. The statement is rooted in a feeling of *lack* or *scarcity*, as if there may not be enough abundance to go around. (It may also be true that your intuition is giving you a strong message that it's a good time to check in with that person, but for a very different reason than to get her to buy something!)

The statement "I want to write, but I don't have the time" contains a mixed message to the universe. The intention of wanting to write is diluted or neutralized by the statement of not having enough time. The subconscious hears that you don't have enough time and works to make that true in your life. One of the laws of life is that energy follows thinking. What you focus on expands in your life. According to the Law of Attraction—taught by many teachers of what is often referred to as perennial wisdom—like attracts like. We attract people and events that match the frequency we transmit. Our personal energy vibration emanates from our sense of self and our beliefs.

RELATE PROPERLY TO WHERE YOU ARE

The point isn't to cultivate one thing as opposed to another, but to relate properly to where we are.

Pema Chödrön, *When Things Fall Apart*

Imagination Creates the Form

VALERIE RICKEL is the founder of www.soulfulliving.com, recognized as a prizewinning site in 2000 by the *Los Angeles Times*. This well-organized site offers a wealth of topics from inspirational authors to healing practices, products, and information on spiritually oriented events. After the death of her father—a catalyzing event in many women's lives—it became clear to Valerie that she wanted more meaningful work. She had had a successful career in marketing shopping centers. She toyed with the idea of becoming a career counselor, since, she says, she loved guiding people and providing information—something her Web site allows her to do in a variety of ways.

Her transition started when two job opportunities fell through (shoulder surgery prevented one move, and a new shopping center was sold before she could take the job). She recalls, "The stress from the death of my father, my surgery, and the disappointment about the jobs all just put me over the edge. Finally, I put a sign on my door that said, 'Stop Struggling. Let Things Unfold.'"

She also began to visualize herself putting her marketing talents to work for, perhaps, a nonprofit organization, such as a university or a science museum. She felt drawn to make her mark in education, art, or science. "It was around this time that I couldn't stop the flow of creativity. My ideas for soulfulliving.com just came pouring out. I was consumed! A month later I was offered a terrific job and a great promotion within my industry by an old boss, who treats me with a great deal of kindness and respect. This allowed me to pay the bills and still have time to develop the Web site.

"I launched my Web site in January. It dawned on me one day that I have *created* my meaningful work. And, oooh, does it feel good! I believe I have found my soulful purpose—to create and share what

I am most passionate about in life: soulful living. All my life experiences have led me right here. The bottom line for me has been to stop struggling and planning, and concentrate on what I want, and let life happen!"

HEEDING THE CALL FOR BALANCE IN WORK AND FAMILY LIFE

ANOTHER STORY of using visualization to effect change comes from a woman I shall call Fran, who is vice president of human resources for a family-owned food business. She sent me an e-mail about the positive effects she has experienced in keeping her vision on the outcome she wanted. She says that for years business was uppermost in her mind. She attended every business seminar and meeting that was offered and threw herself into excelling at her work. "I can't put my finger on exactly when the change came about, because it took place over several years. I just knew that my work was no longer fulfilling me completely, and that I needed balance."

VISUALIZING THE DESIRED RESULTS

FRAN BEGAN to feel a strong urge to be with her children when they came home from school. She started to visualize them jumping off the school bus into her arms. "The biggest part of the change was in how I went about bringing my desire for fewer hours at work to my father and brothers. It was in the 'how' that I could see a change in myself. One day it just felt like the right time to bring up the subject of changing my schedule.

"Instead of going to their offices with a teary, emotional appeal in which I would lose my power, I typed a very professional, succinct letter. I expressed my desire to be home with my boys and said that I wanted them to be in my care rather than a baby-sitter's. I asked for a meeting with both my father and my brothers, because I knew that we had to discuss my salary and how a reduction in hours would affect them. I expressed my appreciation for their commitment to the business and, since I was aware they would be working more than I, I asked for their understanding and mutual respect.

"The morning of the meeting, I began to send my love to the office, so that when I got there I would, in a sense, already 'be there.' My spirit told me to state my desire simply and then be quiet. So that is what I did." The meeting turned out to be even more positive than she had expected. Not only did her family agree to her shortened schedule but her father let her retain her full-time salary.

THANK GOD IN ADVANCE

"SIX MONTHS before, my spiritual mentor told me, 'Fran, if working fewer hours is a desire of your heart, then thank the universe for it in advance.' So as often as I could remember, I would thank God for being able to be with my boys more. I would visualize them getting off the bus and running to the porch, where I would be waiting for them. So it was just a matter of time before what was already happening at a spiritual level manifested itself in front of my eyes. I was a part of making that happen!"

An important point to remember is that you should enjoy the visualization process. It won't have much effect if you do it dryly, without a feeling of happiness.

Be Present—It's Your Life

THE AUTHOR Angeles Arrien writes and teaches about the fourfold path of the shaman (a shaman in this case represents the wise person, one who is self-aware and authentic in expression). According to Arrien, life changes tend to align us with our true path when we do four things: (1) show up authentically in life; (2) pay attention to our feelings, intuitions, and external synchronicities; (3) tell the truth about what we really want; and (4) let go of forcing things to happen in a certain way.

SHOWING UP

THERE IS a different quality to our lives when we are really being ourselves, feeling relaxed, happy, and confident. We show up in life when we know who we are and are engaged in what we are doing. We show up when we really care about something, or when we give our best effort. We don't show up when we are overworked, distracted, resentful, jealous, or fearful of the unknown. We don't show up when we try to *look* as if we are there but do just enough to get by; when we hope that nobody notices that we are not really listening or not fully participating. When we are in a frame of mind that says, This doesn't really count, or I'm just putting in time here, we may be resisting a move into the unknown. We are putting up with something rather than seeing change as beneficial. Why rock the boat, when we're already barely functioning or suppressing our desires?

In what area of life are you really showing up? In what areas of life are you merely putting on a good show?

PAY ATTENTION

PAYING ATTENTION is an attitude of expectant discovery. Perhaps many of us must first notice where we are *not* paying attention, or when we are "tuning out." Generally when we are not showing up in our lives, we also are not paying very much attention to what is actually happening inside us. We feel bored, fatigued, depressed, helpless, or confused. By paying more attention to ourselves and our situation, we begin to empower ourselves. Paying attention allows solutions to become apparent or possible. If we resist our intuitive knowing, we don't really pay attention to those feelings that tell us, This job doesn't fit anymore. I really want to take a creative writing class. Or, It's time to stop the merry-go-round and do something that means more than just existing. Ask yourself, What is on the back burner of my mind? What was that dream I had when I was twelve, or twenty, or thirty? In order to move forward, you must notice what information, idea, or feeling is trying to get your attention *now*—or has been for a while.

Another way to pay attention is to make the decision to notice what catches your attention during the day. Do you tend to read newspaper articles about people who are saving the rain forest or making medical breakthroughs? What do these items suggest for your own life? What kernel of truth might be beckoning to you as a significant indicator of your life purpose?

To increase your ability to pay attention, put yourself "on assignment." Ask a direct question, such as Where should I be focusing my attention these days? Begin to keep a record of things each day that pique your curiosity, make you laugh, or intrigue you, even in the most subtle ways. Your inner guidance system knows how to find the answers you want if it is given a good, strong question.

Notice who you tend to think about during the day. Imagine that there is a reason you thought of this person, and follow through with a quick call or note. You never know why something is being called to your attention, but life becomes more of an adventure when we stop, look, and listen to our surroundings. Your decision to be awake and present in life is one of the most important ways you can stay connected to spiritual guidance. The enlightened person—the shaman—knows that there are no accidents, and that the trail we tread is alive with information if we take the time to look behind the obvious.

TELL THE TRUTH

TO MOVE forward, you first must tell the truth about what you really want. Only then can you begin to attract the right opportunities. We spend a lot of time talking about what we don't want. Over and over again we tell our stories in forms that define us in limiting ways. For example, we've all heard ourselves say something like, "I don't know what I want to do." "I'm stuck in this situation." "I don't know where to start." "If I had money, things would be different." "I have too many responsibilities to just go off and do something different." "I never finish anything." "I'm too impatient." "I'm really frustrated." "It's hard for me to take action." We focus only on the problem as we see it, giving that problem authority over our spirits. The problem becomes the justification for not moving ahead.

When you travel, you have a destination, such as New York City, in mind. You buy a plane ticket or drive there. Your desire to go to New York City is realized through your *intention* to reach your destination. If, however, you say, "I want to go to New York, but I'm too afraid to fly." "The trip will cost too much." "It's too many miles to drive all the way across the country." "Maybe I'll go someday, when . . ." or "I would go, but my boss would never give me that much time off," you are *diluting* or *negating* your intention and will never get there.

We often tell similar stories about moving into the unknown: "I don't know what I'm passionate about." "I don't know what I like to

do." "I'm just trying to pay the rent right now." "I don't have the luxury of finding my true life purpose." Or "I've just retired; I don't
want to get tied down again." Or "I want to get married, but I never
meet any men [or women]."

Perhaps when we were children we received sympathy for being
helpless, or we made ourselves small and insignificant to escape
unwanted attention. Part of our current tendency to stay small or
invisible or to blame others for our failure to move forward is
rooted in this old behavior. When we complain and say pessimistic
things about life, other people may try to cheer us up. So being
negative can become a habit for getting attention without risking
doing anything. Because our self-esteem is low, we tend to think
that only special people achieve success. Or we may be waiting for
some magical piece of information that will make our life purpose
clear. This type of thinking, based more on buying into limitations
than exploring possibilities, keeps us feeling helpless, waiting for
the magic bullet of clarity to hit us before we make *any* moves. We
justify inaction through the excuse of confusion.

Sometimes in my workshops, just to be the devil's advocate, I will
ask a person who says she doesn't know what she wants to do if she
wants to be a truck driver. Does she want to be a chief executive
officer? A mother's helper? A camel driver?

Usually people know very well what they *don't* want to do, so the
reality is that we *do* have some idea of what we want, but we avoid
admitting it for fear we won't be able to make it happen. We are
afraid to make a decision because we see it as an end result that we
will be stuck with forever, forgetting that we keep making choices
throughout our lives. How we tell our stories determines how open
we are to making, or even anticipating, positive changes.

LET GO OF CONTROL

SO FAR, then, you have showed up, paid attention, and told the
truth—which includes taking right action based on your best
understanding and perceptions. At this stage you must learn to let
go of trying to control the outcomes of your actions and trust that
you will know what to do next as you continue to pay attention.
When you send out your résumé, you cannot control where it will
land or how it will be received. When you pop the question, you

don't know if your loved one will dash your hopes or laugh with joy. Whatever the outcome, if your decision or action arose from your best guess or most truthful feeling, you have done the best you can do. The path will continue to unfold—*in its own time*—and you will continue to gather more information for your next decision at your next crossroad. Notice the sense of relief that comes when you realize outcomes are not up to you!

Notice How You Tell Your Story

IN THE poem by Rumi at the beginning of this chapter, the craftsman has already pulled you from the reed bed and cut holes into you. Your holes—a metaphor for your talents and experiences—are what make you uniquely you. Are you lamenting or singing?

A woman named Sue expressed to me her dissatisfaction with her work in the computer industry as a documentation analyst, editor, and designer. She was confused about what she is best suited to do and how to find work in that area. Our correspondence is a good synopsis of how many of us tell a story that keeps us stuck. I have condensed our e-mail dialogue, which occurred over a week's time, and added brief captions to highlight certain points.

RESTLESSNESS AND YEARNING ARE PART OF THE CHANGE PROCESS

Sue: I feel that my destiny is something other than "the ordinary," and the thought of going back into the "money-as-the-bottom-line" corporate workplace fills me with horror and dread. I have never related to the corporate world.

CA: A lot of people feel that they get lost in the corporate machinery. If we want to move forward we need to be able to define what matters to us—even in a general way. What do we want? When we have an idea of what feels good to us, we have something to compare with when opportunities come. Of course, we may also attract opportunities that we never would have been able to imagine, and that's really exciting.

Your statement [about the corporate workplace] is setting a very clear intention for what you don't want. Remember, our unconscious hears all our statements as definitions of what we are focusing on and, therefore, creating. *It does not hear the words "don't want."* It responds only to where we are directing our energy. Therefore, this statement about corporations is sending energy to what you do not want—a dreaded job where the only goal is to make money or else!

LEAN INTO THE RESISTANCE

CA: Let's start with your comment that corporate work fills you with horror and dread. This is kind of interesting. Something about the force of your statement makes me think that your fear about getting trapped in the corporate world is part of a larger fear that is paralyzing you.

One way to get moving on the path might be to go in the direction of your fear. I'm wondering if there is something you need to learn here. Maybe taking a short-term job in a corporation would allow you to resolve your feelings rather than run away. If you chose to work in that type of job, it would be done out of choice rather than making you feel trapped. What if you were to take on a job like that and use it as a mindful spiritual practice just for a certain amount of time—perhaps one year?

Sue: That's a very interesting and inspired suggestion! I smiled a big smile and tingled when I read it. I think you are absolutely right. It resonated with me as well. This gives my job hunt a new meaning.

ACKNOWLEDGE WHO YOU ARE

Sue: I consider myself an artist, both in the sense that I am driven to articulate my inner world (in whatever context that may be) and in the sense that I enjoy creating visually pleasing things out of different media.

CA: Okay. Now you are stating who you are and what turns you on. How much time are you giving to those artistic expressions in your

life? Are you writing? Photographing? Painting? Making a collage to
attract what you want? Are you learning some new artistic form
(ceramics, singing)?

BE SPECIFIC IF IT MAKES YOU FEEL GOOD
WHEN YOU SAY IT

Sue: My sense is I need to give my artistic interests more time and
be around more people I can share them with. Perhaps even rent
some studio space!

I have a deep love for living things, especially animals and green
areas, and in fact would somehow like to facilitate the well-being of
living things.

CA: Could you be more specific? What are three things that you
could do to make money by taking care of animals or property?

Sue: Wow . . . probably choosing just three will be a challenge! I'm
going to look up suggestions in a book I have that lists careers. I
also consider myself a writer-communicator as well as a designer
(giving beautiful form to function) and would like somehow to
make the world a better place.

CA: So now you've articulated several specific areas that you're
good at—and one general desire ("somehow to make the world a
better place"). Only you can know how you feel about your specific
talents, e.g., to be a writer. Do you feel really good when you say
that, or do you feel sheepish because you haven't written anything
in a long while or you haven't been published yet? The feeling tone
underlying your statements is how you feel about yourself. If you
feel somewhat insecure, your intention will be lessened. After all,
why would your unconscious want you to attract something that
makes you feel insecure?

It's best to make *general* statements about how you want to
change your life until you can feel really strongly about the
specifics. For example, "My income is increasing steadily, and I
love all my work." Keep taking small steps that make you feel
good about yourself. In a sense, whatever activity we do—
whether it's building an opera house or giving shelter to a kit-
ten—gives us a chance to change the world. We change the world

by sending out or radiating a positive attitude about ourselves and showing compassion for others. I suggest that you focus on what you love to do rather than worry about how to make the world a better place.

Sue: Good point! That resonated very much. I think that "do-good-ing" for the sake of it—if it does not include something you love—can be kind of empty, although well-intentioned. I am driven to teach or somehow pass on my knowledge and experiences.

CA: Again, can you make this desire a little more specific? Would you see yourself teaching children? Adults? Play with this a bit. If someone gave you a fifty-thousand-dollar grant to teach, what would you want to do with it? What kind of scene do you see your-self in? What would it take for you to educate or certify yourself in order to do some form of education—or community—work?

Sue: Okay! More investigations! I enjoy helping to create the best solutions to problems. Okay, so I know all that, but I don't know what to do with it. My main problem is and has always been lack of action.

AVOID DECLARATIVE STATEMENTS THAT DO NOT SERVE YOU

CA: This sounds like one of your primary beliefs—that your main problem is and *has always been* lack of action. This is a declarative statement that is not serving you. Not only are you sending lots of energy to a limiting belief but you are *eternalizing* it ("is and has always been"). I'm sure you have taken many, many, many actions in this month alone, but you prefer to think of yourself and define yourself as not taking action.

Sue: You're right! Good grief! I have a *really* hard time translating anything into action.

CA: Beliefs die hard, don't they? Your last statement *really* empha-sizes your belief that you don't take action! Your point of view here is also focused in the past. You describe what you don't want and why you can't move forward but don't mention how eager you might be to explore a few things that might be really juicy, fun things to do.

Sue: Hmm. I'm not sure I understand. I do know that I have not pursued any nonprofit work or anything that might give me satisfaction along the lines of my true path . . . whatever that is!

CA: At this point, don't worry about what your "true path" is, because you will be tempted to fix on one thing prematurely. You are currently in the "explore and experiment stage." Your purpose for *now* is to relax, explore, and enjoy what life has to offer. Why not approach this period as simply a time for making new choices—not with a long-term commitment in mind?

It's a good idea to keep a journal during this period. Just quick notes before bed or in the morning. Every day write a clear statement, such as "I want clear directions that are in line with my life path." If you have the idea that you need to take a class or get a degree, make a date by which you will have gathered all the information about it, so that you are prepared to make a decision by the time the class or program begins.

Become more aware of your negative declarative statements. If you write them down when you hear yourself saying them, you will see what your limiting beliefs are, and how they are a lens through which you see yourself and life. Begin to play with rewording them to give yourself support. For example, "My problem is I never take action" could be reframed into "I'm beginning to trust myself to act when it feels right."

STAY WITH THE PROCESS—DON'T LOOK FOR ONE "BIG ANSWER"

CA: The first part of the change comes from seeing what behavior and language and beliefs we are using to create our "reality." The second part of change happens as we begin listening for new insights or ideas. Third, taking action on these ideas moves us forward. The fourth step is taking in the feedback, assessing, and continuing to listen. It's a process that you will never get to the end of. Moving into the unknown is a process, not a destination.

VOLUNTEER AND EXPERIMENT

CA: If you haven't got a clue as to how to get the wheels in motion, start gathering information. Make exploration your intention. For example, check out what's available at volunteer agencies. This is a low-risk way of giving yourself choices to find out what feels good. Or try putting an ad in the newspaper. Write your own job description. If nothing else, it's a great way to express your intention on paper.

Sue: That's a good idea! For as long as I can remember, I have been full of tangible, intense, killing frustration.

CA: "Killing frustration" sounds pretty daunting. Have you gone over this ground with a professional therapist to locate your role models for frustration? Frustration might be a way of stifling yourself, keeping yourself small so you'll be safe.

Sue: I am in fact seeing a therapist at the moment. I haven't heard the statements you just made expressed in quite that way before, though. They hit the mark for me. I'll bring them up with him. . . . I've been trying to fit myself into molds that aren't me.

CA: I understand how frustrated you have felt. This is the work of individuation, of finding out who we are instead of who we agreed to be to please others. It sounds like the time has come to work on these beliefs.

STOP TRYING TO SOLVE IT; INSTEAD, OPEN TO THE UNEXPECTED

CA: I suspect that you feel blocked for two reasons. One is you're afraid of making a mistake, so you do nothing. Two is that you are operating under the fallacy that there is only one right answer to your question. You feel blocked because you don't yet see your path as one of continual exploration. It helps to remember that there is no one right result.

Sue: I do feel I have been working on my beliefs for a while. Is it necessarily a slow process? It feels like it is for me! I haven't been following my true path (whatever that is!). *Help!* [Sue repeats

once again the self-limiting judgment that she has not been following her path and doesn't recognize what it is.]

CA: You know, we always think we should be moving ahead faster
than we are. I see nothing wrong with a slow process. In fact, we
will only move or change at the pace that we can handle anyway.
Give yourself permission to be absolutely as slow as possible and
see how that feels.

Your life is an unfolding path. What you are working on at this
stage (which seems to be a time for healing some of your beliefs)
will be outgrown once you become less self-critical. Of course, new
situations will come along with whole new sets of complexities.
That's neither good nor bad—just more learning, and it's up to you
to make decisions to do things you enjoy.

Sue: Yes, I see. That is just . . . great! I'm excited about doing this.
Actually, intellectually I do see my path as one of continual explo-
ration, but I haven't surrendered to that yet. But I'm working at it!
Thank you.

IF SOMETHING IS IN ALIGNMENT
WITH YOUR PATH, YOU'LL ATTRACT IT

Some people go through life, but don't ask themselves questions
such as

- Do I want to change?
- What's missing?
- What are my values?
- How can I change direction?

Patty Montgomery, *workshop facilitator*

Write It Down

IN PREVIOUS chapters we have talked about ways to create positive change: (1) *visualizing* what you want to produce feelings
of joy and happiness; and (2) *using positive language* that

expresses what we want. Another powerful practice is writing down what you want. Most of us have made lists of what we wanted when we were hunting for a house or a new job—or drafting a personals ad! List making is the simplest form of using writing to create change. The next step might be to describe specific future scenarios that please you. This adds a *feeling tone,* which energizes the ideas on the list. It lets the universe know *why* you want what you want. Last, you can create an *action list* of things to do or investigate. An action or task list does two things. First, it engages the logical mind. Second, it helps free the mind from the general anxiety that arises before you see any manifestation of what you want.

During times of transition it's helpful to deliberately increase your focus on how you want to feel after the transition. Writing down what you want helps set the stage for all kinds of synchronistic support. You can write every night before falling asleep, in essence turning over the task of creation to the unconscious.

Communicating with yourself by writing in a journal allows your interior, and often neglected or repressed, voices to be heard. You can draw these subconscious voices forth by naming them and asking them what they want from you. You might want to take a few minutes once in a while to write in your life changes journal about "What needs to change?" You may be surprised at the ideas and answers that surface.

YOU CAN'T EMPTY THE "IN BASKET"

So many of us live our lives as if the secret purpose is to somehow get everything done.

The nature of your "in basket" is that it's *meant* to have items to be completed in it—it's not meant to be empty.

If I remind myself (frequently) that the purpose of life isn't to get it all done but to enjoy each step along the way and live a life filled with love, it's far easier for me to control my obsession with completing my list of things to do.

Richard Carlson, *Don't Sweat the Small Stuff . . . and It's All Small Stuff*

The trick is not to be bound to your task list by a sense of guilt when you don't get everything done. Actually, you will never get everything on your list done, because life is a continuous process of creating new desires and flowing with an evolving direction. However, writing ideas down is a powerful tool for directing that flow. Many of the most successful people write their goals as a way to focus their attention. Some people mention that having the list on paper takes it out of their heads and frees the mind. Mental freedom helps keep us open to new developments that may be better than the way we were originally going about accomplishing our goals. The point is not to be so task-oriented that there is no space for spontaneous events to happen. For example, if your child gets sick at school, you will probably have to cancel any meetings and attend to that new priority—or find a way that feels right to take care of it. The wise person sees any interruption as a purposeful event that arises to bring something important to our attention. To feel that you are in sync with your life as it changes, you should not be beating yourself up at the end of the day for what you haven't done. The more you can stay in the flow of the present moment, the richer your life is going to be.

Describing in detail what you want as if you already had it—and how you will feel when you have it—sends a powerful message to your subconscious, creative mind that you take these ideas seriously. Be sure to write in present time, using delightfully vivid and descriptive phrases. For example, if you are looking for a new place to live, write as if you were sitting in the chair of your new home, sipping tea and enjoying the sunset after a day of gardening. Write a steamy letter to your soul mate, and tell him how much you look forward to meeting him and creating adventures together! Make the dominant theme your *joy and excitement* rather than how quickly you expect something to show up.

Your writing should uplift you with joyful expectancy, and your best attitude is trusting that what you desire is already on the way.

What changes do you want to promote in your life? In your neighborhood? In the world? Write them down; watch them happen.

MOVING FROM THE COMPETITIVE MIND TO THE CREATIVE MIND

A person can form things in his thought, and by impressing his thought upon formless substance can cause the thing he thinks about to be created. In order to do this, a person must pass from the competitive to the creative mind. Otherwise he cannot be in harmony with formless intelligence, which is always creative and never competitive in spirit.

Gratitude unifies the mind with the intelligence of substance, so that [a person's] thoughts are received by the formless.

Too much stress cannot be laid on the importance of frequent contemplation of the mental image, coupled with unwavering faith and devout gratitude.

Wallace D. Wattles, *The Science of Getting Rich*

Make a Vision Board

WHEN WE "program" our unconscious with powerful visual symbols, such as collages, we accelerate the process of attraction. For example, Melanie Jones assembled a collection of magazine images and words to help her create her dream. Melanie left a corporate sales job because her heart wasn't in it anymore. She now works in schools in a program she created called Speak to the Children. She says, "About ten months before I left my sales job, I made a huge 'vision board' out of three cardboard panels about five feet by three feet. One of the first statements I put there is 'I'm ready for a change.' And 'The adventure is about to begin.' I also liked the statement, 'Take your life into your own hands.' To me, the vision board is like a story you are telling yourself. You get to write a wonderful new story! I firmly believe that putting my thoughts into words and pictures has led me to where I am today, including having a great relationship with my boyfriend. Every single thing I cut out pictures for has come into my life. I keep adding new pictures of wonderful scenes of travel, people, and children."

Vision boards and collages allow parts of ourselves to express our deepest yearnings beyond simple list making or what our logical minds tell us is possible. For example, a man named Joe, in his late fifties, came to one of my workshops. A big change in Joe's life had occurred the year before, when he put his wife into a group home for Alzheimer's patients. As he looks ahead to the next few years, he is beginning to develop a new cross-cultural project fostering dialogue among a variety of community leaders worldwide. His collage expressed what is important to him right now through images of people working together, as well as through words such as *truth, choices, special places,* and *unique people.* He found a picture of a lovely seated woman to represent his wife (he also could have used her actual picture). The title for his collage was *Eternal Man Woman.*

Henry, another attendee of the seminar, was a Catholic priest deciding whether to leave his ministry. His emerging vision is to become a professor, and perhaps marry and have a family. He called his collage *Soft and Strong*. Each picture he selected expressed his yearning for organization (images of bookcases), love (a beautiful woman), speed (a fast car), a warm home, and a good relationship (two people standing together).

Other collage titles from our group were *Light, Air, and Action; The Good Life; Boundless; Focusing in on Me; The Art of Living; Self-Remade CEO; To Marry a Musician;* and *Home.*

THE COMPLETE RESULT

In conceiving what you want, be sure to describe the complete result. This means the whole picture, including the circumstances surrounding its manifestation.

In one workshop a woman said she wanted to be more spontaneous. When I asked her if she had any doubts about having more spontaneity, she thought for a moment and said, "Yes, if I were spontaneous, I'm afraid people wouldn't like me."

"So you want two things," I said. "You want to be spontaneous and you want people to like you. Is that more accurately the result you want?"

> Without hesitation she said, "Why yes! That's exactly what I want. I never thought of it that way."
>
> When creating a vision of what you want, it is important to be in the habit of conceiving the whole picture, not just a small part of it. Therefore, include in your vision what you want to create, the circumstances and qualities of what you want to create, and the full context in which you want it to appear.
>
> Robert Fritz, *The Path of Least Resistance*

Pray

THE OLDEST form of holding one's vision may be praying. Praying is the timeless practice of communicating our wants and needs, our fears and concerns, and our gratitude to our spiritual connection. Prayer is universal, and there is no one way to pray. According to a national survey commissioned by the Unity School of Christianity, 79 percent of Americans believe that prayer and meditation can positively influence their physical health. Eighty-eight percent believe prayer and meditation can have a positive effect on their emotional health.

Rosemary Ellen Guiley's book, *The Miracle of Prayer: True Stories of Blessed Healings,* presents amazing stories of answered prayers. She writes, "The word *prayer* itself means 'to petition,' coming from the Latin term *precarius,* which means 'obtained by begging.' Most of us make petitionary prayers on an almost daily basis, informally, whenever we want something to go right in life or when we want something to change."

The motivation behind prayer may play a role in the results. Guiley cites Daniel J. Benor, a psychiatrist, healer, and leading researcher in alternative healing, who sees three levels of prayer. He says, "The first is an assertion of our will: 'Heal, dammit, heal.' The second is prayer that attempts to understand illness and its underlying causes, and to learn the spiritual lessons from that. The third level of prayer is surrender to God's will." Benor as well as other experts on the power of prayer, such as Drs. Larry Dossey and Bernie Siegel, agree that no one way of praying is more effective than another. If we pray, not just about our own concerns but for the healing of all sentient beings, our prayers may even have more effect.

Prayer connects us to All That Is. When we quietly offer ourselves with humility, gratitude, and trust that all our needs will be met, we are praying. Most of the time we pray for something, but prayer might also be a time of simply sitting still and feeling our inner connection to something larger than ourselves.

Our prayers are fields of energy that go out into the universe, affecting circumstances and people, just by our simple act of thinking about them. Our prayers signal to higher beings in the spiritual realm that we are in need of aid. The response to our call comes in the form of synchronicities.

A woman named Rebecca wrote me to share an encounter with a stranger named Bob, who seemed to come into her life at just the right time to give her a message about the importance of prayer and love. She had just been reading about prayer fields and their effects in James Redfield's novel *The Secret of Shambhala,* a sequel to *The Celestine Prophecy.*

Rebecca says, "My fiancé and I have recently embarked on a new adventure together. We are partners in a small bar and grill, something I have always dreamed of doing. We took our chances and created our dream knowing that it would be long hours, hard work, and a great deal of responsibility. The money and success didn't flow immediately!

"I was feeling discouraged, stressed, frustrated, lonely, and fearful of being unsuccessful. One Saturday afternoon business was very slow, and I was tending the bar. A man walked in whom I had never seen before. He sat down with two of the regulars, and I began to listen in on the conversation. Half an hour later they left, and only the man remained. He said his name was Bob, and he began to tell me how incredible his life was becoming. At first, I really didn't want to hear any of that because I was caught up in my own fears and a bit jealous. He told me how he had started working for a very wealthy man, moving his furniture, fixing up his house, et cetera. After about a year of his doing odd jobs for this man, the man sent him to school to learn corporate financing. After Bob finished the course, the man hired him into his company because, he told Bob, he liked his enthusiasm.

"Bob said that within the year he was going to become a millionaire. He couldn't believe that all this was happening to him and was still astounded and in shock. Once, when he was very poor, he told his mother that one day he would buy her a house, and now he can!

"I told him about starting my own business, and my feelings of being a bit overwhelmed. He congratulated me on my upcoming marriage and told me that I could get through anything as long as I have love in my life. Bob also said that the greatest thing that got him through his troubled times and that brought him to this point in his life was prayer. My heart skipped a beat," Rebecca writes. "A few days before, I had started reading *The Secret of Shambhala* and was beginning to understand about prayer fields. Bob told me to keep praying and to keep love in my life. His words accentuated the truths in the book. I knew this was a synchronicity, and it opened me to a part of myself that I had been missing for quite some time. This complete stranger woke me up!"

RISK THE UNKNOWN

There is risk, but life itself is risk. For a higher life there will be higher risks. You move on a dangerous path. But remember, there is only one error in life, and that is not moving at all; that is, just afraid, sitting; just afraid that if you move something may go wrong. . . . This is the only error. You will not be in danger but no growth will be possible.

Osho, *The Path of Yoga*

The novel *The Secret of Shambhala* describes beautifully the power of prayer, and the main character learns how to control and strengthen his energy field. According to Redfield, there are four levels or extensions of our energy fields, which can not only affect our own situations but in small or large ways can also effect positive change on the entire human race.

FIRST LEVEL

IN THE first extension, through experience we realize that this energy is real. We begin to notice that our prayers are often answered. As we grow in spiritual understanding, we realize that each of us exists within a field of living energy that connects us all.

We actively desire to improve the quality of our personal energy field, by nourishing ourselves with pure food, good thoughts, positive expectations, and a desire to contribute to the betterment of conditions wherever we find ourselves. We make changes in our lives, such as Rebecca and her fiancé did, in moving toward what attracts us—a new business, a new field of investigation, or other arenas of self-improvement. A sign that we are in a higher state is seeing beauty in our surroundings and feeling connected to something larger than ourselves. Our behavior becomes more loving, understanding, open, and responsible.

SECOND LEVEL

IN THE second extension, we deeply desire to move with the synchronicity of life. We enhance this level by staying in a state of conscious awareness of signs, messages, information, or opportunities. Our prayer energy field extends even further as we align with universal flow. Because we are consciously looking for signs and signals from universal intelligence, our flow state increases.

THIRD LEVEL

IN THE third extension, we automatically expect that the best course is to keep our energy as positive as possible, both for ourselves and for others. Instead of feeling that we need to control people and circumstances, we are more willing and able to go with the flow, trusting that a better plan is working out, with better timing than what we had originally thought. When we encounter others, we realize that it is in our best interest—and the others'—to be uplifting in our attitude. When we extend our energy in a positive way in *any* interaction, each person involved automatically has easier access to his or her higher intelligence.

FOURTH LEVEL

THE FOURTH extension happens when we do two things simultaneously. First, we must maintain our positive outflow of energy, even in angry or frightening situations. This ability involves setting the tone for ourselves *before we get embroiled,* rather than letting others' moods or behaviors set the tone for us.

Second, this extension involves something of a paradox. We must be able to maintain an attitude of neutrality toward results while still trusting and *expecting* that the process is working for our highest good at all times. It is like saying, I'm hungry and want an apple, but I'll be willing to eat whatever shows up. Even without immediate fulfillment, we are able to maintain a positive expectation that the process is working.

> ## CHANGE IS JUST ANOTHER PATCH
>
> The Amish keep the borders of their quilts closed. Mine must remain open.
>
> If the quilt is to come to life, if my life is to come to life, I must leave room for the unexpected.
>
> The biggest surprise—and it came as a great revelation—was understanding that whatever happens, no matter how catastrophic or wonderful, it's just another patch.
>
> Sue Bender, *Plain and Simple*

Trust requires that we maintain our intention for success in the face of a present moment that does not look like what we want. For example, you want a mate, but at present you are not even dating. The tendency here is to fixate on the fact that there is nobody in your life (that's what the present moment looks like). However, by fixating on what is lacking, according to the Law of Attraction, you will attract more lack. This attention on lack creates a negative prayer field. At the fourth level, you learn to hold the vision of what you want in the face of the contradictory reality without losing your positive anticipation.

Sometimes we notice that change happens (for example, we

meet our mates) when we least expect it. This occurs when we have not been focusing on the lack of a mate in our lives. Lessening the worry-victim vibration allows our original desire to be met. The spiritual challenge is to continue with our prayer extensions while avoiding critical thoughts about ourselves, others, or our situation. Our spiritual helpers, angels, and guides cannot inspire us or help us when we radiate negativity.

CONCENTRATION

Concentration is like a diamond, a brilliant focusing of our energy, intelligence, and sensitivity. When we concentrate fully, the light of our abilities shines forth in many colors, radiating through all that we do. Our energy gains a momentum and clarity that allows us to perform each task quickly and with ease, and we respond to the challenges work offers with pleasure and enthusiasm.

Tarthang Tulku, *Skillful Means*

My friend Dianne Aigaki recently accompanied five Tibetan high lamas on a teaching and healing tour in the United States. She kept me informed of some of their engagements, which included creating sacred sand mandalas, conducting meditations, and demonstrating a variety of sacred art techniques. Most interesting were the healing ceremonies conducted for people who were quite ill. For example, one woman explained that she had cancerous tumors in her brain, liver, and other organs. She had not pursued allopathic treatment and was extremely ill. Dianne suggested that she create a strong support circle for herself by bringing to the ceremony as many of her positive friends and family as she could.

On the day of the healing, the senior lama began by asking the woman *why* she wanted to be healed. To what would she dedicate her life if she regained her health? he asked. The monk explained that she would not necessarily be healed of her illness unless she included in her request healing for *all* who suffer. He explained that it was most important that she not ask for these blessings just for herself or even her family but that she widen her request for compassion to include all beings.

A week after the ceremony the woman's doctor could find no malignancies in her brain or her liver, and the only remaining tumor had shrunk to a small dissolving spot.

It might be inferred from healing stories that if healing does not occur there is something wrong, or we have not "prayed right." During illness we must remember to be compassionate with ourselves. Regret and blame are not healing vibrations. We must always remember that there is a time for everything. There is a time for healing and a time for letting go. We may pray for someone to be healed and instead she dies because her time has come to leave this plane of existence. Death is not a failure but a rebirth into spirit. When we love people and want to assist them, we can always pray for them to receive what is in their highest good. We can pray that their suffering be lessened and ask for whatever is right for them to come into their lives.

Books on vibrational healing, such as Larry Dossey's, *Healing Words,* Deepak Chopra's *Quantum Healing,* and Bernie Siegel's *Love, Medicine, and Miracles,* document many case studies on directed, heartfelt prayer. According to Rupert Sheldrake, author of controversial books on the collective mind such as *A New Science of Life* and *The Presence of the Past,* there are universal morphogenetic fields that are extensions of our individual minds, accumulations of mental ideas and behavioral patterns. Sheldrake hypothesizes that these patterns organize mental fields, accounting for simultaneous discoveries and inventions as well as evolutionary shifts in human and animal consciousness. These fields function as connections between people, animals, and the nonphysical world. Sheldrake posits that prayer works within these mental fields. We might ponder the idea that our own individual life changes may be triggered by or linked to evolutionary life changes in the whole human race.

Stir the Pot

ANY TIME you are researching a subject, making calls on behalf of someone you know, or checking in with people you haven't talked to in a while, you are stirring the universal pot, which will eventually deliver exactly what you need. If you have a goal, put it in front of you, and give life (or the morphogenetic fields!) a chance to fulfill it.

DEVELOP A MAGNETIC CENTER

The influences that come our way are in large measure determined by the magnetic centers we develop within ourselves. For example, if we want material success, we would develop a magnetic center capable of bringing more opportunities for financial growth.

The way we spend our focused time—the groups we belong to, the hobbies we pursue, the films we watch, and the literature we read—establishes the frequencies to which each of our magnetic centers is tuned.

If we are immersing ourselves in superficial, mindless activities, we will attract lower-frequency influences that may keep us asleep.

David Samuel, *Practical Mysticism*

If you are looking for a major life change—a new job, new apartment, new dancing partner, or a ride to Las Vegas on a certain day, why not put a small classified advertisement in a local newspaper? State exactly what you are looking for, and see what happens. Use your intuition when and if you receive a response, and also do some logical left-brain checking to make sure your incoming information or contact is on the up and up. Posting your need in the newspaper is a powerful affirmation and intention statement, even though what you want may ultimately come from a completely different avenue. Stirring the pot in one area activates your entire life field—since all life is interrelated.

Cherish the Gift of Life

THINK OF the most precious things in your life. Are they seemingly dichotomies, such as material comfort *and* spiritual development? Freedom *and* security? Routine *and* adventure? Family relationships *and* personal time? At the root of each pair is a connection to what matters most to you. As you feel that connection, you are in touch with deeper levels of life.

Yearning, longing, intending, and desiring bring forth new life energy. When you feel your connection to others, to nature, to beauty, you are in touch with your spiritual roots. These times are the seedbeds of your next life stage. Your beliefs and thoughts are the roots of the next experience, and the routes of life and change.

Cherishing what you already have opens your heart. If you are looking to make positive changes, take care of yourself in the smallest ways. Your unconscious stores everything you encounter or learn—*even when you don't know you know*. Your intrapsychic repository will provide exactly the right inspiration, solution, or comment *when the time comes*. All the ideas and stories that you have read in this book, and all the books that you have ever read, are available to you without your having to do anything else. Every experience, every conversation changes you.

Make time to imagine your vision. Enhance the feeling by listening to your favorite music, whether it is a love song, a symphony, the meditative sound of a waterfall, or the singing vibration of a Tibetan bowl. Feed your inspiration by reading great literature, or revisit a movie that reveals the change of a character over time as he or she follows what has heart and meaning. Be still. Open to the mystery.

SEEKING PLEASURE

The wind blows across my bare arm
the hairs move, touch each other, stand up even!
the air flows down the corridors of my arm-hair forest,
sending ten thousand tiny gusts of wind-turned-nerve-waves
through me
and if I pay attention I wonder
is this coolness?
is this pain?
is this overwhelming?
is this soothing, or chaotic, or pleasure?

or is this
a me I didn't know?
If I stay and follow
I go to the start of wind
and where the wind winds up:
home

Penney Peirce

6

❦

Watch for Answers

And it may also turn out that in searching for this one bit of information, something else will turn up that you absolutely could not have known would be out there waiting for you.

ANNE LAMOTT,
Bird by Bird

Align with Guidance

WE KNOW that life moves in mysterious ways, and as we awaken to that mystery, we sense that it moves *us* for a purpose. To align with our purpose, we continuously look and listen for universal wisdom and directional signals.

If you are wondering what your next step is, ask to be given clear signs. The musician Steve Cooper, for example, almost seems to have a conversation with life in everyday synchronicities, such as the following "license-plate messages." Steve writes, "My health insurance company went bankrupt last week, and I had a meeting with an agent to get different coverage. As I was driving away, I was wondering if the company would decide to insure me. A few minutes later I saw that the car in front of me had the license plate INSURED. A few minutes later I heard on the car radio what a bad day the stock market had. I thought this might be the end of a long bull market. Within a minute, I saw a plate that read BULL MRKT.

"The third instance that day related to my having been looking for a production company at a theater where I'm putting on a concert. I looked it up on the Internet but couldn't find it. I looked under the name Center East Theater but couldn't find anything. As I was driving home, I saw the plate CENT N RE (I don't know what the car owner meant by that), but I realized that the Center East was really spelled Centre East. When I got home I looked it up, and there it was!"

On another day Steve saw two license plates in quick succession. One tag said DOGS and the other said MARY E. The first reminded him that he needed to take his dogs to the vet. The second, that he needed to buy a present for his wife, Mary Ellen. These occurrences could seem rather inconsequential or random. However, when synchronicities become regular phenomena, one has to wonder at our connection to universal intelligence.

Answers Are Everywhere

STEVE COOPER has become a master at asking to receive guidance and finding synchronistic answers everywhere. By following his intuition he has made contacts he could never have accomplished by a logical plan. It may be an advertisement on the radio that gives directions to the business he just happens to be en route to when he's forgotten how to get there. It might be watching a promotional video at a sales meeting, which happens to show the bass player of a band that just that day he wanted to know more about. Other synchronicities have catapulted Steve's career to a new level. Amazing coincidences enabled him to meet people representing the estate of his late musical hero Lawrence Welk. These contacts led to his being offered rare opportunities to study Welk's original arrangements, and even to meet and work with some of the old band members. Steve's synchronicity stories show the magnetic power that lies in being devoted to a passion and maintaining an intention.

These examples may seem insignificant when taken individually. However, every small question we have is a part of our questions about our larger life purpose. Each choice we make changes us and the course of our lives. Our purpose is inextricably woven into the tapestry of everyday actions.

To accelerate the occurrence of synchronicities that could help you make positive changes—especially when you feel stuck—get into the habit of writing down a simple question that has an answer you will be able to recognize when you have received it. Then wait expectantly for relevant information to show up.

GO WHERE THE ENERGY IS

ALIGNING YOURSELF means noticing what lifts your energy and going in that direction. Sometimes the beckoning path is tinged with anxiety or outright fear. However, if you take the time to search your heart and go in the direction of your fear, you will most likely be aligning yourself with your best interests. Life is rich with false starts, regressions, retractions, impulsive moves, first impressions, calculated waiting, and panicked What have I dones? This is all part of the creative flow of life—to be enjoyed, rejoiced in, and wondered at.

> *Cherry blossoms, yes*
> *they're beautiful . . .*
> *but tonight*
> *don't miss the moon!*
>
> So-In

Put More Heart into Where You Are

IT'S HUMAN nature to want something different from what we have. However, it seems that there is always a natural logic to, and reason for, our current situation. Therefore, if you find yourself frustrated by your circumstance, give some thought to *leaning into* the situation rather than resisting it, by putting more heart into what you are doing. You can make friends with the situation exactly as it is, knowing that you are there for a purpose. This practice of acceptance, however, would not apply if your situation is causing you to suffer abuse of any kind.

WORRYING IS NOT THINKING

When I worry, I feel cut off from my life—and this sense of being cut off from life is practically a definition of loneliness.

The future simply cannot be seen with the egoistic or anxious mind. We are on earth to do things that only human beings can do, but none of them can be done until we are able to think as a grown-up man or woman thinks.

Jacob Needleman, *Time and the Soul*

A woman named Ava left her home in the United States and moved to Mexico with her husband. She writes to say that all the time she lived in Mexico City, she kept searching for what her next career would be. Looking in the wrong direction kept her from seeing what was right in front of her. She writes, "When I landed in Mexico City, I was stripped of all the trappings of pride and success that had previously formed my identity. I left my career, my reputation, and my stuff. There ensued a period of two years of wailing and gnashing of teeth over two big questions: Is it enough for me to 'just' be a mother and a housewife? What should I do about my career?"

She now understands that she failed to see clues to the answers to her questions in her circumstances. For example, she lived in a house on a street called Fuente de la Escondida (Spanish for "the Fountain of the Hidden One," with the article *la* implying that the hidden one is feminine). At the entrance to their neighborhood there is a huge fountain of a woman frolicking in the water with her children. "It's a well-known landmark"—Ava laughed—"but I did not get the significance of it in terms of my question for two years! I was the *Escondida* in hiding. I couldn't acknowledge the big, truly meaningful and joyful piece of my purpose in my role as mother to our son. Right at the entrance to my home was a visual representation of what joy and meaning I could have had all along, had I taken it out of hiding."

Ava struggled to find what she would do for a career and "forced her will," as she put it, into technical writing. She also took on volunteer financial roles and scoured the want ads for appropriate jobs. She complained that all anyone ever advertised for was teachers of English as a second language. She wanted real work. With time she has begun to see exactly why she had been placed in Mexico, and how she could facilitate the often difficult relocation process for other newly arrived foreigners. She has reached the other side of her query and is now returning to Minneapolis and enrolling in a program to become certified to teach English as a second language. "For three years, hands-on training and experience were graciously offered to me on a daily basis by my situation, and I couldn't see the grace," she says.

OPEN YOURSELF TO NEW INFORMATION

Be particularly receptive when you think you know what to expect, because that is when you are most inclined to overlook new clues. This is especially true in family situations or with people you have spent a lot of time with. Ask yourself what has changed, not if anything has changed. . . . This process will keep you interested, present, and connected.

Charlene Belitz and Meg Lundstrom, *The Power of Flow*

Do Something Different

WHAT CAN you do when your child is having problems learning and you have no idea how to improve the situation? Jamie and Tim Saloff's son Mark had not been doing well in school from the beginning, but by fifth grade his failure to read and write, his angry outbursts, and his increasing withdrawal were tearing the family apart. The Saloffs tried everything they could think of to help Mark, whose behavioral and learning problems were blamed on attention deficit disorder. He was given prescription drugs, tutoring, and psychological counseling, yet nothing seemed to change his downward spiral. "School was like a war zone," says Jamie. "The teachers and principals were bending over backwards to help, but they couldn't give Mark what he needed."

Synchronistic information began to show up as Jamie and Tim

prayed for guidance. One of Jamie's friends recommended a book by John Holt entitled *How Children Fail*. Holt, a former teacher, argued that it wasn't the *children* who had failed but the *system* (not to be confused with the teachers themselves). Even the most respected forms of schooling were, Holt said, hindering kids' innate desire to learn. "Over the next couple of years," says Jamie, "I read every book Holt wrote and began to think more and more of teaching Mark on my own, but I was afraid. What if I failed to teach some vital skill? What did I know about education?"

NECESSITY FORCES A SEARCH FOR SOMETHING DIFFERENT

THREE IMPORTANT things happened to change Jamie's mind about her perceived limitations and force her to look for answers in another direction. The first was when school officials suggested that Mark might not graduate from high school. The second was when one of Jamie's good friends decided to home school her own son. "While my son struggled through his fifth-grade year—the worst he'd had yet—she was telling me how her boys were excelling," says Jamie.

The third motivating force was the daily arguments and threats that made family life miserable. "Each night Mark and I fought and struggled to complete homework, which neither of us saw as valid assignments," says Jamie. "Each day Mark would leave for school, not with a hug and a smile but with threats from us. In school he'd be excluded from his favorite activities as punishment for not completing work. Finally, my husband said, 'You have to do something different, this is tearing our whole family apart.' At that moment I made the decision to home school Mark the next year."

The last major turning point occurred on the evening of the eighth-grade graduation of the Saloffs' older son, Matthew, when a student shot and killed a teacher. The aftermath was devastating to all the families involved. "If ever I needed confirmation about home schooling," remembers Jamie, "that was it."

Jamie filed the papers to home school Mark despite the doubts of her husband. The decision, however, proved to be the right one. In Mark's first year of home schooling, he read over twenty books, and wrote two stories, a miniscreenplay, and a letter to the mayor about vandalism at a nearby playground. He stopped taking all medications and became calm. By the second year Jamie said that Mark exhibited a sense of being at peace with who he is. "He learned how to use the sewing machine and made his own 'uniforms' after his favorite cartoon characters," says Jamie. "He wore them everywhere and didn't seem to care if he looked different from the other kids. In fact, the younger kids looked up to him as a mentor, older kids trusted him as a leader, and adults respected his opinions, which he was rarely afraid to express."

THE PAST DOES NOT DEFINE THE FUTURE

Cradles of Eminence, a delightful (and well-documented) report on the childhoods of four hundred famous modern persons, states that three fifths of the subjects "had serious school problems."

Thomas Edison said, "I was always at the foot of the class." Albert Einstein wrote of his middle school: "I preferred to endure all sorts of punishments rather than to learn gabble by rote." Winston Churchill, at Harrow, "refused to study mathematics, Greek, or Latin and was placed in the lowest form—in what today would be termed the remedial reading class."

James Hillman, *The Soul's Code*

Creativity flowed as Mark experimented in his free time recycling unused items. He made a working video camera by combining parts from two broken ones and then taught himself how to make stop-action movies by watching stop-action cartoons. "Learning comes best when we are doing something valuable and in line with our own interests," says Jamie.

Eventually the Saloffs' older son asked to be schooled at home as well, even though he was doing well and had many good friends at school. Jamie says she was shocked at first by his request. His learning style was very different from Mark's, and she wasn't sure how she could help him create a curriculum that would meet his interests—which at the time centered on Star Wars and Japanese cartoon animation. "I gave him a piece of poster board and asked him to write in the center, 'How can I complete my education and fulfill my highest purpose and goals?' He wasn't even sure what a 'highest purpose' was, but I told him that didn't matter. I told him just to write down everything that came to mind, and not to worry if it went with education or not.

After about forty-five minutes, he handed me the board, which was sparsely filled in with ideas like eating and cooking Italian food, meeting chicks, interest in space, Greek gods, and wanting to own a card shop someday. I asked myself how I could use these interests in his education, and I found an entire year's worth of curriculum. For example, I gave him Syd Field's *Screenplay: The Foundations of Screenwriting* as a text, along with Scriptware, a script-writing software. I told him to write his own animated cartoon script, which he loved doing. Since he had written that one day he would like to own a card shop, I bought *Business Plans for Dummies* as a textbook, which served for his math requirements as well as teaching him what it takes to run a business. This book, coupled with his job at a local card shop, taught him more than he'd ever learn in a typical high school business class."

The Saloffs feel that home schooling has turned out to be a huge success for the entire family, bringing them all closer together. The boys are learning real skills, expressing themselves creatively, and getting along with their peers, and they are happy.

This story is a good example of how in what seems like an insurmountable problem the answers arrive one by one. Gradually doubts dissolve as the intention to have a happier life draws us forward into the unknown. For the Saloff family, the answers unfolded as they began to explore the unknowns of home schooling. Necessity brought them to a new level of risk taking. The answers showed up as they moved forward with the intention of meeting their boys' special needs and regaining harmony in the family. As a result, transformation occurred for everyone.

Jamie says, "One of the great things in home schooling is how different kinds of support seem to come into your life at just the right moment. For example, while my husband was recovering from major surgery for three months, he was able to work with Mark on his math, and Mark's math went to a whole new level. We are learning as a family, and it's really brought us together."

Jamie recommends Debra Bell's book, *The Ultimate Guide to Homeschooling* (published by Thomas Nelson), which suggests that parents write a letter to themselves defining important goals and values for home schooling. "Whenever I doubt myself as an educator (which is common for a home schooling mom) I reread my letter and stop worrying about what my children haven't learned and reassure myself in what they *have* learned. I believe my children will have received the most important thing in education, which is not being good at memorizing the contents of textbooks, but is knowing *how to learn and enjoying learning.* This type of self-motivated learning naturally develops leadership and a sense of authenticity."

FIND ANOTHER WAY

There's an old saying: Nothing is as dangerous as an idea when it is the only one you have. We are all prisoners of our limited point of view and we have a tendency to think our point of view is the only correct way of seeing things, especially when we are upset. So, when you are stuck or unhappy, find another way of looking at the situation. Think of it from another angle.

Bill O'Hanlon, *Do One Thing Different*

Be Impeccable

FRANCINE KELLY, editor and publisher of *Conscious Living Magazine* and owner-director of the Center for Conscious Living, made a huge transition from her dissatisfying life as a New York copywriter and journalist a few years ago. "Looking back, I don't feel my changes were so much voluntary as they were guided," Francine says. "It was while visiting the Monroe Institute in Virginia in [a research center for the exploration of accelerated learning and expanded consciousness founded by the author and researcher Robert Monroe] in 1998 that I was guided by Spirit to cocreate a retreat center." Francine describes some of the influences that promoted her interest in healing and spiritual study. She had grown up in an alcoholic family, where she was often told she was stupid and incompetent. During her thirties and forties, Francine worked as a journalist and ghostwriter in advertising and medical copywriting. "I didn't believe in what I was doing," she says, "and when jobs started drying up, I kept pushing my will to make them happen. The more it dried up, the more I pushed my will. Obviously, I wasn't getting the message I shouldn't be doing this work any-more."

Her own alcoholism prompted Francine to go into recovery sev-eral years ago. When she hit bottom emotionally, she says she made a deal with God to be of service to others.

As her discouragement grew, Francine's interest was piqued by a new field. She happened to find a newspaper focusing on health and personal growth, which led to a stint selling advertising for the publication. Although her first try at New Age advertising did not turn out to be the best opportunity for a long-term focus, it did put her on the path to being hired by a national magazine. Even though she won an award for her work, however, the situation felt abusive.

"After this experience, I made the decision to start my own news-paper, *Conscious Living*," Francine says. "At first it was a free local tabloid, then we became a national magazine with subscriptions. The first issue paid for itself, which is almost impossible in the mag-azine world. To start a magazine, you usually need between one and three million dollars. We had no money, and we were leasing the computer! Obviously, Spirit wanted this project to succeed."

Francine believes that, at the beginning of any project, the two keys to success are having a strong dedication to one's mission and being businesslike, in that order. Dedication is another form of intention. It attracts synchronistic opportunities in alignment with the focus. Dedication comes from doing the inner work of choos-ing things that really mean something to you, rather than just doing what seems lucrative. Trust, patience, self-esteem, and integrity are also part of dedication.

The second key, being businesslike, involves having the com-monsense habits of checking facts, following through, delegating and, again, working with integrity in all one's relationships.

How do we handle our fears and self-doubts when starting a new project? "I have to say," Francine continues, "trusting Divine guid-ance is how I handle the inevitable fears that arise in new territory.

My 'ego-based will' presents itself very differently, which is to say that it feels more self-centered. Divine will is about doing the right thing. We do know the right thing to do, but the fear comes in to block us from following God's will. We tell ourselves things like 'This won't work.' Or 'I'm going to lose money.' Divine will says, 'Something will work out,' even though it may seem to be impossible at the time—especially when everybody tells you it's impossible! I like what a friend of mine told me. She has decided from now on to hire just the unemployed angels!"

EXPRESSING THE VISION AND FOLLOWING CLUES

WHEN FRANCINE decided to start a retreat center, she asked her inner guides in meditation where the center should be. One day while she was in a bookstore, a magazine rack attracted her attention. She noticed a publication called *The Sedona Journal of Emergence.* "I knew Sedona was supposed to be a very spiritual place. It felt like a good place to start my investigations, so I booked a flight," she says. Before leaving for Arizona, she discussed qualities of the location that would be necessary with her husband, Bruce, and other colleagues at the magazine. They made a list. Bruce said the center would have to be near a national forest so no one could build around them. Others mentioned having enough acreage, and how nice it would be to be on top of a hill.

Francine says, "When I arrived in Sedona, the miracles continued. While I was looking at a real estate magazine, my eyes were guided to a picture of the property. I looked up at my broker and said, 'What about this place?' It turned out that *this place* had been recently owned by a drug dealer who is now serving time in prison. Although it was a place with a past, the ranch had a swimming pool, sauna, hot tub, Jacuzzi, and it was in foreclosure, so the price was right. It would be a perfect place for weekend workshops and for spiritually oriented people to stay when they were visiting God's country." The property also met the parameters they had listed, and more.

Francine signed the papers on her fiftieth birthday. After a lot of hard work cleaning up the place and finding the right staff, the Center for Conscious Living was born. "A friend of mine keeps reminding me that you have to be impeccable, absolutely impeccable when you are following Divine guidance," Francine says. "You can't manipulate and you can't lie. The law of cause and effect will always show you what you need to pay attention to. For example, one month I didn't take care of my printing bill, and I had all sorts of problems in other areas until I cleaned it up. Another time we were having difficulties, and I realized that it was probably linked to the fact that we were using mailing software we had bootlegged and not paid for. We couldn't pay for it, so we stopped using it and did all our mailing by hand. After the decision not to use it, everything started going smoothly again."

IMPERMANENCE IS WHAT MAKES TRANSFORMATION POSSIBLE

If we practice the art of mindful living, when things change, we won't have any regrets. We can smile, because we have done our best to enjoy every moment of our life and to make others happy.

Thich Nhat Hanh, *The Heart of the Buddha's Teaching*

Francine says her life has completely changed since she started following her inner guidance. She feels that she is now working at her life's mission—at least what the mission looks like at this stage of her life. "Since my recovery, I have the confidence I never had as a child. I look to Spirit, and Spirit tells me there is nothing to fear because I have my guides. I really trust my feelings about the energy in any project now. I try to discern the energies of people I work with in business and, if it feels uncomfortable, I move away from it, instead of pursuing it any further." [Francine has moved the Center for Conscious Living to Hawaii.]

FRANCINE KELLY'S TIPS FOR MOVING FORWARD

- Be honest with yourself. Don't deny who you are and what you feel.

- When you see things you don't love about yourself, acknowledge them, accept that you can change, and move on. Don't stay stuck in judging yourself.
- In new situations, be discerning but not judgmental. Recognize that people are where they are in life for a reason, and it's not your business to change them. Don't get embroiled in other people's issues.
- Follow the guidance that comes to you even in the most unlikely times and places.

SEEDS OF CONSCIOUSNESS

What is important in each of us is the seed of consciousness which is released in changes and transformation. As long as we hang on to our ego, our personal problems, we can't hear the voice of the universe.

Joseph Campbell, *The Power of Myth*

7

✥

Trust the Process

Do not be afraid to make a sudden and radical change if the opportunity is presented and you feel after careful consideration that it is the right opportunity, but never take sudden or radical action when you are in doubt as to the wisdom of doing so.

WALLACE D. WATTLES,
The Science of Getting Rich

Learn to Live with Uncertainty

ONE OF the biggest limitations to creating the change we want is that we want to be sure of the outcome before we start, so we can (1) avoid making mistakes; (2) not waste time; (3) avoid feeling fear or anxiety; and (4) not look bad to others.

Most of us are convinced that we must take action based on a plan, and that the plan must be logical and under our control. The desire to rid ourselves of uncertainty comes from the ego. Being willing to tolerate a certain amount of uncertainty, however, gives us the benefit of flexibility and, in the long run, allows our lives to unfold with almost effortless ease.

LIVING WITH UNCERTAINTY

I've learned that you have to be willing to live with a certain amount of uncertainty. Wanting to know how everything is going to turn out is too much like trying to control everything. You can't possibly know everything and you have to trust the process.

I've learned that when something wants to emerge, I go through a period of feeling uncomfortable inside. When I feel unsettled, then I know there is something I need to pay attention to. I used to want to jump on it and do something, but you don't have to do anything but wait, and let it show itself.

Blaise, therapist and performer

A woman named Laurie wrote that she finally got a much-needed divorce. "I've found it helpful to let things go in flight for a while. I tell myself not to push too hard. It's amazing when you resign as the puppeteer of your life, miraculous things start flourishing around you. In the midst of chaos, I've had people drop like angels out of the sky to help me, in every capacity."

Slow Down and Wake Up

THE SINGLE greatest lament of most people, next to a desire for more money, is lack of time. We ask each other, How are you? The answer is usually Busy.

Often keeping overly busy is a way not to face the uncertainty of stopping and examining where we are going. When we are in a hurry, we are less likely to follow up on a relevant suggestion or even notice something that speaks to what we are searching for. Our bodies may be aching from hunger or fatigue, but we still try to squeeze in one more activity before we end for the day.

Time for reflection is essential if we are to stay attuned to where life is taking us. Without time for solitude, we are little more than productive (or unproductive) robots headed for meltdown. A meltdown may be the only way we wake up to the changes we need to make; frenetic activity usually obscures—not clears—our vision.

During the years it takes to accomplish life goals, we may suddenly realize that we are living dreams we've outgrown. They might be dreams we watered down or put on hold because of family responsibilities, feelings of unworthiness, fear of failure, or sense of resignation. Whatever our life circumstance, slowing down is a healthy and wise thing to do, so that we may consult our inner voices and see who is crying for expression. We also need time to integrate the ideas and influences that we absorb every day. We must allow ourselves time each week to regather energy, mend, and germinate. Nature, music, rest, and silence are great healers.

I recently received a phone call from an old acquaintance. She told me that her best friend, a lawyer, sought medical help about a pain in her leg, which she thought might be a result of her running. The doctors found advanced cancer in several parts of her body. The woman's first action after the diagnosis was to close her law practice. She told my friend, "I have always hated practicing law." Thirteen weeks later she died.

When we unconsciously deny our inner voices and desires, we may not realize the extent to which our thoughts can create drastic shifts in our lives. What is the cost of our addiction to a fast-paced life, in which we cannot take time to eat a proper meal, relax with friends and family, or enjoy the moment?

NURTURE YOURSELF AS MUCH AS YOU CAN

COLEEN, A nurse, writes in an e-mail, "Last year my husband of twenty-three years told me he was thinking of moving out. The next day when I came home from a difficult meeting at work, he was packing boxes into the pickup. Even though *I* had wanted to leave *him* many times in the last eight years, I was obviously taken aback by his sudden departure, leaving me with three teenagers, two of whom are troublesome.

"Because of the problems with the kids, I asked to step down from my evening nursing job, where I had worked faithfully for twelve years. They would not give me an on-call job. Within a few weeks I lost my husband and my job, while my son got into trouble and now has felonies on his record. Your basic dark night of the soul.

"Thank God I had already started down a path of healing, and studying healing touch. I made an altar at the foot of my bed, which I had wanted to make for two years but didn't for fear of recrimination from my husband. I started to do things that nurtured me, like taking long bubble baths and enjoying good chocolate without guilt. I brought more order to my house. Old stuff got tossed out or passed on. Room by room my house started to feel more alive and so did I. I took a painting class from a local artist, which brought new life to my style of painting. I meditate more, have slowed down, and enjoy a beautiful sunset. I thank God every day, several times a day, for how my life has been reordered, and I can truly see Divine hands at every turn. My only fear is that when I start working again I will get caught up in the thick of things. But at least I know how free this life feels, and it will be worth the challenge to keep my load light. I have learned not to make hasty decisions, to take my time to let the dust settle before jumping into something and starting to run again."

Hope Connects, Expectation Separates

THE BUDDHIST teacher Pema Chödrön says, "The spiritual journey is not about heaven and finally getting to a place that's really swell. In fact, that way of looking at things is what keeps us miserable. Thinking that we can find some *lasting* pleasure and *avoid pain* [italics added] is what in Buddhism is called *samsara,* a hopeless cycle that goes round and round endlessly and causes us to suffer greatly."

Another teacher, the yoga master Osho, writes, "The mind that hopes is nonsense, it leads nowhere. It simply closes your eyes, it intoxicates you, it never allows reality to be revealed to you. It protects you against reality." While it seems Master Osho is advising us against hope, we may add here that *expectation* is the limiting form of hope. We must be clear in our understanding that we can always hope that life is worth living, that bad conditions can change, and that things will improve. It is desire to control others or to avoid growth and pain, to live only with our eyes on the future, that takes us out of life and its richness. Spiritual development comes from keeping our minds open, our hearts open, and having an attitude of gratitude and trust that what we need will arrive in the perfect time.

Teachers of positive thinking tell us to imagine ourselves playing tennis with a perfect stroke and to see the goal of success. Olympic coaches train by showing videotapes of exceptional performances to ingrain the images so that the body will follow on the field and in the match. New Thought authors advocate setting an intention and setting the right tone, so that results will be attracted in line with desire. All teachers recommend surrendering our will to the greater intelligence of Divine will, allowing the results to flow in, according to the most perfect lesson we need at the time.

TODAY

You are hoping something is going to happen tomorrow—some doors of paradise will open tomorrow. They never open today, and when tomorrow will come it will not come as tomorrow, it will come as today, but by that time your mind has moved again. You go on moving ahead of you; this is what dreaming means.

Osho, *The Path of Yoga*

It's a Dance

ELIZABETH JENKINS, author of *Initiation: A Woman's Spiritual Adventure in the Heart of the Andes,* defines the dynamic between setting an intention and receiving fulfillment as a dance. In an interview she says, "It's a call and response. You have to have an intention, otherwise there is no creation. Your job is to focus on something you want and put out a call. The thought pattern goes out like a wave into the universe. Then the universe responds. It's like a dance between you and the world. The trick is not to give up your intention too soon, just because you don't see any immediate response, or because it doesn't come in the way you expect."

Intend your deepest dream, untainted by fear and doubt. "The shamanic way," says Jenkins, "is to hold an intention, let's say for attracting your soul mate, or for right work, or for meeting great people, or just for everyday happiness. Then trust that the universe is going to respond. You have to hold it longer than you think you should. When you want to give up, don't. *Releasing* your intention and letting go signals the universe that you trust what you need will be provided. *Giving up* is collapsing into doubt."

Jenkins recalls reading about the great theosophist and clairvoyant Alice Bailey, who described watching the energy field of a man sending out an intention. "She saw the thought form go out, and then she said she was able to see the responding wave of energy, the answer, coming toward the man from the universe. At just that moment, the man gave up his focused intention. Alice Bailey saw the two energy fields diverge instead of coming together. They were almost coming together when he gave up. This made a big impression on me."

INTENTION KEEPS INFORMATION ORDERED

Our intentions are the force that keeps information in consciousness ordered. Each person allocates his or her limited attention either by focusing it intentionally like a beam of energy, or by diffusing it in desultory, random movements. . . . Our experiences shape themselves according to our expectations and beliefs—often reactions to the past—combined with the direction of our attention in the present.

Jane Katra and Russell Targ, *The Heart of the Mind*

Receptivity Is the Sister of Intention

IN THE old times, those of us who were the tribal hunters prepared ourselves before the hunt by retreating into silence, praying, conjuring images of the game, and purifying ourselves until we felt in alignment with the Great Will. We followed the signs of nature, watched, listened, and waited. When the game was within striking distance—taking advantage of that quarter inch of opportunity (as Carlos Castaneda called it)—we pounced. We were ready, and our hunt was successful.

"If you know what is going to make you happy," says Jenkins, "then you have to go with that. Your soul is connected with what you want and what you truly need. If you can align the needs and wants of your soul, then you are in flow. For example, when I came back from my shamanic training in Peru, the conventional thing would have been to go on with my counseling practice, but that felt dead for me. I felt a call or command from my soul to write a book about my experiences. However, my beliefs about my writing ability and my self-image up to that time did not allow me to even consider that. I thought it was grandiose, but I was miserable. My misery was like the sand in the oyster. I think a lot of people give up in that misery instead of bursting the bubble of the small self-image. I wrestled with this for four years. One day I just started writing, and I wept hysterically for several hours. It was the physical breakdown of that constricting self-image, and the release of the fear. You have to grow, but it may hurt, too."

Every single thing
Changes and is changing
Always in this world.
Yet with the same light
The moon goes on shining.

Priest Saigyo

Synchronicity Answers Clear Questions

WHEN YOU have a life question, the universe will inevitably bring you an answer, if your question is put forth clearly. "I don't know what to do" is not a clear question. It's a statement of doubt.

However, when you make a clear but open-ended request, such as, "Show me how to have a happy relationship with my mate," you've given notice that you are looking for specific information. For example, you may begin to gain insight on how to communicate about where the relationship has broken down, how the two of you are evolving, and what the options for change are. You might become aware of how you need to change your attitude or take more responsibility for your own happiness. You might get clear that you both need to let go and move on.

When we hold attitudes that we want to change something but are not willing to look at what steps must be taken, we feel stymied. There is nothing more draining than not taking the steps you know you need or want to take.

A woman named Patricia, who is now, at age fifty, a Catholic chaplain and director of pastoral services at a hospital, has had very intense spiritual experiences all her life. "Something intervenes for me that is much greater than myself when I really need it," she says. "When I was six, we lived in a poor little house. I was never alone. I watched the movie *The Inn of the Sixth Happiness,* and I knew that's what I wanted to do with my life—rescue poor children.

"I used to pray over a map of the world. When I was twenty-nine, a friend asked me to go with him to China to smuggle in Bibles. At first I didn't want to go at all, but in the middle of the night, I had the strongest desire to go. For inspiration, I opened a book, and got the message that the money would come so that I could go. It did.

"On the flight from New York to Los Angeles, I heard them announce the name Morton Sunshine, and I laughed a little. The man in the seat next to me said, 'That's a funny name, isn't it?' Then he said, 'You're probably too young to remember this, but have you ever heard of the movie *The Inn of the Sixth Happiness*? I'm the producer of that movie.' " Patricia told him that she was on her way to China, and that that movie was the reason she was going. It happened that he was going to visit Ingrid Bergman, the star of the movie, because she was ill and probably dying of cancer. "He asked me if I'd like to write her a note, and in the note I told her that God had used that movie to speak to my life."

Deadlines Intensify the Process of Attraction

A YOUNG man named Jason wrote that he was under consideration for a job as a production assistant on a film. His friend Bob called and told him he could give him the job if he had a safety traffic control certificate. Jason says, "I phoned different colleges to see if there were any seats left for this course. Everyone told me there wouldn't be an opening for another month. I needed to get the certificate before the twelfth or I wouldn't be hired. As a last resort I decided to phone a college that I didn't really think would hold this kind of course. As it turned out, they had just started to offer it, and there was a last-minute cancellation for the class starting in three days. I rushed down there. What weird luck, I thought!

"The traffic job was a cinch, and now Bob has other plans for me. He needed a production coordinator, and we put together a video in five days. It will air in two weeks, and we have two more videos coming up by the same artist. In August I'll be a production assistant on a major television show. The budget is over a hundred million. The real cool part is that I'm exactly where I've always wanted to be—or at least at the beginning of where I was meant to be—behind the scenes, helping others, and creating a name for myself."

Gratitude and Appreciation Raise Your Attracting Frequency

GIVE THANKS regularly for what you already have. Gratitude is one of the best ways to raise our spirits to a higher frequency. Acknowledging every large or small success, daily kindness, or blessing paves the way for continued positive events.

Pass that energy along to others. For example, if you want to find a new office space or home, look for every opportunity to help someone else find space. Make room for friends at the cafeteria table, help someone move, or assist someone who is looking for an apartment. Don't talk about what you are doing, just be willing to assist others in their efforts.

YOU ARE A BLESSED RECIPIENT

Develop an awareness of yourself as a recipient rather than as a victim. Virtually everything that you possess in your life is because of the efforts of others. Your furniture, automobile, home, clothes, gardens, yes, even your own body are all, in some way, gifts from others. . . . Just remind yourself of this fact each day and gratitude will begin replacing cynicism.

Wayne W. Dyer, *Manifest Your Destiny*

The Ten Principles of Flow

WHEN WE are tired, frustrated, discouraged, and disheartened, we typically blame outside events for keeping us down ("I have bills to pay!" "Corporate life stinks!"). We secretly fear that we are doomed to mediocrity, or that we lack the assertiveness or cleverness to move forward. When we are drained by jobs that are dull and unful-filling, we feel as if we are doing something wrong. It helps to see the present situation as one moment in an *ever-changing flow*.

Flow is a process, not a destination. One day in a workshop I was helping a young actress write a statement of purpose. She wasn't comfortable making an affirmation such as "My acting career is a great success!" It didn't feel successful enough yet. However, when I asked her if she could feel that she was in the *flow* of acting— since she was indeed auditioning, taking classes, and meeting actors and film people every day—she immediately said yes. Her statement of purpose became "I am in the flow of my acting career." Her affirmation is a good example of an open-ended, broadly envi-sioned purpose. Since she can really feel the truth of it, she feels good. When she feels good, she is relaxed, open, and enjoying the process. No matter what happens down the road, she is in the flow of what makes her happy. She is not trapped in waiting for a result.

F	= Fun	Focus
L	= Love	Listen Learn
O	= Open	Opportunity
W	= Willing	Wit Wonder

The first principle of being in the flow is feeling you are having *fun*. Fun is on the same feeling continuum as passion (if I could spell *passion* with an *f,* I would use it as the first principle, but I couldn't, so I had to get creative!). When you're having fun, you automatically connect to a part of your life purpose. What's fun and necessary for one person may not be fun or useful to another. But fun is an internal indicator that something is resonating positively. Life also changes when you have fun. You are uplifted and you uplift those around you. Fun is its own reward and is a necessary part of everyone's life. For example, I find it a lot of fun to look up the definitions of words in the dictionary. That's one indicator that writing is part of my life purpose. It's fun for me to move into the unknown world of words and the blank page in order to write. For somebody else, like yourself perhaps, this activity might be terrifying and unthinkable. So don't go there—unless you have to, and you know in your heart that writing is the next stage of your development!

Focus on what makes you feel good. Don't waste another minute of your life energy talking about the problems you have no intention of changing. To adjust your focus, begin to notice how much energy you give to something you wish would go away. Allow it to solve itself or just dissolve as you stop feeding it with your words and thoughts.

Love what you do and do what you love. If you are doing something you don't love very much, how could you shift your attitude about it? What adjustments need to be made to increase your satisfaction? Commit to finding more ways to love, and notice that the unknown suddenly seems more exciting than fearsome.

Listen to your intuition. What have you been putting off? What has been bubbling away there in the back of your mind? Listen to the persistent ideas that seem to energize you, even though another part of you pooh-poohs them as pie-in-the-sky or scary. Make a list of these abiding but unrealized thoughts. Notice what kinds of signs and signals appear in the guise of a friendly phone call or a book that falls into your hands. Just for fun, read through the local classified ads and see what leaps out at you. Let the tiny pulsations from the unknown become a drumbeat that stirs your blood toward freedom and self-expression.

Open to new ideas as potential *opportunities*. Review obstacles for their possible potential. If your budding idea or even your greatest obstacle were part of the plot of an intriguing movie, what outrageously fabulous outcome could you imagine? Draw a circle on a piece of paper, draw or write that outcome inside, and tuck it away for your inner producer to stage for you in a moment of transcendent, mind-blowing synchronicity. What have you got to lose? Only the obstacle.

Finally, be *willing* to do whatever it takes to make the changes you want. Have the *wit* to open to the *wonder* of life. When we wonder and marvel at life, we are alive, open, and spiritually connected. Wonder and curiosity increase creativity and positive change. When I moved to Santa Fe, New Mexico, for example, I knew no one at first. I was willing to take any kind of work to make a living. I worked as an artist's model for a short time; I learned how to work silver, which led to managing a shop; and I waited tables at two cafés. To support myself when I went to graduate school a couple of years later, I cleaned houses all over the county, learned to run a restaurant kitchen, and taught basic cooking techniques to a housekeeper who worked for the large family of a movie director. (She knew less about cooking than I did!) Before this I had never cooked professionally, nor had I taught cooking. Necessity is a wonderful Muse.

You Always Have a Choice

"YOU NEVER know when a person is going to be ready to change," says Terrance, director of a homeless shelter and substance abuse program. "I realized I could help people not by preaching but just by showing up at meetings. Sometimes only one or two people show up, but I keep doing it because I figure I want to be there when someone is ready."

Terrance, fifty-two, has hepatitis C and was recently diagnosed with liver cancer. He drove trucks for twenty years because trucking paid more than social work. "By the time I got out of high school, I was addicted to alcohol and was dependent on marijuana, psychedelics, barbiturates, speed, heroin, cocaine, and crack cocaine. I'm amazed I could do all that, because I was also addicted to sports more than drugs and alcohol," he recalls. He looks back and sees a skinny little kid who craved attention and would do anything— lying, stealing, and cheating—to get it. He was arrested for selling cocaine and went to prison for a year and a half. All prison did was teach him not to get caught again, he says.

For thirty-two years he drank and used drugs. These habits were so much a part of his life he didn't even recognize that his behavior was not normal. At twenty-six he married and had a son; a second marriage gave him a daughter. "At no time did I realize that I had a problem with drugs and alcohol. Toward the end, because I was drinking about a half gallon of vodka a day and smoking pot, I started losing touch with my kids and not showing up for events. That really started to bother me."

One day, a day that was seemingly no different from any other day, Terrance had bought a new bottle of vodka. "I had just taken a sip, and my brother-in-law came along. I told him to take a sip and keep it. That was something new, because I never shared anything with anybody. After that I went over to a detox unit and checked in. I still don't know why I did that. I think my higher power helped me take this step. Even when I was in the unit, I had no desire to recover, just to get my drinking down to a half a pint of vodka a day. I'm just amazed that I could have been led to make these changes.

"In order to stay in detox, I had to go to recovery meetings. A couple of guys I had known in my old life were sober now. Both of them were clean, and they had sparkling eyes. I was struck by their cleanliness and presence. On two occasions they both told me, 'You are really sharp. You could help a lot of people. You don't have to live this way. You have a choice.' Really seeing that I had a choice was the turning point. I had never realized that I had a choice and that I could change how I was living my life. Recovery opened my eyes."

Within three weeks of finding out he had liver cancer, Terrance also had a car accident and was forced to leave the job he loved because of his health. "At first I felt scared and upset," he says about his diagnosis of cancer. "It caused me to question my faith. Why me? But I believe that I still have a lot to contribute, and I know this disease is another experience that I can use as a teaching tool to help others. It's an opportunity to really live what I talk about," he says. "People must have told me years ago, but I don't remember being told that I had a choice. Now I make it a point to tell young people that you can choose to stay where you are and continue doing what you're doing, or you can choose to do something different."

> *A mantra is a word or series of words*
> *that you repeat over and over again.*
> *A phrase that has a deep spiritual meaning*
> *—"Our Father who art in heaven," for example,*
> *works well to quiet the mind.*
>
> —Anonymous

POP QUIZ ON MASTERING FLOW

Rate yourself on your willingness or present ability to live the principles we've been discussing. Use a scale of 1 (low or rarely) to 10 (high or frequently).

Principles for Attracting Life Changes	1 to 10

- **Desire Creates Change**
  How would you rate your level of desire for what you want?   __

- **We Create with Every Thought**
  How often do you think about the result you want *as if you already had it?*   __

- **Hope and Expectations**
  How willing are you to let go of expectations and stay attuned to the present?   __

- **It's a Dance**
  How able are you to state how you want to feel and then listen intuitively for where to take small steps forward?   __

- **Trust**
  What is your level of trust that the universe always provides?   __

- **Synchronicity Answers Clear Questions**
  How much do you believe that there are no accidents?   __

- **Deadlines Intensify the Process of Attraction**
  How often do you schedule time to do what brings you joy?   __

- **Imagination Creates the Form**
  How often do you visualize what you want?   ___

- **Gratitude and Appreciation Raise Your Attracting Frequency**
  How much time do you spend on average each day noticing
  good things?   ___

- **The Principles of Flow**
  What is the general level of fun in your life?   ___
  How much do you focus on the positive in conversations?   ___
  How often do you act on your intuition?   ___
  How excited are you about something new you are learning?   ___
  How open are you to taking new steps toward a goal?   ___
  How easy do you think it's going to be to attract what you want?   ___
  How attractive do you feel?   ___
  How ready are you to deal with the challenges of a new life
  change?   ___
  How willing are you to do whatever it takes to change your life?   ___
  How much curiosity do you have?   ___

- **Accepting Uncertainty Keeps Us Flexible**
  How well do you tolerate uncertainty?   ___
  Are you willing to let go and just see what happens while waiting
  for opportunities to take action?   ___
  How patient are you?   ___

- **You Always Have a Choice**
  How easy would it be for you to make a choice about changing
  something important?   ___

                                                        TOTAL POINTS   _____

Scoring	Interpretation
23–69	**_Resistant to Change._** You tend to see outside circumstances as holding you back, or believe you lack what it takes to move forward. Change will come slowly, and is likely to bring difficulties that require you to (1) stop blaming others; (2) release the past; and (3) notice that your beliefs are interfering with your desires.

What to do:

- Choose one of the principles that most appeals to you and practice it until you lose interest in it.
- Write down your goals and imagine yourself feeling the way you would feel if you had those goals now. Do this for 60 seconds every day.
- Look for evidence of the tiniest positive things happening to you every single day.
- Find ten things to be grateful for every day before sleeping.

70–120

Ambivalent About Change. You may want something consciously but may be afraid that you will be asked to change in ways you don't think you can. Change tends to come slowly because your doubts dilute the intention to change.

What to do:

- Follow all the points under "Resistant to Change."
- Decide to go somewhere new, do something different in your routine, or work specifically to improve yourself (take one semester of Italian; take singing or dancing lessons; learn a hundred new words; practice yoga).

121–166

Thriving on Change. You've had changes that have brought the good and the bad, but you trust that things generally get better. You're impatient for changes and sometimes get ahead of yourself. You are active and generally positive but may need to slow down in order to listen to your intuition more.

What to do:

- Write down your goals and imagine yourself feeling the way you would feel if you
  had those goals now. Do this for 60 seconds every day.
- Remember every day to wake up and set
  a positive tone, asking for good people to
  come into your life and for perfect timing
  in all things.
- Review your problems or obstacles for a
  silver lining.
- Make an outrageously fabulous goal, find
  a picture that represents it, and put it on
  your refrigerator.

167–230   *Mastering Change.* You easily move through life
because you understand that everything hap-
pens for a reason. You are actively pursuing personal and spiritual growth, and have a strong
desire to communicate and teach others. You are
ready!

What to do:

- Acknowledge that your intuition is prompt-
  ing you to take on new challenges that will
  take you far.
- Know that you have a fairly well developed capacity for change, and remember
  the importance of:
  —doing what feels important to you
  —trusting your gut instincts
  —keeping a sense of positive outcomes
  —being willing to do whatever life asks of
     you.
  —being grateful for what you already
     have and know.

Each of us has a different capacity for handling change. To understand how we might differ in this ability, let's say people tend to fall

into four categories by which they see and handle life. I generally refer to these four categories as the *thinker/analyzer, intuitive/ visionary, pragmatic/doer, or nurturer/connector*. Obviously, each of us may operate from any or all of these positions at some time, but often we do approach life from *predominantly* one perspective.

The *thinker* needs data to make or handle change, and likes to review what he or she already knows or what has been done before. Thinkers need to make a logical plan in order to feel confident about instigating change (even though the plan may never unfold as they planned). Because they usually feel a need to defend their decisions, they tend to keep stockpiling information until external conditions or deadlines necessitate action. Change may happen more slowly for them—driving their action-oriented colleagues or partners crazy—but they are less upset if change is orderly and pre-dictable.

Intuitives prefer to keep as many options open as possible. Change that requires decisions on their part, therefore, may be dif-ficult for them as they tend to view any choice as a limitation of their potential or freedom. Their big complaint is narrowing down options in order to concentrate on one direction. In reality, their emotional priority is not to *develop* but to *expand and explore*. They actually spend a lot of time envisioning how the world could change for the better. They tend to believe in the importance of personal development, such as overcoming blocks and changing internal patterns.

Active, *pragmatic* people prefer change of any kind as long as it seems to advance efficiency, order, and create a positive, tangible outcome. They don't like lengthy discussions of change, especially from nurturers who bring up ideas such as "what will people think?" Change may be easiest for them—as compared to the other three types—as it usually releases the tension of inaction. However, efficiency-oriented pragmatics may also act too quickly on little data or leave themselves out on a limb with no contingency plan!

Nurturers are often concerned about what others think and how their actions will affect their circle of friends and family. Therefore, if a nurturer has a strong need to please others and be accepted, change can be very stressful and painful. They may feel that changes will somehow bring a loss of love or connection. To avoid this unconscious conflict, they may downplay their need to grow and move in new directions. They may even feel they need to get "permission" from a partner or spouse to make a life change. In order to avoid conflict, they may make a surreptitious decision, which they don't announce until it's already done, for fear of being talked out of what they want to do.

By recognizing our predominant approach to life, we will be better able to understand why we handle change one way and why others are so inexplicably not like us.

8

Let Yourself Evolve

The mantra, like a
Mountain stream, purifying
Whoever chants it.

KENNETH VERITY,
Awareness Beyond Mind

The Driving Force of Change—Personal Growth

AS WE look back at what we have done, where we have been, and the things that caught our attention, we might ask, Is anybody directing this show? In spiritual terms, part of the answer is that *our life purpose* is shaping and directing our attention, as well as presenting specific challenges for us to handle. In the language of cinema, it's the *character arc,* how the character changes from the beginning of the movie to the end.

In psychological terms, this developmental process is *individuation*. Individuation means we are not just getting older, we are becoming more differentiated and developed. More of our facets are being polished and are shining through. Individuation is like an internal engine that drives us to take risks, to reach out, to learn, to satisfy our curiosity, and to forge into the unknown. The tests and challenges of the individuating person, like the trials of the heroes and heroines of myth, shape us into what we are becoming. Individuation is one of the premier psychological life forces that attracts change into our lives.

What tend to limit our individuation are the declarative statements we make about ourselves that keep us small and safe. For example, have you heard yourself say something like "My problem is inaction." "I'm confused." "I don't know what my life purpose is." "I'm tired of fitting myself into a mold that doesn't fit, but I don't know what else to do"? These statements are all variations on the fear of making a mistake. They signal to the unconscious that you fear the unknown because you don't think you could handle what might arise.

Personal growth is inevitable. Shifts in our focus can happen even when we are at the peak of success.

Calling

PEADAR (RHYMES with "rather") Dalton, fifty-two, was born in the west of Ireland and ordained a Catholic priest at age twenty-three. Today he lives in Marin County, California, with his new wife, Margarita Ramirez, and has a busy psychotherapy practice and a ministry which includes spiritual mentoring and wedding and memorial ceremonies. Between 1970 and 1987, as Father Dalton, he served in a parish in Mobile, Alabama. His career skyrocketed in the way of careers of brilliant, committed, empathic people who have truly found their calling. His métier was life—the meaning of it, the launching of it, and the transitions of it—from high school seniors leaving home through engaged couples facing a lifetime commitment to the sadness of death or divorce. Within his scope lay the ability to initiate dialogues on the meaning of God and of family; discussions of doctrinal issues such as guilt, confession, and reconciliation; and social activism. By the age of thirty-five he had achieved an enviable work life that was meaningful and sustaining. And yet, at the top of his career, he began to feel another kind of calling.

No matter our level of success and achievement, there may come a time when the force of life purpose demands a step into the unknown. Those who knew Father Dalton would never have expected his successful life path to require any kind of change. "When I noticed this gnawing to look within," he says, "I recognized that my workaholism was a resistance to that call. It masked a fear of intimacy, of not knowing how to cope with who I might find I was. I thought I was doing a good job by working all the time but, ironically, didn't take the time to develop a deeper intimacy with myself and the Divine within."

After taking a sabbatical from active ministry, Peadar applied to graduate school for clinical social work at Tulane University in New Orleans. "When I first heard about the concept of individuation, I almost fell in love with the word. *Individuation* is a key term in family therapy, basically meaning a process by which individuals come to understand themselves as differentiated from others and the whole social system in which they were raised. This must happen if we are to be truly who we are, and be able to authentically contribute to life. If our awareness of the authentic self doesn't grow, we will always hold back for fear of rejection, or from the fear that we're not entitled to follow our own path. True spiritual growth is about developing our potential. *Individuation* is a word that constantly inspires me and increases my capacity to love and be more consciously communal."

After stepping aside from active parish ministry, Peadar, for the first time in his life, had to face the unknown realities of living alone. He says, "For example, I suddenly had to become fully responsible for all financial matters. I began to understand what it was like to compete and be part of a workforce without getting the entitlements I had as a priest. I always had room and board, a guaranteed job, retirement, and reputation, public recognition, and validation. Holding a public office is very attractive. I had enjoyed being in a position of persuasive authority and having people come to me at profound moments of their lives. I had the opportunity to speak to a captive audience five times a weekend. Priests are generally given instant trust, which isn't as true with therapists. Of course, I didn't think through all of the consequences of this decision, and it has not been an easy transition. Is there an enticement to go back to that? You bet there is. However, I would return with a much more mature understanding of ministry and, of course, with a wife.

"But upon leaving, I was pushed to a deeper layer of self-understanding. I began to date and experience the opportunity to develop relationships with women, which helped me to understand a little bit more what it is to care, to feel, to love, to be anxious, to be unsure of myself, to come to understand integrating sexuality rather than compartmentalizing it. I hadn't realized that my understanding of many of these issues was limited.

OWN WHO YOU ARE

"IN MUCH of my pastoral work [counseling others]," says Peadar, "I was trying to help people find answers to their spiritual questions in order to enhance who they were as people. I encouraged them to do a bit of chewing rather than swallowing. I saw how important it is to *own* your spiritual path, even though it may cause you, paradoxically, to move away from the Church. Ultimately this allows you to return as a freer and more aware person."

FACE FEARS OF DISLOYALTY

"NOW, AS a licensed therapist, I frequently find that people who protest too strongly about their misery are actually resisting moving on from this misery. They cannot imagine the joy that would be theirs if they did move on. Frequently people remain in belief systems and family systems that continue to bring them only pain and suffering. They remain entrenched in the belief that any kind of movement away from family or Church would be disloyal. Instead of wanting to have more joy in their lives, they protest they don't want it. The first step is recognizing the pain or disconnection. The next step is simply questioning their beliefs and considering what other avenues might be available. But, all too often, it seems to be too high a risk to cross that threshold to simply questioning.

"Many times I saw how confession was an opening for major life changes," says Peadar. "People would come who hadn't been to church for thirty or forty years, and they'd have a long list of things to confess. I'd say, 'Stop the clock. Forget the list. What would you like to see change in your life? God is totally aware of what has gone wrong. He's more interested in what would make you *joyful*.' That particular question would help them to get more clear. Suddenly they would come up with something like 'I need to be more loving to my wife.' 'I need to be less racist at work.' I would then get them to talk about this pattern. It amazed me how people might first be concerned about missing mass on Sunday or masturbating and later realize that they were ripping someone off in business on Monday. I felt very blessed to be part of those pivotal changes.

"I miss being involved in that particular capacity today. What drove me to make such a huge life change?"

NOTICE WHAT IS MISSING

"FROM MY mid-thirties to mid-forties, something was missing for me. I went into therapy on and off. I saw a licensed psychotherapist, a Jesuit priest, and later a Jungian analyst who happened to be a nun. This was the beginning of a conscious quest for a deeper inner journey. To put it in a nutshell, I was beginning to become aware of a sense of myself that wasn't exclusively related to being Father Dalton or to being the compliant Peadar Aloysius Dalton back in boarding school. Something was waking up within me, and even though I was very fulfilled in my life, I needed to step out and look back. But at the time I had no clue about where that inner voice would take me!"

GROWTH COMES FROM REFLECTION

"AS A priest, I've heard hundreds of people who had to tell their partners, 'I need to move on.' I think it's a very universal feeling when confronting change to feel like 'I'm not entitled to do this.' 'My life is overall pretty good; I'll just put up with it.'

"Growth doesn't necessarily come from just accepting or rejecting anything. It comes from reflecting on the questions that living and maturing present. So many times husbands or wives would come in and say, 'You know my wife (or husband) is a good person, but I have to get out. It's not there for me anymore.'"

CALLED TO ANOTHER REALM OF GROWTH

"PEOPLE FREQUENTLY asked me why I did what I did [leave his ministry with the Church]. I found it hard to communicate that I was being called to another realm of growth. I think most people struggle with developing a strong sense of self. There's a temptation, particularly for Christians, to think it's selfish or egotistical. But I'm talking about a strong sense of self that allows me to interact at a deeper level with self, others, and God.

"I see now that from the beginning in my family of origin, my nature was to be compliant and a people pleaser. The family, boarding school, seminary, rectory all implied that you were part of the system. In our culture, disagreeing with authority, whether it is the parents or the local priest, could be considered disloyal."

Individuation, then, is that stage when you begin to recognize your own stamp on the world, your unique way of believing and seeing. It is the force that propels us, like the mythical hero or heroine, to set out for the unknown.

Each of us is influenced by various ideological and social systems, but turning points come throughout life when we must examine what has true value, what makes us happy, and what allows us to be who we were meant to be. Peadar says, "I am more aware now of my own gifts and vulnerabilities, which is a strength and not a weakness.

"Did I have any clue about all this at thirty-eight years of age? None. Do I believe there was a power within me that allowed me to discover this truth? Yes."

Where Are You in the Process of Individuation?

FATHER DALTON'S story of moving forward into the unknown of his developing life purpose outlines the universal challenges we must undertake when we face the next steps in our lives. Which of the following questions do you intuitively think you are working on right now?

- Am I really owning my unique interests, passions, and talents as important and valid?
- Is there someone I am afraid of letting down?
- Am I afraid of seeming disloyal by being more honest?
- What is missing from my life?
- In what new way would I like to blossom?
- What *exactly* is it about the future that worries or frightens me?

Usually, when we are able to bring to awareness the questions and fears we have been suppressing, we open up new streams of energy and unexpected answers. If we let the question lead us, we receive more than we could have imagined.

Stop Struggling

WHEN LIFE feels like a struggle, it is sometimes because we are pushing and forcing, not attracting and flowing. Sometimes we have conflicting desires, such as, "I hate going to parties, but I have to go out and meet people in order to date," or "I want to change my life, but I'm too busy making a living." We forget that, although we *can* make things happen by taking assertive action, *better* opportunities may come through the Law of Attraction.

"I've been in private practice for eight years," said Blaise, a fifty-seven-year-old therapist who is developing his own one-man performance as a female impersonator. "Last year I began to have some dissatisfaction in my work, as well as in my lack of a primary relationship. During therapy sessions I found myself thinking, Oh, God, if I have to listen to one more story! On a personal level, my own little inner voice kept saying, 'What are you doing wrong that you don't have a relationship?' Since I left my wife several years ago, finding a good relationship has been a major preoccupation. This year I got fed up. Making an *effort* to meet someone seems like a waste of time. Instead, I decided to just have fun and expand, and add more things to my life that I enjoy. Through that I'll be more likely to meet somebody. I've shifted from searching to doing more enjoyable activities for their own sake."

Blaise struggled with an inner conflict about his sexuality for years. During his marriage he came to realize that he was gay. After he and his wife split up, he began to explore a whole new dimension of life. He talked about the continuing journey into the unknown of self-discovery. "I am becoming my own man, not anyone else's definition," he says. "When I encounter external judgments, they remind me of how important it is to follow my own heart. I try to be even more gentle with myself and stay grounded in what I know has value to *me*."

GO WITHIN

So when such challenges come, as they always do, make it a habit to go within at once and focus as much as you can on the inner energy field of your body.

Eckhart Tolle, *The Power of Now*

When life is a constant struggle, it usually means that we have not awakened to some part of ourselves that needs recognition. Struggle almost always appears to come from *external* forces, but if we look deeper we see that the struggle reflects a deeply held conflict *within* us.

Blaise, in his role as therapist, says, "When the inner voices come up, challenge them. Talk back to them. Don't shrink from them. I listen to hear if they remind me of anybody, like my mother, father, minister, teacher, or whomever. These voices are tremendously powerful in their effects on how and where we choose to create change."

To stop struggling, the first step is to notice that you *are* struggling. We are not meant to live in constant conflict. One thing you can do is identify your contradictory voices by writing them down. What are they saying? What do they want? What are they tired of?

Struggle comes from seeing things in black-or-white perspective. Limiting decisions to *this* or *that* keeps us paralyzed and out of the flow of other possibilities.

Blaise says that for him the urge for self-expression became irresistible. "I'd been going to a summer camp for gay men and women for six years," he says. "Every year we have a talent show. In my third year I heard a little voice say, 'I want to do something in drag.' I heard a bigger voice in me respond in horror, 'What do you mean, drag!' But every time I tried to dismiss the first voice, it kept coming back." The persistent voice of intuition began to nudge Blaise into the unknown. Of course, the ego continues with criticism, logic, and social conventions: What will people think!

EFFORTLESS ACTION

Notice any excess effort or willpower you're using today. Whenever you're pushing or pulling at life, your intuition will be blocked.

Penney Peirce, *The Present Moment*

"The first step I took when I decided to create the female impersonator act," recalls Blaise, "was to buy a shimmery blue top. I felt incredible shame buying it, but I bought it anyway. I went home and said, 'Okay, what is this about?' I realized I'd really wanted to buy it. I loved the color, and I thought, This is the beginning of a beautiful costume. The next step was to buy another piece. Then I started performing at home and watching myself to see what was emerging. Boy, the voices that came up on that! But I just kept working with each voice. It all boils down to learning to accept yourself.

"There are so many aspects I enjoy about preparing for a show. I love the design, the lighting, how to perform the songs, thinking about the progression of the songs. I used to do things like this as a kid. I loved to design costumes, put on plays, entertain people, work with color, create an atmosphere, and help people enjoy themselves. I love using my imagination."

Blaise watched the stream of beliefs and old judgments emerge in this process of self-growth and began to see how hard he tends to be on himself, how meanly he talks to himself (which is common to many of us). "Those mean thoughts," he realized, "generated the fear."

Going toward joy and taking new steps that feel good begin to dissolve the struggle. The joy that comes from exploring and creating is so energizing, the struggle fades. By not attacking the struggle head-on but instead going toward something that is energizing and fulfilling, we gain the solution. The key is to notice what gives you positive energy (buying a shimmery blue top) and move toward that energy source.

Meditation for Dissolving the Struggle

READ THROUGH this meditation a couple of times to familiarize yourself with what to do. Then, when you are ready and won't be disturbed, put on some quiet music and begin your visualization.

1. Close your eyes and induce a feeling of relaxation and contentment.
2. Notice any areas of tension in your body.
3. Imagine softening those areas of tension until your whole body feels as relaxed as possible.
4. Imagine your conflict or struggle as an object, symbol, sound, or feeling state.
5. Imagine that the symbol of your issue is gently dissolving.
6. Imagine the pieces of the struggle falling apart and being carried gently away by a flowing stream.
7. As the image dissolves, allow yourself to become even more still and relaxed, breathing quietly.
8. Feel your face relax, and feel the quiet joy of being free and at peace.

Whenever you're ready, open your eyes and carry this peaceful feeling with you as long as you can. At your next meal eat slowly and with attention to and appreciation of the smallest detail of your food. Act as if your previous struggle is a thing of the past and all has been taken care of for you. At bedtime give thanks for all the things you are grateful for today and for the support that is already on the way to pave your road to success.

This simple meditation, done over time, can work miracles. Trust that your inner self is generating and attracting an appropriate and positive solution for you.

Accept Who You Are

RECOGNIZING THE truth about ourselves liberates us to follow the "left-hand," or unconventional path. As a teenager, Victoria was shy and somewhat a loner. Now nearing forty, Victoria has had a suc-

cessful career as an actress, producer, and director in adult entertainment. At the time of our interview she was living in a long-term
ménage à trois. (Victoria has since moved out to live with another
partner.) The development of her personal and professional life
required risk taking, courage, determination, and the commitment
to be authentic in order to follow her dreams and fantasies in the
face of social conventions and prejudices. The beginning of her
career in the sex industry was closely linked to a strong and supportive emotional home life, which she established with Gene and
Danielle, who were in a committed but open relationship when she
met them.

"I knew I didn't want to live a traditional life, and I didn't want to
live in the closet," Victoria says. "I met Gene at a café where we both
worked in 1980. He told me about his really cool girlfriend, and the
first thing he told me was that he was nonmonogamous. I was
attracted to both of them for the kind of relationship they were able
to maintain. I wanted that knowledge. Gene and I started dating,
and they both moved into my house two years later. The three of us
have been together as a family since 1982. In theory we can see
other people, but most of the time we don't."

EARLY FREEDOM TO BE DIFFERENT

FROM AN early age, Victoria was exposed to radical thinking about
sex and gender roles. In the 1970s her parents, both seekers, practiced Zen; her mother, a former scientist, is currently the abbot of a
large urban Zen center. "I came home at the age of ten and told my
father, 'I'm an oddball.' I don't know why I said that, but I was
already realizing my own alienation. I was lonely, socially awkward,
and usually retreated into books. I was a geek of the highest order.
I didn't date in high school, but I got involved in theater and did the
costuming. I knew I was bisexual by the time I was fourteen, and
luckily, growing up in a liberal family, I never felt shameful."

EARLY INTERESTS POINTED TOWARD EDUCATION
AND HEALING

VICTORIA FOLLOWED an early interest in health and science and
earned a bachelor's degree in psychology in 1985. That background

in psychology has evolved into a vocation in sex education, which includes everything from live sexual acts onstage to educational sex films. She says, "My duty and job and vocation is to help people realize their sexual potential and overcome feelings of shame, ignorance, awkwardness, and guilt. Sexuality is my life's work."

Once we are clear about how we want to feel and take responsibility for who we are, we make better choices. Self-understanding, however, does not occur all at once but requires a periodic review. Victoria suggests we ask ourselves, What can I do to become even more whole and loving—more of who I am?

A sign of growing maturity is how willing we are to accept what we cannot change about ourselves. Victoria remarks, "I'm never going to be an organized or neat person, or really good at the nuts and bolts of business. But now I accept that I am really good at being a feeling person, a communicative person, and a good counselor. It's about accepting your shortcomings and accepting your strengths and successes, too.

"You change by sitting alone with yourself and being quiet and looking at your life. It all comes down to deciding that you are going to take 100 percent responsibility for yourself 100 percent of the time—for your emotions, your behavior, and your attitude. I practice what I call compassionate awareness. You have to be able to sit with your feelings and not run away. If you want to change something about your sexual life, you need to understand how you got to where you are.

"You have to feel compassion for yourself. I have finally become the woman I wanted to be: confident, kind, sexy, competent, and comfortable in my skin."

WHAT PART HAVE YOU LEFT BEHIND?

So many men have told me they faced the same dilemma around fifty. They'll say, "I wish I could be a writer or a theatrical producer or work with the volunteer fire department"—whatever their passion happens to be—"but there's the mortgage, the kids aren't finished with college yet . . ." This is the signal to stop and do a life review. Contemplate: Where is my missing piece?

What part of me did I leave behind that desperately wants to find expression? What old wound or musty anger is locked up inside? Can I now let it go?

Gail Sheehy, *Understanding Men's Passages*

Accept Your Strengths as Purposeful

IS IT possible to solve one of the world's most ecologically devastating problems by simply talking to a friendly stranger in a restaurant? David Samuel seems to have done just that. The author of the book *Practical Mysticism,* David became a millionaire at the age of twenty-eight. A native of Montreal, he already had three jobs by the age of thirteen—photographing weddings, teaching photography, and working in a Hallmark card store. From an early age he was clear in his intention to make a lot of money in order to be free to pursue a spiritual quest.

David developed eight companies, encompassing retail stores, a real estate development and management company, a brokerage firm, and a trading company that bought goods in China and sold goods in Russia and South America. He recalls, "I came to a point where I said, 'Okay, that's enough.' I sold everything. People thought I was crazy."

Buying an open ticket to travel around the world, David started in Japan with no idea where he might end up. His motivating thought was to find teachers of Eastern traditions, such as Buddhism, Zen Buddhism, and Sufism, and the works of esoteric masters such as Gurdjieff and Ouspensky. He stayed in monasteries in Japan, India, Thailand, and Istanbul, crossing paths with many teachers and masters, as well as profoundly wise strangers. David remembers, "I was on a bus traveling in India, staring out the window feeling slightly depressed. A man sitting next to me who obviously owned almost nothing was eating his small lunch. He cut his banana in half and handed it to me, and said, 'It's okay if you have troubles as long as you share them.'"

But as David traveled the globe in search of truth and wisdom, many teachers told him in one way or another that he was not destined to be a monk. "Even though I met so many wonderful masters, I was never happy. My goal to be a monk and find God made me depressed. Something was wrong. I felt sadder and more lonely," he recalls. His teachers told him that he was supposed to be *in* the world—that he was to work with businesspeople and share spiritual teachings.

Finally David came to accept that his success in business had been purposeful, that his business acumen was a spiritual gift. "I gave in to my destiny," he says. "I now know that I am supposed to teach people how to be in business and make money, and yet not lose their spiritual orientation and values. We can be spiritual no matter what we are doing. Like a lot of people, I thought that we have to go off and devote ourselves to some esoteric spiritual practice, when in reality we can brilliantly live our truth as a cook in a restaurant. We have to find our own destiny and do that. Mine was to be in the Western world of commerce, not the Eastern world of a renunciate."

Be Open-minded and Prepared to Act

DAVID, WHO applies the principles behind disciplines such as tai chi, chi gung, and archery, consults with entrepreneurs. He teaches that all material success stems from the work we do on character. "The wisdom of the ages is right in front of us. If we choose to learn it and use it, we can become abundant and successful," he says. "When we refine our characters by being generous, honest, and conscientious, we create from our highest selves. Operating by these principles can tremendously increase our business. It's difficult for people in the West to realize that doing for others can bring such great benefits."

In 1995 David's brother saw an ad in a magazine for a new retreat center in Crestone, Colorado. Wanting to know more about it, David went for a visit. Little did he know that following his curiosity would lead to a series of seemingly random meetings that would ultimately lead him to collaborating with the physicist Paul Brown.

WAYS TO INCREASE YOUR ENERGY LEVEL

- Know when to eat.
- Lighten your load. Carry less in your pocket or purse. Weed out clutter.
- Do less.
- Associate with inspiring people.
- Delegate tasks.
- Be on time.
- Speak less.
- Exercise.

David Samuel, *Practical Mysticism*

While having a cup of tea in a restaurant in Crestone, David struck up a conversation with a friendly stranger. In line with his desire to be of service, David offered to visit with the man's friend, who needed some business advice. This contact led to another person who also needed some help, all of which David offered for free. Through a series of continuing synchronistic meetings in which David freely offered his business expertise, he eventually met a group of people interested in starting a company to develop clean energy devices.

At a conference in Phoenix, David met Paul Brown, a nuclear physicist who had come up with a better and faster method of stabilizing toxic waste from nuclear power plants. At present this radioactive waste, which poses a risk of contamination for thousands of years, is usually transported to an isolated area and buried. "Basically, Dr. Brown had the idea, and I had the capital to get the company started," David recounts.

Needless to say, this project could have a far-reaching outcome— and it all started from the tiny event of one man sitting in a restaurant drinking tea and talking to a stranger. "I didn't even find the article that got me there," says David. "It was my brother who pointed it out to me. If it's truly your destiny and you missed your delivery, the gods will find a way to bring it to you. You just have to be open-minded and prepared to act on what comes to you. Everything has a potential to guide you. I take the attitude that I learned in my spiritual search: Whether you are ruling an empire or cooking a small fish, you do the same thing."

CHANGING FROM THE INSIDE OUT

- *Ask yourself, What is missing in my life?* People often make changes, but they don't know what the real problem is, so the changes don't work. Don't move too fast until you see what's wrong.
- *Never say never.* For example, my businesses were working great, but I thought I needed to get away from business and be a monk. No. What I needed was to get more into business. What we think we need may not be what we need at all. For instance, when I was young I worked in retail stores and said to myself, I'll never work in retail again. But I wound up with three stores and made most of my money in them.
- *Reflect on what you really want.* When you want to make changes, it's tempting just to make changes in your outer world—like moving, divorcing, working harder—but that isn't necessarily the best way to change something. It's more effective to look within and see who you really are rather than trying to measure up to some external standard or ideal.
- *Rest, relax, and take care of what is in front of you.* Paying attention to what is interesting and following up on so-called chance encounters could have the potential to change your life or change the world.
- *Don't judge what's important or not important.* Life will bring you what you need. Just be open to all of it. Realize the perfection of life just as it is.
- *Stay in the present.* I like the Sufi saying, "He never thought of anything more than the one step he was taking."

David Samuel

Limitations May Be Strengths

IS FAILURE always a bad thing? Or is failure a signal to look again at what we thought we wanted?

Roy Iwaki, a sixty-five-year-old Japanese American, says that he failed miserably as a young man at his original goal of becoming an architect. After barely getting a degree from the University of California at Berkeley, Roy found his first job in an architect's office. He was fired after one month. Devastated, he spent several months looking for another position. After months of unemployment he gradually came to realize that his desire to be an architect was not a good fit with his true nature. Recognizing that his slower learning style and work style did not suit a high-profile, competitive career, he found work that was more aligned with his strengths, which included patience, ability to follow through on tasks over time, problem solving, and manual dexterity. Choosing the less glamorous occupations of carpenter, electrician, and remodeler provided him with a long-term successful vocation. Roy says, "My construction work gave me the time and the resources I needed to develop my avocation of paper sculpture. My paper art has been my true source of self-esteem and artistic fulfillment." This unique form of art, which Roy created from his own experimentation, could have been developed only by someone of his patience, spatial understanding, and determination. His ability to see possibilities, to explore unconventional ideas, and to take all the time he needed without pressure to perform—not qualities appreciated in his first job—turned out to be exactly what would make him a successful and original artist.

Follow Your Passion(s)

BEING TRUE to ourselves is the eternal recipe for living an authentic life that brings joy and success. Nancy Rosanoff, intuition consultant and author of *Knowing When It's Right,* demonstrates what happens when you (1) know how you want to feel; (2) know and focus on your strengths; (3) put out a strong intention for what you want; and (4) let go of any sense of struggle.

Rosanoff says, "About two years ago I decided not to market myself anymore. I thought to myself, You know what? I'm not good at marketing myself, I don't like it, and it's not working.

"I also came to the conclusion that the work I want to do is not a whole thing in itself. I need to be part of a larger fabric, working as one part of a team of people who have other kinds of expertise. Rather than do things I'm not good at, such as trying to force myself to market my skills, I decided to do what I do best as part of a larger group. My original intention was that I wanted to affect three areas: world leadership, business, and health care."

VISION INSPIRES ENERGY

The minute you create vision in your life—and that's what we're talking about when we talk about discovering what matters most—the energy comes back.

Hyrum W. Smith, *What Matters Most*

Within a few months of making that decision (setting her intention), Rosanoff was contacted by three consulting firms that had heard about her work from other colleagues. These contacts have provided her with steady training work. It is interesting that each of the companies with whom she is collaborating is focused on leadership, business, and health care. For example, one of the companies hired her to teach intuitive decision making to hospital executives and doctors.

Rosanoff continues to stay in the flow of her original intention to let go of the struggle of marketing and concentrate on increasing her skills and contacts. "Last week I got a call from one of these companies and was invited to become part of a very large project which is incredibly lucrative and which focuses on using exactly my skills. It is right in line with where I am and what I want to do, and it's happening with effortless ease. What I've realized is that the more I've focused on getting better at who I am, the more opportunities come to me. In the past, when I've tried to force things to happen, I end up doing work that isn't even appropriate. It's a waste of time and money."

Rosanoff's commitment to be prepared to follow up on leads that come her way is an important part of this process. Most of the time when we are thinking of the future and the great unknown, we assume an unnecessary burden of thinking that we have to do everything ourselves, and we have to figure it all out. Going with the flow, however, does not mean that we do nothing. We are working on whatever is at hand that requires attention. We learn. We do our inner work, and we take action when it feels right. We are willing to risk, to explore, to ask. We are not inactive but always alert for what is our business to do.

Your Evolving Self

BEING TRUE to ourselves is like looking for clues. The clues to our identities are often found in the specifics of our early environment and our early dreams.

EARLY CLUES TO DESTINY

CYNTHA GONZALEZ-KABIL, a thirty-seven-year-old transpersonal counselor, was born in Detroit to an upper-middle-class family. Her mother was Anglo American, her father Mexican. She says, "When I was six, I announced that I was going to be a nun and a doctor. The way I translate that now is that, at that time, nuns and doctors were the only modern women role models I had to express my desire to be on a spiritual path and be a healer. These two archetypes—the spiritual woman initiate and the healer—guided me."

Early Mixed Messages May Remain as Contradictory Inner Goals

"AT AGE fourteen I read a book on psychology and became convinced that 99 percent of illness is psychosomatic. That blew away my desire to be a doctor, and I became fascinated by psychology. At seventeen I attended a Buddhist meditation group that changed my thinking again about the wisdom of getting a doctoral degree in psychology. Everybody said I'd end up waitressing with a Ph.D."

Like most of us going into adulthood, Cyntha was bombarded by suggestions from members of both sides of the family to become a professional—doctor, lawyer, or engineer. She was to be the first woman in either family to go to graduate school, and everybody wanted her to be self-sufficient and financially independent. "It was a mixed message," says Cyntha. "On the one hand they urged me to be independent, and on the other it was 'go do what we tell you to do.' They weren't urging me to go after my passion of spirituality and psychology." When the University of Michigan offered her an engineering scholarship, she succumbed to the pressure and rationalized that she would make money as an engineer, then go to night school to become a psychologist!

"Four months later I was in the engineering school, and the day before exams were to begin, I had a major psychosomatic breakdown, which was my body's way of saying, No, this is not your right purpose. It really felt like a death-rebirth experience. I couldn't bat an eyelash. I was literally paralyzed with illness. I couldn't go to most of my exams, and I flunked a key determining one. There was now no choice."

Cyntha's story so far hints at something we need to consider as we examine our own destinies. How are we as individuals, making life changes one by one, contributing to the evolution of ideas and paradigms in our culture? In Cyntha's case the family messages were shaped by strong values of independence and striving for education to better oneself. Her individuation process involved choosing how to listen to her emerging life purpose and still maintain family relationships. At a deeper level one might conclude that Cyntha's dilemma was part of a larger shift in the collective unconscious, one that can be played out only in individual lives. Her interests in the feminine, healing, and spirituality are major trends that would become much more mainstream twenty years later. As we know, in the 1960s and '70s, American culture underwent a radical shift, with the diverse influences of social unrest, civil rights, personal freedom, Eastern philosophy, and spiritual teachings. Those shifts had to have happened to millions of individuals, *waking up one at a time.*

WAKING UP OVER TWO GENERATIONS

The first generation of the consciousness movement was focused on what might be called *personal waking up*. Its questions were individual . . .

By the 1980s and 1990s the second generation of the consciousness movement was growing into what might be called a *cultural waking up*. . . . This has been the work of the second generation of the consciousness movement: to see and feel and bring awareness to their own lives and to help to heal our world.

Paul H. Ray and Sherry Ruth Anderson,
The Cultural Creatives

AN AFFIRMATION COMES TRUE

DURING THE next few years, Cyntha studied transpersonal psychology and cultural anthropology. Her passion for shamanism took her to Brazil and Peru, where, synchronistically, many doors opened for esoteric study and mystical experiences. "When I entered the graduate program on transpersonal psychology at California Institute for Integral Studies in San Francisco, I had to fill out a two-page statement of what I would do with my degree. I wrote, 'I want to live in a major international metropolis and give seminars and workshops, bridging allopathic and complementary medicines.' Five years later I was doing exactly that in France. I became a full-time consultant on auric healing and the power of intention, as well as dance and art therapy, for the mainstream French Cartesian medical establishment."

While attending a conference for the International Transpersonal Psychology Association in Brazil, Cyntha met her future husband, Yahia, an Egyptian medical doctor. Married within months, they lived in England for a while before moving to the United Arab Emirates with their young daughter. Cyntha, continuing to evolve through her early Catholic, Buddhist, metaphysical, and traditional shamanistic explorations, now lives in a primarily Muslim community. "The theme of my life has always been bridging different worlds, starting with my Mexican father and Anglo mother. My current interest is in writing a book that extends the boundaries of what we think is reality—whether it's a cultural reality, a healing reality, or paranormal reality."

LET THE CALLING LEAD YOU

Change can bring the absolute terror of dying or of being consumed. You will feel engulfed by the unknown and feel out of control. But you have to trust that inner calling. It's there. Follow your passion. Do your passion.

Cyntha Gonzalez-Kabil, transpersonal counselor

Build on Your Strengths

MARTY DEAN, fifty-five, has been searching for her life purpose for as long as she can remember. Searching, observing, listening, and using her intuition were all keenly honed skills during the thirteen years she worked in the security department of the Hotel St. Francis in San Francisco, California. Starting as a guest services security officer, Marty eventually became manager of the department—a lone woman in charge of the team. In her role she met numerous heads of state and dignitaries, such as the former King Constantine of Greece and Henry Kissinger.

A CATALYZING ENCOUNTER

MARTY NOW realizes that her life began to shift the day she escorted Mother Teresa in the elevator of the hotel. "I was the security supervisor at the time, and we were waiting for the elevator to go from one floor to the other," she recalls. "All of a sudden I felt a hand making little circles on my shoulder blades. I turned around and looked down, and she was just looking up at me, smiling. I smiled back, but we didn't exchange a word. We walked into the reception for her, and the flashbulbs started going off. I never got a picture of her, but that image has stayed with me."

Sometime later the hotel was sold, a new regime came in, and Marty eventually left. She spent six months traveling, took an intensive career training program, and put together a new résumé. "It's always tempting to put too much emphasis on our weak points when we are making life changes. For example, I could have felt limited by not having a college education. But I learned in my process to focus on my strong points instead. I realized that my work over the last thirteen years had brought me extremely strong relationships in my community. I had to trust that this was a big advantage."

PAYING ATTENTION TO WHAT HAS ENERGY

"NONE OF my interviews for corporate jobs felt like a fit. By this time I knew that I needed to be free to follow whatever it was that I was trying to birth, and a corporate job wouldn't have given me that much freedom.

"About this time I came across an article in a national magazine about a man who was granting final wishes to terminally ill adults. That caught my attention because the two things I was looking to accomplish were number one: to stay connected to the liaison community from the hotel, and number two: to help people, but I didn't know in what capacity."

Following up on what had caught her attention, Marty contacted the man in the article and sent him her résumé. It turned out he was not interested in expanding to the San Francisco area. Disheartened, but still feeling a strong attraction to this idea, Marty decided to take another route and met with the director of Make-A-Wish Foundation, which grants wishes for children. In that interview she told the director about her desire to work with terminally ill adults, although there was no existing organization doing that. The director asked her if she had considered doing it herself. "I would never have thought of starting a foundation on my own, but after doing some research, and a lot of reflection, I found that I kept thinking about it. I was continually drawn to the idea and kept gathering more information. I knew it fit in perfectly with my resource of community contacts and my desire to help people. I began to think seriously about creating a nonprofit organization, which I eventually did. I named it Beyond Dreams Foundation."

LIFELONG TALENTS BLOOM IN DIFFERENT PERIODS

"I FEEL like the seed for this new direction was planted years ago. I had gone to a couple of psychics who told me that I was a healer and clairvoyant. At that time I didn't have a *clue* as to what that meant because I was working in the security department. But I did relate to the fact that I was unusually sensitive to the feelings of people and to the energies in certain spots. For example, I've often been able to feel a presence when I walk into a room or house and then later have it corroborated. A series of synchronicities helped me realize that I had a gift for working with healing energy. I started looking at things differently and did a lot of reading about personal and spiritual development. A few years later I met a woman who became a very good friend and who is my mentor in this area of healing energy."

Trusting her increasing interest in the spiritual life, making creativity a priority, and following her intuition, Marty has worked to make her vision a reality. "For me the juice is in understanding the value of the time of transition between life and death. I want to bring joy to the lives of those who don't understand the transition and are fearful. I just want to make their journey a little easier."

TRUST YOUR INNER STRENGTHS

- Listen to and follow your intuition.
- Keep focused on the vision, and see what happens.
- When you connect with someone or someone gives you something, follow up on it. Don't let it sit there. Do it when you're in the flow of receiving it. Things come to you for a reason.
- Build on your strengths. Let go of defining yourself by what you think you lack.

Marty Dean, founder and director of
Beyond Dreams Foundation

9

Develop Mastery

And that band was best that played the best *together*. That band, it would know its numbers and know its foundation and it would know *itself*.

You had to have a reserve of knowing how to play anything with a lot of feeling and understanding. And one thing—that one thing you just can't describe—the feeling there was to be a good band that made it able to do anything better than the next band, knowing how to do something without being told.

SIDNEY BECHET,
in *Creators on Creating*

Develop Your Edge, Expand, and Integrate

WHEN YOU look back on your life changes, chances are you will evaluate them in terms of (1) what you gained; (2) what you lost; (3) what you accomplished; (4) what you felt; (5) who you met; and (6) what you learned. Often it's the learning that stays with you and takes you to a new level of self-esteem, strength, honesty, and courage.

When you hold the vision of what you want, there are four essential points, three of which we have already discussed.

1. *Law of Attraction*. It is easier and more organic to *attract* change rather than to force changes to happen.

2. *We Attract from Our State of Being*. Our state of being is an energy field that radiates and connects to universal energy. Our state of being is how we feel about ourselves in the moment. It combines all of our past experiences, our sense of the future, and our basic sense of self-esteem (which may fluctuate but will have a general tone).

3. *Like Attracts Like*. Whatever vibration of energy we offer to the world (which is based on how we feel about ourselves) will return to us as a like vibration.

4. *Developing Mastery in Anything Raises Our Level of Vibration and Self-esteem*. In order to keep working upward in the spiral of life changes, we need to grow and expand and deepen self-esteem. How do we do that? By learning. Whenever we learn something new, even something as simple as changing the oil in the car, planting tomatoes, or learning to use a new software program, we gain in self-esteem.

Our movement into the unknown is greatly assisted when we have reliable information and skills. Therefore, if you are confused about your next step, ask yourself what subject or skill would be interesting to learn. What book calls out to you when you are at the bookstore? What class do you notice when perusing listings? What have you always wanted to know? When you define and hone the essential you, you gain mastery. Mastery is an intrinsic reward. Start anywhere. Stir the pot.

Continue to Go for the Vision

A WOMAN named Lee writes from South Africa, "As a child I used to live in my own fantasyland, and this made my mother very cross. After she passed away six years ago, I was finally free to reach for my dreams and make them a reality. All my life I wanted to do some form of artwork but was always told that artists were no-good people. I rebelled over this but believed in myself and knew that I could do it.

"I started taking ceramics classes and did well. When it was no longer a challenge, I got bored. I knew I had to do something else, so I started chancing my dreams. It all became a reality last week when I finally opened the doors of the shop which I have wanted for so long.

"I sell my own and others' arts and crafts from a little shop in my home. I knew I was going to have to give up a lot to get what I wanted and, yes, I did sacrifice a lot. First of all, I sacrificed my freedom because now I run a shop from 10:00 A.M. till 6:00 P.M. every day, Monday to Saturday, and on Sunday from 2:00 P.M. to 5:00 P.M., *but* . . . I'm finally happy. I don't mind not having time off because I'm doing what I love. I have also just discovered that I love to write, and now, when I have a free moment, I write poems. This is all I ever wanted in life, and now . . . I have it."

ELEMENTS OF WELL-BEING

Those who put energy into several areas of their lives, such as work and family, were more satisfied than those who put all their eggs into only one basket, such as work or family. The ability to invest in several aspects of life results in a "sense of mastery," a feeling of being "important and worthwhile, and finding life enjoyable." . . . The combination of mastery and pleasure is what generates a sense of well-being.

Nancy K. Schlossberg, *Overwhelmed*

Commit to Life Not Just Security

IF YOU are not happy, it's probably because you are doing things that don't feed you energetically. If you are not happy now, the unknown might seem like more of the same—or worse! Before taking on more commitments than you already have, look at what needs to be completed or released. It's very liberating to free up your time *before* you head out to tackle the unknown. As your time opens up, you might just make room for something to pop in that was waiting in the wings of the unknown future.

Get into the habit of reviewing your commitments from time to time. What is your level of energy around each one? Many times we agree to do things for the wrong reasons. Some commitments happen at a moment when

- We don't feel we can say no
- We want approval
- We put the pressure of others' needs before our own
- We decide to do more of what is not working.

Lifelong commitments inevitably evolve and change as we grow and individuate. Danielle, partner of Victoria, the sex educator and porn star in Chapter 8, embarked on the left-hand path in her twenties, when she realized that the known world—working an administrative job with no future and living with her parents—didn't hold a lot of promise. Like Victoria, Danielle decided early to live life on her own terms rather than by the rules of the socially proscribed setting in which she grew up.

She says, "I grew up in Indiana and and started working as a medical office assistant in my early twenties. It was a narrow, circumscribed life, living at home because I couldn't afford my own apartment. After seven years in the same office, I got the last raise I would ever get, and it was so small I couldn't even move out of the house on it. I couldn't see any future for myself. I decided the only thing to do was go back to college."

INDIVIDUAL GOALS SHIFTED TO COLLECTIVE ACTION

"MY PARENTS were role models for changing and governing the community—they were active in most of the town's community organizations, from the PTA to the church to the Elks. My dad even ran for mayor. I wanted to transform society, and I was in the heart of the antiwar movement in the 1960s," recalls Danielle. "I got involved with union organizing through my boyfriend, Gene, who has been my companion since 1972. I was active in the state women's committee for the union, and head and chairperson of the metropolitan district. Suddenly I had a constituency that would listen to what I had to say. I was negotiating contracts, and I felt very empowered creating better working conditions for people. I forgot about the idea of just changing *me* to have more money and a bigger life. I just started doing what was in front of me to help people work together collectively. Organizations are begging for someone who will make a commitment to do something. The best way to get involved is to volunteer in something you have some interest in."

Leaving Indiana, where Danielle had meaningful work and political influence, to live with Gene in California, where nothing was yet established, was a huge decision. Agreeing to live together non-monogamously, Gene and Danielle soon enlarged their relationship to include Victoria, then a psychology student. "Yes, we had our struggles," Danielle recalls. "I had to really confront my principles and beliefs, and move from an intellectual acceptance of Gene's relationship with Victoria to a deep-down feeling of being truly okay with it. With that the relationships among us worked. I had to be open to the changes, and realize that if it's right it will be okay.

"Once Victoria felt secure with our relationship, she wanted to explore her own fantasies. She started performing and stripping in clubs," Danielle says. "Her decision forced me to examine once more my feminist principles that say you can do what you wish with your body. But to go into that in the world was a scary thing. When I wasn't sure where I stood, I stood with my principles rather than with my fear."

DOING WHAT MATTERS GIVES US STRENGTH

DANIELLE'S POINT here is well taken. If we are committed to something that matters to us, that principle can furnish the support we need to move out of our comfort zones into new learning. By holding fast to a life committed to expanding rather than shutting down because of fear and traditional limitations, Danielle changed her life in very unexpected ways.

"Synchronicity brought in some movie opportunities for Victoria, and she made her first film in 1984. Suddenly we had a ministar in our midst! Life changes push you to move along. Her success and notoriety put our life into whole new levels of turmoil. I'm enough of an activist that I became aware of the changes that were going on in our society, and the dangers to people in the sex industry because of the religious right. In the 1980s the religious right was attacking abortion and pornography, although it was still quasi-legal in most places. There had been several prominent arrests of actors in well-known movies, and I could see it was easy for an individual to get chewed up by the system in a cultural war. I didn't want that to be Victoria's fate.

"In part to defend sexual freedom of speech and to defend her, I cofounded a statewide coalition of citizens against censorship. That moved me into ten years of anticensorship activism."

Danielle's continuing commitment to make the world a freer place has come to the fore several times in the last few years. Her advocacy work expanded to include a diverse spectrum of individuals and groups of artists, feminists, gays, lesbians, and sex workers. She has been able to garner enough support from these diverse interest groups to affect major changes in the law at the federal level on issues of sexual expression. She says, "I was vindicated in the initial direction I had chosen for my life."

IF YOU WANT TO CHANGE SOCIETY

- Don't wait for someone else to do it.
- Don't be afraid to bite off more than you can chew. You'd be surprised how much you can do in little steps.
- Society changes by the accumulation of all those people who stand up.

Danielle, activist

Rediscover Your Center When Things Go Wrong

WHEN OUR lives seem stuck, the easy way out is to justify our joylessness by saying, Well, that's just the way it is. If we feel helpless and can see no way to make a change, we just assume *we* have to adjust. Maybe the answer is somehow to be a "better person," but we do nothing. Our motivation disappears, and we begin to operate on automatic.

FINDING BOTTOM

RENEE, FORTY-THREE, had been married for twenty-one years. She and her husband, Hugh, had two sons. "I woke up one morning and my life seemed as bad as it could get," she recalls. "My teenage son, Bob, was into all kinds of drugs, and it was hard to be in the same room with him. He dropped out of school and left home. Hugh was drinking heavily and isolating from me. That morning I seemed to have some kind of clarity, and I knew I had reached my bottom. I told Hugh I was leaving him. I moved to Santa Cruz, California, for six months."

WHO AM I NOW?

DURING THIS period Renee started reading, meditating, and taking workshops and classes to rediscover who she was. "I didn't even know what I liked anymore," she recalls. "When my sister took me out to dinner, I wanted to keep going to the same place because it didn't have a big menu. I literally couldn't make a decision about what to eat."

One of the first things Renee remembers doing is deciding to let go of the toxic people in her life. As feelings began to surface, she realized that she felt worse rather than better, after visiting with some of her friends. The superficiality of the relationships added to her despair.

KEEP ON KEEPING ON

Many people are knocked flat at some point in middle life. What's important is not how you get knocked down . . . it's whether or not you can pick yourself up.

Gail Sheehy, *Understanding Men's Passages*

BUILDING A NEW FOUNDATION

RENEE TOOK a job organizing corporate events, which allowed her to support herself, regain a feeling of self-worth, and make new acquaintances. At the beginning of their separation, she told Hugh she preferred not to have any long telephone conversations with him. After a few months she asked him to write her letters. "This was really hard for him to do. I received two long letters, and he told me that he was starting to see some things about himself. It was beautiful. He wrote that he had started meditating and stopped drinking. I think he started going to some Alcoholics Anonymous meetings, even though that wasn't the main route of his recovery."

When Hugh came for a visit, Renee says, "It was like coming home. Just seeing him I felt, This is the man I love. It was a soul mate feeling. On his next visit he brought a camper that he had just bought, and we went camping. This was a new interest for him. He was really getting into finding out what he liked and what he wanted. We had a wonderful time, and I knew then that I wanted to go home with him."

For Renee, Hugh, and Bob, sobriety continued to demand that they define themselves, and how they were going to relate to each other, in new ways. Changes in their family life were hard-won with lots of counseling. A major agreement was to keeping the lines of communication open and current. Renee explains, "A big change for me was that now I was dealing with someone who was sober and available, and who wanted to be with me. Up till then all the men in my life—dad, uncles, brothers, and all my boyfriends—had been alcoholics. I knew what to do and how to behave with people who had a drinking problem. Now I was with a man who was sober and available, and who had an opinion about the bathroom towels! It's hard to explain, but I had always been on the periphery of his life, and now I was in the spotlight."

INDIVIDUALS FIRST, THEN PARTNERS

A MAJOR key to the positive changes in the family was the personal development of each of the members. Hugh began to explore and develop some interests that had lain dormant for years. He started spending time with men friends instead of staying home and drinking. He became an interesting person again, says Renee, and reemerged as the man she fell in love with. "I think our identities become too enmeshed in the focus of the marriage," Renee comments, "and we lose the focus on ourselves. As individuals, we become casualties to the marriage."

Renee and Hugh committed to finding out what each of them liked and didn't like. They learned how to talk to each other about what they were feeling. For example, Renee said they created a safety zone at the dining room table, where they would agree to sit for an hour, sometimes sitting in silence for thirty minutes before the conversation began to flow.

A HAPPY FAMILY

AFTER HUGH stopped drinking and his recovery was fairly well established, Bob started his own recovery. Strong family ties helped when Hugh was diagnosed with colon cancer. Renee is grateful that he is healthy after a successful operation. "That painful, unhappy family no longer exists," she says. "But I don't want to close the door on that scenario either, because it helps me stay on track today. Hugh's work takes him out of the country, but now he wants me with him. We have such a fun and romantic time. Even though he works long hours during the week, we spend all our time together on the weekend. We even go grocery shopping together, and do things we never used to do. When I look back, if I hadn't hit my bottom and recognized it and moved out and found myself again, I don't think Hugh and Bob would ever have started looking at themselves."

HEALING CHANGES

- Recognize your bottom.
- Trust those moments of clarity and act on them.
- Instead of trying to fix other people, put the focus on yourself.
- Start today being available and loving with your children.
- Avoid making constant critical comments to your kids.
- Encourage your family members to be their own people, then respect them even if you don't agree with them.

Renee

Freeing the Self

THE INNER drive to become who we were meant to be is always at work. Sometimes, however, certain things may have to occur before we can blossom. Kathy, a therapist in the Pacific Northwest, had a patient named Caroline, a seventy-nine-year-old woman whose symptom was severe depression following the death of her forty-three-year-old retarded son. During therapy, Kathy says, Caroline's biggest realization came as she saw that her entire seventy-nine years had been spent being there for everyone but herself. She never learned to say no. In order to gain approval, because she never felt good enough, she continually rescued everyone around her.

After a few weeks of intense therapy, Caroline admitted she had always wanted to be a writer. She had been writing since childhood but had never showed anyone her work. She felt that her writing was not good enough, and she feared ridicule.

Kathy asked Caroline to bring her writing to one of their sessions. She brought in poems scribbled on backs of envelopes, and the beginning of her life story in bits and pieces on yellowed scraps of paper. Caroline beamed when Kathy offered to type up some of the writing on the computer. The two of them made a book of Caroline's poems in a three-ring binder. Kathy remembers how proud Caroline was to see her work typed up in the binder.

Since that first step of becoming more accepting of herself, Caroline has written more poems, and had one published. She is now active in a group that meets at a local coffeehouse to read poetry, play music, and tell stories, and she also plays her violin at the meetings. She has discovered that she is a terrific storyteller and is now in demand to tell her stories, not only at the coffeehouse but also at her church. Kathy writes, "Caroline is now eighty, and talent is still coming out all over. She is working on her book, and I would imagine that it will be finished before too long. It has been very interesting to see how the grief from the death of Caroline's son resulted in her finding out who she really is."

MEETING OUR OWN TRUE FACE

There is something in us, an urgency to meet the teachings on the other side, that gnaws at our ignorance, that desires to meet our own true face, however lazy and comfort-loving we may seem to be. This something was working in me, albeit slowly, and often underground.

Natalie Goldberg, *Long Quiet Highway*

Keep Getting Better: Your Best Decade Might Be the Ninth

BARBARA KINGSOLVER, the author of several novels, was recently interviewed for an article in the *San Francisco Chronicle* about writers over the age of fifty. Noting that creativity is an ever-growing drive within us, she spoke of the eighty-four-year-old screenwriter Horton Foote, who wrote *A Trip to Bountiful* and *To Kill a Mockingbird*. She had been astounded to hear Foote remark that he was planning to do his best work in his nineties. Age, for the writer, she mused, only lends greater depth and understanding to one's work. Kingsolver says, "I always explain to young writers that getting published takes time, and there's a good reason for it. We are artists of the human condition, and simply by slogging through another year of being human, we know more about it. We may accelerate the process somewhat by keeping our eyes wide open, taking good notes, and taking risks that broaden our experience of life—but [we] should bear in mind that any risk prone to shorten life is a bad trade-off, in actuarial terms. The surest path to greatness for a writer is probably this simple: (1) never stop paying attention, and (2) live to be old."

TAKE YOUR TIME

In a five-decade career, Al Purdy, one of Canada's greatest poets, published thirty-three books of poetry and won the Governor General's Literary Award in 1966 for *The Cariboo Horses* and in 1986 for *Collected Poems, 1956–86*.

"His poetry came out of the ordinary—trees, animals, loggers, workers," said poet Patrick Lane. "His was the voice of the common man and common woman."

According to Purdy's publisher, Howard White, he was a high school dropout and served an undistinguished term in the air force. "He said himself that his first book, which he self-published, was atrocious," White said. "For a lot of years, it was hard to look at this writing and say there's anything original or promising. And yet, he suddenly became the most original of voices at age forty."

Associated Press obituary, April 2000

Life never stops changing, and we always have options. Education in later years is bound to become a growing trend as our population grows older and lives longer. According to a recent article in the *San Francisco Chronicle* by the staff writer Sam Whiting, retired people are flocking back to school in several institutions in the Bay Area. The Emeritus College at College of Marin, in Marin County, California, has three thousand students, and many of the popular art lecture classes have over eighty students. Stanford University's enrollment in continuing education has doubled in the past few years, and they receive four times as many applications as for their master of liberal arts program. The Fromm Institute for Lifelong Learning at the University of San Francisco was founded twenty-five years ago by Hanna and Alfred Fromm, German emigrants who ran a family wine business. Once she retired Hanna realized how boring life had become. She hired six retired professors to teach seventy-five students in classes that have grown to include fine arts, art history, literature, music, and history. Classes such as Why Are We Here?, discussing the works of various great writers on life purpose, became so popular that enrollment is by lottery.

As we contemplate moving forward, learning is often the first step.

Align with Your Values

WHEN YOU feel dull, trapped, or adrift, you are out of alignment. Being in alignment means being aware of whether you are feeling good or bad and feeling that what you are doing makes a difference in the world.

Your feelings are your inner guidance. How can you get back into alignment? If you are trying to make a decision about something right now—whether it's a job change, marriage, or travel plans—use this alignment continuum to find out exactly what your feelings are. Rate how you feel on each of the quality continua by marking where you think you are currently sitting.

ALIGNMENT CONTINUUM

Think of one issue in your life that you are questioning. Mark an X on the line where you think you stand on each of the qualities concerning this issue.

On this issue of _____ , I feel _____ percent

Committed _____ Ambivalent

Passionate _____ Dull

Open _____ Overwhelmed

Trusting _____ Skeptical

Optimistic _____ Pessimistic

Connected _____ Isolated

Grounded _____ Defended

Honest _____ Manipulating

Discerning _____ Unclear

Receptive _____ Shut Down

Courageous _____ Victimized

Mentally Stimulated _____ Bored

Flowing _____ Stagnated

Relaxed _____ Uptight

Motivated _____ Depressed

Happy _____ Sad

Spirit-full _____ Lonely

Now that you have described how you feel on each of these continua, you may want to write a juicy and fun statement of intention to shift the energy. Let's say you are deciding whether to move to Seattle. Rate each feeling in relation to the decision about moving to Seattle.

Where do you see a block (low energy) to what you are proposing? What does your intuition suggest that you need to do or rethink? In writing your statement of intention, you might affirm to yourself, "I'm open to and excited about seeing what adventures lie ahead in Seattle, or in an even better choice if one arises."

DEEP DOWN

The outer situation of your life and whatever happens there, is [like] the surface of a lake. Sometimes calm, sometimes windy and rough, according to the cycles and seasons.

Deep down, however, the lake is always undisturbed.

Eckhart Tolle, *The Power of Now*

10

Be Open and Present

If life were not impermanent, it couldn't be the wonder that it is.
Still, the last thing we like is our own impermanence.
Who hasn't notice the first gray hair and thought, Uh-oh.

CHARLOTTE JOKO BECK,
in *Radiant Mind*

Life Is Both a Seesaw and a Spiral: The Eight Worldly Dharmas

HAVE YOU just lost your job? Has your rent increased unexpectedly? Have you lost a loved one? Has your reputation been tarnished? Did you think you'd be further along in life by now? If so you are probably blaming yourself for not being more in control! Any and all of these so-called setbacks teach us that we cannot control the change in our lives, we can only control how we handle that change.

Each change is a specific, and apparently necessary, step that allows us to reshape ourselves. Over and over we dip down on life's seesaw, feeling the ground hard under our bottoms. Pushing off again, we hover momentarily on the neutral balance point. Then, without warning, we shoot straight up to the apex, and we laugh with surprise. Inevitably, the board evens out again and we continue the "fun." Children naturally love the surprise of the seesaw. As adults we gain in maturity as we realize that each stage holds value.

Buddhist teaching reminds us that life continually shifts between opposite conditions—or the eight worldly dharmas of pleasure and pain, loss and gain, praise and blame, fame and disgrace. Without the perspective that life *is* constantly changing, and is *supposed* to be constantly changing, the unknown may seem bleak and pointless. If we think we have lived well only if we have avoided the experiences of pain, loss, blame, and disgrace, we lose sight of the fullness of life.

The eight worldly dharmas exist only in our minds: We create the judgment that something is good or bad. Our natural instinct is always to want the positive sides of these worldly coins and to live in pleasure, gain, praise, and fame. Freedom and wisdom arise when we decide to be present with what *is,* to learn from any situation, no matter how it looks or feels. How do we do that?

WISDOM IS KNOWING WHEN WE ARE HOOKED

We might feel that somehow we should try to eradicate these feelings of pleasure and pain, loss and gain, praise and blame, fame and disgrace. A more practical approach would be to get to know them, see how they hook us, see how they color our perception of reality, see how they aren't all that solid. Then the eight worldly dharmas become the means for growing wiser as well as kinder and more content.

Pema Chödrön, *When Things Fall Apart*

Curiosity about ourselves and the events in our lives is a helpful trait to cultivate in order to work creatively, rather than reactively, with the eight worldly dharmas. When we remember that any event could be good or could be bad, we can let go of the drive to control, since we can never really control events anyway. With curiosity, we can gather information on how we feel about something. We can begin to notice when we are in pain. How do we feel when we have suffered a loss? How do we feel when we have been blamed or criticized? Often we jump into a defensive reaction that covers up how we feel. Curiosity allows us to open a place in ourselves where we might decide to drop our attachment to the drama and see instead what we have to learn.

To shift from creating a limiting story of injustice or taking defensive postures born of fear, begin to notice what goes through your mind when a life change happens. Do you become afraid and close down, or do you assume there is a reason for what's happening and open up to it?

Stay Attuned

THE CHICAGO bandleader Steve Cooper is almost consistently upbeat and open about life. He says, "I just keep thinking that life is magical if you are open to it. So many people are negative. You can look at things and see them as getting worse, but I believe that more people are becoming more aware and compassionate. I try to stay open to seeing the positive.

"If I try to analyze the synchronicities that happen to me, I think it shuts off the flow. It's kind of like playing a musical instrument. You can't think about it too much. When things don't happen the way you want, you have to let it go.

"Six or seven years ago none of the ballrooms would hire us. I kept wondering, How could I get them to hire our band? Instead, I found a place and rented it myself, and we started out on our own. Then all the other ballrooms started calling us, and now we're working so much we need a vacation. Sometimes I lose money, but I often get other benefits and contacts, so now I don't worry about the money at all."

As long as we immerse ourselves in the flow of life—just by *accepting* the flow and doing what comes naturally—we seed the field for synchronicities to bring us gifts. When we go with our flow, and are open and prepared to act, we are in what is called effortless ease. We may work hard, but the work makes us feel uplifted and fulfilled, so that there is a sense of ease and rightness in our transitions. We are tapped into the power of the present moment.

Be Open to Unexpected Help:
Anything Is Possible

WE NEVER know where help will come from. A woman named Christina writes that for years she had worked as a waitress. After moving to Florida three years ago, she fell back on waiting tables and was doing quite well financially but felt dissatisfied and unhappy. "I enjoyed interacting with people in the restaurant, but I felt truly alone," Christina says. "To compensate, I began working as much as I could, seven days, sixty hours a week. Even when I became run-down and got sick, I kept working. One day I was with a friend on my way to work, and we stopped at a convenience store. The next thing I knew I was in the hospital. Because of my collapse, I never made it to the bank that day. When I came out of the hospital a week later, I had a big stack of bounced check notices in my mailbox.

"I was so confused as to what I had in the account and what fees I owed that I went to the bank, sat down with an officer, and asked for help in sorting it out. She refunded all the fees to me, and I remarked how grateful I was since waitresses don't typically have medical insurance, and I was facing a costly hospital bill. She told me I should find a part-time job with medical benefits. I said, skeptically, 'Who would hire a waitress who never finished college for a part-time job with full benefits?' She said *they* [the bank] would."

Christina filled out an application that day and has been working for the bank ever since. This job turned out to be a boon in other areas of her life as well. Working daytime hours freed her for social events in the evenings, which resulted in her meeting her husband. "I know the bank is not my ultimate life path," she says, "but I feel it is a step. I am now starting to get restless and dissatisfied again, but it is not because I feel alone. It is because I see so much at work that isn't right, and I know I really have more to do." Looking back over the recent changes in her life, Christina says, "I would have never gotten this far if I had made it to the bank that day and made my deposit!" Her story is another good example of the principle Who knows if it's good or if it's bad?

CENTER YOURSELF THROUGHOUT THE DAY

Pay special attention as you arrive home today. Use it as an
excuse to center yourself.

Penney Peirce, *The Present Moment*

Practice Peaceful Waiting

KATHY, THE therapist we met in the previous chapter, has learned
that even slow periods have a purpose. A new venture may not
reveal its true purpose if we look at it from only one perspective—
for example, from the bottom-line question of Is it making enough
money?

Kathy writes, "I left an eighteen-year career at a hospital to start
my own counseling practice in 1998. In my heart I felt this was the
right move. I'd been reading [spiritual authors such as] Deepak
Chopra, James Redfield, Wayne Dyer, and others. Even though I've
had fewer patients than I anticipated, and as a result less money,
those clients have taught me more than I could ever have imagined.
My biggest concern is staying on track without becoming discouraged while I wait for my next move to become clear. It's a mixture
of peace and occasional discouragement."

While Kathy has had fewer patients than expected, what *is* happening is a deep level of interaction and learning that might not
have been possible if she were swamped with patients and less
likely to have time for integration and reflection. She concludes, "I
have experienced a great deal of change—divorce, entering college
as an adult to pursue my R.N., remarriage, illness, career change,
reentering college, and setting up a new business. Making changes
is much easier now that I have learned to meditate and listen in the
quietness for my answers. My old manner of prayer was asking and
talking to God. My new method of prayer (meditation) is knowing
that God/Spirit already knows what my needs are."

INCUBATION

What are the conditions for creativity? First of all, one must be living in the medium. People are not creative in some medium with which they have no real contact.

. . . The spontaneous element is really out of the person's control. Yet, though it comes unexpectedly, spontaneity does not come without certain conditions being satisfied:

- Study. Prepare the ground.
- See how it fits together *in your mind.* Don't write anything down yet.
- Find what's missing and do more investigation.
- Don't come to a solution prematurely.
- Keep the groundwork fluid so there can be a transformation.
- When you are ready for the next level, *you must ask yourself a clear question.*
- Don't think about it. Empty your mind of all that you know about it. *All that remains is the need to find an answer.*

Adapted from J. G. Bennett, in *Creators on Creating*

We Shape and Color Events

WHEN WE are on the "wrong side of the coin" with the eight dharmas, we have two choices. When things are not going well, we can either try to power our way through, or stop and reflect about what is really going on. Assuming that everything happens for a reason, what might we see as a contributor to our dilemma? Consider if any of these five possibilities might be the hidden purpose or the root of your setback or problem: (1) projection, (2) timing, (3) karma, (4) personal growth, (5) bowing to a higher intelligence.

RECOGNIZING OUR PROJECTIONS

WHEN SOMEONE in your life is giving you trouble, it's an opportunity for you to become aware of your own beliefs and attitudes. We think *they* are the problem, of course, and if only *they* would change, our life would work better. However, during these times, perhaps we should play with the idea that the other person is serving as a teacher who is reflecting something in our own nature that needs balancing. How might those big, ugly, unacceptable aspects you see in another person be an unacceptable part of yourself that you need to recognize and change? What could you do to improve your situation without asking anyone else to change?

An interesting phenomenon happens when you start to think about doing something different, such as quitting a job or starting a new venture. Some people will think it's a good idea and be supportive; others will give you strong advice not to do anything too risky. Often those negative comments coming from other people are actually reflections of your own self-doubts. You will notice that the more deeply committed you become, the fewer negative admonitions you get from others.

TIMING

IF THINGS are not happening the way you want, it may simply not be the right time. You may mistakenly be pushing. At such times we tend to accuse ourselves of inadequacy—of not taking the right actions or of not being clear enough about what we want. If the universe has its own timing—which it does—you may do better to relax and accept the situation and yourself just as you are. Keep your focus on creating positive energy in every moment, recommit to attracting positive change, and surrender to the idea that a greater intelligence than yours is at work. Surrendering allows Spirit to have a free hand to create for us.

Further along in this chapter is a description of the nine-year cycle of growth that influences events in our lives to an often astonishing precision.

KARMA

EASTERN PHILOSOPHY teaches that every thought someone has had continues to exist in the universal field. It also teaches that every action has a reaction. Therefore, an inexplicable setback or turn of events may have no visible root cause because its actual cause is too far back in time. The notion of karma is helpful in explaining why some terrible events—such as accidents, untimely deaths, and murders happen to innocent people. If you realize that time really has no meaning in the largest sense of life, and that you may live many different lives whose actions have not yet been balanced, it makes more sense that your present life is an opportunity to work out some of those outstanding debts or conditions. You need not worry constantly that something bad is just around the corner. There is no way to anticipate "bad karma" arising—nor is knowing your karma useful or possible. The reason that we forget our life purpose at birth is that each life must start afresh. There would be little joy or creativity if we continued to drag our past along! However, when something bad does happen, the only question is how are you going to respond?

PERSONAL GROWTH

WHEN YOU feel stymied, confused, or chastened, it may be that your character needs to be examined, refined, and developed. A "negative" life change may be the catalyst for you to learn how to forgive, to trust more deeply, to develop patience, or persevere in the face of adversity. It is from dealing with what we don't want that spurs us on to greater accomplishments and understanding.

BOWING TO A HIGHER INTELLIGENCE

SOMETIMES OUR current situation indicates that it is time to grow not only in personal ways, but also in psychospiritual understanding. We are forced to search more deeply and to take responsibility for how we need to change our thinking or behavior. We see that we have little or no control over what happens, yet we are tied to the inevitable fluctuations of life. Yesterday we were lauded. Today we are forgotten. If we can be open to living life exactly as it is today, and not attached to needing life to be a high plateau of excitement or needing others to behave the way we want them to, we are truly free.

Bowing to a higher intelligence does not mean doing nothing, but it may. Surrendering to the inevitable, and accepting circumstances that you cannot change is wisdom.

Nonattachment is not about being in denial or being uncaring, but about keeping an open mind. It is about learning, as we move *toward* life with questions and curiosity. Openness encourages us to anticipate help from unexpected places. It softens and enlarges us. When we grow larger and can tolerate more uncertainty, life becomes less threatening. Through curiosity and openness we begin to see how we are seduced by our fears and insecurities. We are able to sit equally with change or no change.

The Nine-Year Spiral

WE LIVE in spiraling cycles, usually bringing us similar challenges but at different levels. Having studied numerology for years, I find that it helps me to know what personal year cycle is influencing me.

Numerology is an ancient system of esoteric knowledge that describes who we are and what we came on Earth to do. There is evidence that people in all civilized countries have used forms of astrology and numerology to guide them in everyday decisions and to help them cope with the unknown. These systems demonstrate underlying foundations that give structure to what might seem random or chaotic. Numerology helps us orient ourselves to lessons we need to learn. I have found it a very accurate and relatively easy system to use.

THE NUMEROLOGICAL PERSONAL YEAR

BY USING your birth date as a reference, you can find out where you are in the nine-year cycles of development from the birth of a new direction (a 1 personal year) though the foundation-building time (the 4 personal year) and the harvesttime (an 8 personal year) to the completion time (9 personal year).

To find your place in the nine-year numerological cycle, all you have to do is write down the month and day of your birth and add it to the full current year. Let's say your birthday is November 28 and the year you are asking about is 2002. You would write, 11 28 2002. Add all the numbers together $1 + 1 + 2 + 8 + 2 + 0 + 0 + 2 = 16 = 1 + 6 = 7$. You are in a 7 personal year.

Here is a very brief description of what to expect in each personal year. The important point to remember is that if you are near the end of the cycle—in the last few months of an 8 year or at any time in a 9 year—your actions are more about ending and completing things than about starting a new venture. It's best to wait until you are in the new 1 year cycle to start important ventures or make decisions with long-term consequences. Note: The personal year changes to the next consecutive number each January no matter when your birthday occurs.

Characteristics of Personal Years

1 Planning, launching, moving, beginning, new opportunities, clarity, choices, independence, originality. Favors mental activities, writing, designing, directing, starting a new business. Challenges: Arrogance, timidity, confusion, fear, low self-confidence, distractions, listening. Action Months: April, September

2 Relationships, partnerships, cooperation, coordinating, consolidation, details, slow change, receptivity. Favors love, integration, taking care of the self, opening the heart, negotiating. Challenges: Fear, patience, sluggishness, overlooking details, oversubmissiveness. Action Months: March, August, December

3 Good luck, spontaneous social events, creativity, teamwork, help from friends when needed, self-improvement, general well-being, short trips, conception or birth, spending time with young people. Favors imaginative endeavors and sales. Challenges: Overoptimism, distractions, jealousy, hyperactivity, depression, extravagance, possible job layoffs. Action Months: February, July, November

4 Planning, laying groundwork for future payoff, building, revitalizing health and image, taking care of business. Favors reorganizing, investing prudently, making personal and business commitments, repairing, gardening, producing. Challenges: Health concerns, debts, too much stress or pressure to produce results, restrictions and red tape. Action Months: January, June, October

5 Sudden changes or decisions, new opportunities, freedom, love affairs, changes in the body, public activity. Favors fre-

quent travel, selling, promotion, multiple projects, vitality, sex, changes for the better. Challenges: Overextension or speculation, distractions, uncertainty, resistance to change, lending money, adrenal exhaustion. Action Months: April, May, August, September

6 Responsibility, many duties or support of others, marriage or divorce. Favors social events, feelings of love and security, teaching, improving the home, voice or speaking lessons, paying back loans, community work or teamwork. Challenges: Feeling like a victim or martyr, resentment, guilt, overextension, deadlines, money spent on necessities rather than pleasure, work preventing recreation. Action Months: April, August

7 Reflection, spiritual connection, choosing to withdraw from negative people or uninspiring scenarios, sabbatical. Favors education, more meaningful choices, time spent in nature, analysis, research, writing, composing, personal and spiritual growth, meditation. Challenges: Self-deception, skepticism, pessimism, suspicion, burnout, loss, deceit. Action Months: March, July, December

8 Taking back power where you have relinquished it, recognition, achievement, career advancement, property investments, licensure, increased income. Demands being absolutely clear and businesslike about finances. Favors editing, sports, buying or selling property, harvesting results of the last eight years. Challenges: High financial stakes, legal matters, power struggles, life balance, overextension. Action Months: February, June, October, November

9 Completions in all areas, changes for the better, increased opportunities, expansion, increased intuition. Favors emotional and physical healing, education, long-distance and international travel, spiritual development. Challenges: Emotional roller coaster, loss, grief, forgiveness, tolerance, letting go, confusion about the next step. Action Months: January, May, September, October

Dismembered

LEIGH, A fifty-year-old advertising director, attended one of my workshops with her stepdaughter, with whom she had had a recent reconciliation after several painful years of separation. Leigh, like many of us, has lived through the eight worldly dharmas of being on the high road and the low road.

At the age of fourteen and a half, Leigh had already started college. At fifteen she had sung at the Metropolitan Opera in New York City and was expected to have a brilliant career. Within months, however, she came down with a serious bronchial infection. After several surgeries her vocal cords were stripped to prevent a mucus buildup that might have suffocated her. Her condition forced her to leave New York City, and she moved to Puerto Rico to heal in the high heat and humidity. The illness turned out to be the death of her career. "I don't think I've ever stopped looking for the reason why it all happened," she admits. "The search led me to deeper spiritual study."

Leigh eventually developed a second career in advertising and married a man who had children. She became very close to her stepdaughter, but through a series of misunderstandings the two grew estranged and the daughter moved away from the family to start a life on her own.

HOPE LIES IN UNCHARTED TERRITORY

When you attempt to hang on to the past, you are in the greatest peril. The future is uncharted territory—but it is where hope lies. There are no guarantees. The risk is great. But if you want to be fully alive, quite simply, you have no choice.

Carol Orsborn, *The Art of Resilience*

During this period of estrangement, Leigh became seriously ill. The dormant anaerobic viruses from her previous disease took hold of her system, and she nearly died. One day in the hospital, a rabbi told her, "You know, Leigh, if you are holding on to any negative energy, you should really let it go because it will kill you. You need all your strength to get better." Leigh knew without doubt that the issue she needed to resolve was the one with her stepdaughter. By this time she was no longer interested in who was right or wrong. She was determined to repair the estrangement and move on.

Leigh called her stepdaughter, and the two met and had a heartfelt reconciliation. "I feel like a different person," Leigh says. "I have my daughter back. I have my family back. I have my life back. I feel so much lighter. There's still a lot to work on, but it's not a negative burden."

The long-dormant virus that stripped Leigh of her place in the opera world also created a healing crisis that sparked the insight to reach out to one she had lost. A story such as this gives us a hint of the complex web of forces—past, present, and future—that pull us through life.

"Never give up on the resolution of an issue," says Leigh. "Don't try to control it, but trust that it's all happening in the way it's supposed to unfold. Even though I didn't have a lot of faith in a positive resolution at first, I see now that the heaviness in my heart was a symptom that there was something to work on. The heaviness reminded me of where my work was. You can't just banish people from your life. You have to finish it one way or the other."

We Have Guardian Angels

BEING OPEN also means asking for help when you need it, and being receptive to nonphysical interventions.

In *Angels and Companions in Spirit,* the authors Laeh Maggie Garfield and Jack Grant make a distinction between angels, who are considered exalted beings, and those guides who we generally refer to as guardian angels. They believe guardian angels are more like invisible helpers and comforters, mentors and companions. They report one instance of spiritual communication in which spiritual guides say, "A relationship between a guide and a human being is a two-way phenomenon. You may be attempting to contact us, but meanwhile we've been watching you for years and years, long before you were aware of our existence. . . . Although we may not hover continually by your side, we are with you in your hours of deepest trouble, and we stay tuned to your life situation. You are never alone. Throughout your life you'll have company in everything of significance that you do. The universe may scatter its children far and wide, but it doesn't abandon them."

These beings point out that when they are able to help us achieve something, it is an achievement for them and their development as well. Our lives, our choices, our struggles, and our accomplishments are part of a scheme much larger than we ordinarily consider. Their presence may be felt when we receive flashes of insight, dreams, and chance encounters. They are probably present when we experience a renewed commitment or when we feel reenergized to tackle our problems or when we regain any power we have relinquished to other people. The silent encouragement of guardian angels may shift our attention in a way that helps us to develop contentment, faith, love, creativity, joyous self-expression, and the flow of abundance. *Our* work is to become open, willing, and ready to *allow* these and all other positive qualities to manifest.

YOU ARE NOT ALONE

Having an open connection to the intuitive plane is like having a terrible day and then remembering that there will be someone at home who loves you no matter what. It might be your dog, cat, fish, or lover. This can make the worst days bearable.

Nancy Rosanoff, *The Complete Idiot's Guide to Making Money Through Intuition*

The angels or guides do not take away our free will or our responsibilities. Giving thanks and praising our unseen helpers is affirmation that helps keep the communication flowing between the two worlds. Asking our guides for *specific* help in manifesting intentions and our highest good is powerful. To begin to feel your connection to your guardian angel, it might be helpful to imagine a threshold or gate between our world and theirs. Each time you affirm and avow your beliefs in the reality of the spirit world, you open this gate a bit more and your beliefs start to "bloom into revelation and knowledge." Whenever you feel lost, abandoned, or at odds with your life, you can approach this threshold by prayer, meditation, love, and forgiveness.

When you feel down, you will notice that you are thinking about either the past or the future. You can receive the inspiration of your guardian angel when you allow yourself to become present in your body wherever you are. When you become present you are connected to the living energy stream of *now*. Specifically requesting help from your guardian angel is more effective than simply hoping that things will turn out well.

Deborah is a career waitress who loves her job so much she can't wait to get there each day. She recalls one morning in La Jolla, California, when she was working at the Surf and Sand restaurant. Suddenly sirens from every direction screamed through the peaceful morning. She looked out to see a bright blue, homemade one-seater airplane sitting on the Pacific Coast Highway. An old man about eighty years old was sitting on the curb. "I believe I could almost see a guardian angel sitting behind him," she said and laughed. "I don't know how he even was able to get this thing in the air, but he landed it on the highway without hitting any cars. It was a miracle no one was hurt or killed. He thought it was a landing strip, and he thought the Pacific Ocean was Lake Elsinore, which is actually about two hours away. At the moment he landed, the cross traffic happened to be waiting for the red light, but there are *always* cars on this busy highway. Nobody could believe that he managed not to hit anything. He didn't crash, he just landed. I guess it wasn't his time to go."

Our Paths Are Lighted When We Ask for Help

A STORY from a woman named Tammie provides a simple, mundane example of how our guides step in when we need help. Tammie lost her car key at a baseball game. She looked in her handbag and around her seat at the stadium, and even searched the rest room. The key was gone. While she and her family walked back to the parking lot through a grassy field, Tammie was trying to figure out how she could get the spare key from her house. "I looked around the grass for just a moment in case I had dropped it there, but the idea of locating it in the dark seemed like looking for a needle in a haystack. We were all standing next to the car when suddenly an overhead light came on. It startled us just enough so that we all looked around. And there it was! My key was in the grass, about ten yards away, shining in the light. We all saw it at nearly the same moment. We were awed by the luck of that light coming on at just the right time. I am still amazed by it."

DOES YOUR GOAL RING TRUE?

Once our goal/priority is set we then ask, "Am I at peace with my goal? Does it ring true? Does it make me want to get up early in the morning and get right to it?" If our priorities are still couched in "shoulds" and "oughts," we do not really move with them.

Rick Jarow, *Creating the Work You Love*

Who Knows If It's Good or If It's Bad?

STRUGGLING AND trying to stave off the inevitable is a definite red flag that we are going along our paths in the wrong way. A man named Jack wrote to describe how he fought the very thing that was trying to open up a new path for him. He jumped through hoops in order not to get laid off in the big reorganization that swept his company when profits began to dwindle. He worked late without extra pay. He ate at his desk rather than taking an hour to have lunch and a quick walk. He took over another manager's job for no extra compensation and generally ran himself into the ground trying to control what turned out to be the inevitable termination.

A year later Jack looked back on those months of fear that caused him to work against his own best interests and shook his head in wonderment. The layoff he tried to forestall turned out to be the best thing that could have happened. Within two months of looking for new work, Jack ran into an old friend who ran a boatbuilding shop and needed someone to run the business end of things. Today, relaxed, happy, and working with his friend out at the docks, he's thrilled to have landed in a safe harbor with good prospects for growth. This serendipitous meeting and life change wouldn't have happened if Jack hadn't lost his job or taken an afternoon stroll down by the water after a job interview.

PERFECTION IS OVERRATED

Another lesson I have learned along the way is that perfection is highly overrated! I have struggled for years to "get it right," only to discover that 90 percent of the time my struggle was self-created. It is so true that the number one person you need to make happy is yourself.

Shawn, on becoming a second-grade teacher

Time usually reveals the larger picture of our unfolding destiny. A woman named Sarah writes, "I studied biology at university, but my marks plummeted from those I'd had in high school. No matter how hard I studied, I couldn't bring them back up. I figured I was not supposed to be studying science and looked around at other programs. Massage therapy just jumped out at me. I had thought about it in high school, but different circumstances turned me off of it. As it turned out, my year and a half at university, regardless of how bad my marks were, put me above the rest of the applicants at massage school. So everything is working out."

What are you facing right now that seems bad or difficult? How might that hold a hidden treasure? Begin to notice how your peace of mind begins to expand when you step back a little and become the philosophical Zen master who says, "Hmm, who knows if it's good or if it's bad?"

Body, Mind, and Spirit Always Communicate

SEAN CASEY LECLAIRE was once a successful, overachieving advertising executive who traveled more than 250,000 air miles a year and worked eighty to ninety hours a week. At the age of forty-four, he is now a life coach, teaches yoga six hours a week, and is writing a book about accessing soul-based values and life-affirming leadership. This man who formerly lived mostly out of a suitcase at five-star hotels now lives with his second wife about an hour's drive from Boston in a quiet, wooded area of rolling hills upon which cows graze. He defines himself as a poet and yoga teacher who helps people learn how to reconnect with their bodies and become more aware of their bodily experience. He has definitely slowed down. His story reminds us that we are always receiving messages from our inner selves about how to create joy and balance. Sometimes the only way we can make needed changes is to stop the merry-go-round completely.

Sean says, "At thirty, I started my own business in event marketing. It was successful very quickly, probably too quickly. My wife and I were partners, and we joked that we didn't have a baby, we had a business. What happened for me is that God (or what I like to call good, orderly direction), started to show its face inside me. The mask started to crack.

FIND NEW FRIENDS

My wife and I divorced, and we are learning to live our individuality. My life change now is letting my being feel free, to come out, and be myself. I guess I've lived a life that was not mine. My difficulty now is not being able to share all this with many of my friends. They just want me to go back to my original structure.

Therapy has helped a lot, but I realized I also needed a more spiritual approach. Meditation has been an ally. It's a straight way to find peace, to let yourself go with your instincts and intuition.

Sergio, Buenos Aires

"It's interesting that poems started to come to me in the middle of the night. They literally woke me up. I was beginning to have this split kind of thinking. For instance, during the night I might hear the words 'Advertising changes simple wants into dire needs.' The next morning I might be scheduled as a keynote speaker on how to develop brand image in a foreign country.

"I was living in Vancouver, Canada, then. I started walking every day and also began to do yoga every morning by myself. I started to really see myself—a thirty-five-year-old man, two hundred pounds, holding it all together with *tension*. I started to unravel inside myself. The gift was that I could *see* it happening."

As Sean began to awaken, he became curious about his feelings. He moved toward the numb part of himself and started to write. He says, "I started to thaw. I started to feel. I wrote about the deaths of three friends, and I wrote about my feelings about my own adoption for the first time. I started some addiction therapy and a recovery program. I started reading poetry—Sappho, Rumi, and Rilke. After about a year of doing all these new things, I felt the energy shift." Like Leigh's, Sean's recovery involved reclaiming and resolving locked-up energy and developing a stronger connection to his real values.

"I decided to sell my business," Sean continues. "I sold all my tools of the corporate warrior—cell phone, fax, and computer. I'm a Scorpio; we go to extremes. This was a painful period with lots of uncertainty. I thought, How am I going to pull it all together? I had a strong sense of being Mr. Not-Good-Enough."

When we make drastic changes, we must be willing to skid off the road at the times we hit those frozen patches of fear and insecurity. When as babies we fell down learning to walk, our progress may involve moments of regression.

"After selling the business, I traveled for five years," Sean says. "I met and lived with all kinds of yogis, monks, and shamans. I was meeting all sorts of people I wouldn't have met in my life as an advertising executive. I became passionate about yoga, and practiced four hours a day. I studied with various masters. I see it as a long journey into feeling."

Sean spent the next nine months learning to be comfortable being alone with himself. During this time he frequently wrote in his journal and healed stored-up wounds from childhood. At one point he lived virtually in silence in his van, staying for a while in New Mexico, California, and Arizona. He wrote poetry and hung out in old bookstores but rarely spoke to people. After this period of reflection, he resettled in Vancouver and opened a yoga studio. He started writing poems and essays.

He continues, "If I had met a psychiatrist, he probably would have said my ego had dissolved and I was in a psychotic state. It felt to me like I was in a space between two spaces. What helped me through was meeting a good woman who was my match. I am blessed to have wise and kind-hearted friends in my life today and I have come to know a deeper peace within, to have a partner who helps me see that being different is okay, and that there's room for both of us in this relationship."

BEING PART OF THE NET

When you finally wake up and see the extent of your connectedness, you will feel an immense peace. After all, how could you ever fall through this immense net when you are part of that very net? But the peace will not last, for soon you will realize that part of what this net of relationships contains is pain as well as pleasure, suffering as well as delight, and that the narrow part of the whole that resides in the body with your name can as well find itself in the pits as well as the heights. Enlightenment will not keep you from crashing if you don't fly right.

So in one sense nothing changes. . . . But at the same time everything is different.

James A. Ogilvy, *Living Without a Goal*

It took Sean five years of wandering to stop using what he calls "my grasping Western eyes." He says, "For years I thought I had to be someone great and special. Mother Teresa once said, 'We can do no great things. Only small things with great love.' I've given up the chase for greatness.

"The biggest change in my life is that I *choose* to be time prosperous. I live simply. It's only by working from a place of your own integrity and vision that you can begin to feel more connected to everything you are doing. At the moment I'm passionate about counterbalancing the drives and pace of technology with just the simple movement of our bodies. I can feel how ungrounded people are, and the place from which they are making decisions.

"Our bodies have become slaves to machines. I want to help people become aware of their relationship to these machines and to the technology in their life, and to know they can make some choices about how they use that technology. Technology is a tool like a garden hoe.

"The work I do integrates all my experiences. My work is about helping people to slow down, to feel, and to expand their awareness. It's a combination of classical yoga and somatics. Somatics is the study of bodily experience, and becoming friendly with sensation, image, impulse, energy movement, streaming, and pulsing. Every day the average person receives three thousand messages from advertising. You talk to people, and they want to be more spiritual, but often there's a kind of frantic serenity. You ask people how they are, and they say, 'I'm busy.' Busy is not a feeling. It's a choice.

"I believe what Robert Frost said, 'There's absolutely no reason for being rushed along with the rush. Everybody should be free to go very slow.'"

Here are Sean's tips for implementing positive change:

- Bring your awareness to the feelings in your body. Follow your breath and wait. No matter how changed the feelings, they will pass and change.
- Around sunrise, wake up and lie on your back with a bolster under your knees and watch your thoughts, sensations, and feelings for one-half hour everyday. This will change your life.
- Trust in good orderly direction. Trust the GOD that lives inside you.

IF I STOPPED

If I stopped for a year
to read the classics
what would happen to my life?
If I stopped for a year
to visit art galleries and museums
would I ever work again?
If I stopped for a year
to dance and climb mountains
would the boardroom bell not sound for me?
If I stopped for a year to teach
would I learn who I was in the angry
eyes of our tender youth?
If I stopped for a year
could I feel the seasons change
and hear the ants talk?
If I stopped for a year
would I learn how to breathe
and love the senses I have
long since forgotten?
If I stopped for a year
could I remember the birth canal
and the bright, white light called life?
If I stopped . . .

Sean Casey Leclaire

BUDDHA NATURE

Aspiration, in the context of practice, is nothing
but our own true nature seeking to realize and
express itself. Intrinsically we are all Buddhas,
but our Buddha nature is covered up.

Charlotte Joko Beck, in *Radiant Mind*

11

Give and Receive Support

Be prepared to give up your models of the path as you travel it.
There is no shame in admitting your mistakes.

Mahatma Gandhi once led a protest march in which many
thousands of people left their jobs and homes to endure great
hardship. As the march was well underway, Gandhi called a halt
and disbanded it. His lieutenants came to him and said, "Mahatma-
ji, you can't do this; the march has been planned for a long time
and there are so many people involved."

Gandhi's answer was, "My commitment is to truth as I see it
each day, not to consistency."

RAM DASS,
Journey of Awakening

Reach Out to Others in Places Where *You* Need Help

A WOMAN named Debra e-mailed her thoughts to me on how to
accelerate positive life changes. "While home recovering from a
hysterectomy, I had more time than ever to think, six weeks to be
exact. What hit me is that we should reach out to others around the
very issue that we find is a void or weakness in ourselves.

"A year ago when I realized that I wanted to write more, I started
a writing group. Prior to that when I noticed that I wasn't reading as
much as I wanted, I started a book discussion group. This month
because of my need to be enriched within my own community, as

opposed to going to another area of town, I met with the local bookstore and started a lecture series. Somehow in some really spirit-filled way, when we reach out to help others in the areas where we need help, we seem to get all of the resources necessary to make great things happen."

Sean Casey Leclaire, the overachieving business executive in Chapter 10 who quit to become a poet and yoga teacher, recalls a time when he did volunteer massage on the hands of people in a retirement home. "One time," he says, "I was massaging an elderly woman's hands and humming an old Scottish tune. Suddenly this rather frail woman started belting out that song. We both began crying. I was so touched. I was amazed at how present she was with me. I had just thought I was doing a favor for *her*. Here I was trying to do massages in order to be a good guy, but I didn't exactly have the good orderly direction (God) behind it, which is the sense of God in everyone. That's what fills you up and makes you feel good inside yourself."

THE OPPORTUNITY PATROL

Once you have affirmed your intention, take a few moments to identify the specific needs of your company for today (or for this week). Write down the needs and keep it somewhere where you will see it all the time.

Every time you're on the phone, meeting with someone, having lunch, or buying something at the grocery store, keep your list handy. In every conversation you have, mention at least one of these needs.

Of course, the idea is not to be obnoxious about asking for help all the time. Be sure to return the favor by asking about their lives and seeing if there's a way you might be able to help them.

Nancy Rosanoff, *The Complete Idiot's Guide to Making Money Through Intuition*

Actively Support Yourself

A WOMAN named Sofia wrote that she walked out of her job after three and a half years and took a loan to support herself for four months. She wanted to give herself time to get to know herself better and explore options. Giving herself this kind of active support, she writes, was a big change. "I have followed the 'automaton' route up to now, and in the end have come to feel like an automaton. I know I'll have to pay the loan back, and that I'll have to start earning in four months. But I got to the point where I needed an opening, I needed some space and some unknown aspects around me. I needed *the benefit of uncertainty and chaos* [italics added] in order to stimulate a new path and a new existence. I really felt that I had begun to decay spiritually, and now for the first time I feel a breath of new possibilities. I am focusing on Deepak Chopra's *Law of Infinite Possibilities.*"

Sofia reports that an important turning point happened when she started to understand that her mission was already "written into every part of me." With time to tap into her current life interests, she says, "My mission as I know it now is to help take the art and science of ethical leadership forward. To think that just a few weeks ago I was wondering and wondering what I should do! It was there in me all the time."

With the heightened awareness that often comes to us during times of stress and change, Sofia began to see that her biggest enemy was her own limited self-perception and her self-criticism. "I have been very tough on myself, despite my knowledge of positive thinking. I made such a big effort to 'break free,' and then I put a lot of pressure on myself to earn money, to be successful, even to 'realize myself.' I was making my new-earned freedom quite difficult to live with.

"I finally realized that it wasn't working to pressure myself like this, and that what I needed to do was to actively support myself, in tiny ways as well as big ones. I listened to Louise Hay's tapes and really saw how every moment counts. What I think of myself really counts. Actively changing my thoughts about myself has radically helped. I actively love myself more, and am more able to laugh at my challenges.

"I am realizing the benefits of being nice to myself, on a simple but deep level. I look in the mirror and view myself in a way that gives me a chance. With the negative images and thoughts I was having before, I really had no chance. My beautiful, luxurious freedom was disappearing into my own self-depreciation.

"I really feel like I've made a breakthrough. I think that it may have come because I identified my passions, which gave me the drive to say, 'I'm not letting this disappear. I'm willing to do whatever it takes.' I am sure that being nicer to myself, no matter what, will send me in a better direction. I will have allowed natural universal intelligence and synchronicities to come through."

FIND INSPIRATION IN THE MOMENT OF NEED

I hate logical plans. Myself, I should find it false and dangerous to start from some clear, well defined, complete idea and then put it into practice. I must be ignorant of what I shall be doing and I can find the resources I need only when I am plunged into obscurity and ignorance.

Federico Fellini, in *Creators on Creating*

In a similar vein of active self-discovery, a woman named Lorraine talks about ending her twenty-two-year marriage. "The only thing that got me through this time was my family, and being able to withdraw and write for hours at a time. I journaled and wrote poetry, pouring out every guilt-laden self-doubt, every despairing thought, every ounce of righteous anger, every prayer, curse, torturous self-exploration, and finally every sad good-bye.

"I have now come to another crossroads in a new relationship. I am enduring another separation in order to try to understand the lessons that I need to learn in this situation. My suggestion to others is . . . try to be very, very quiet, . . . turn off your TV and your CD player. Learn to say no. Listen to your inner voice, your intuition. Face the hard truths about yourself and make necessary changes in order to be as honest as you can be. Become mindful of everything you do and every place you are. Get lots of exercise, be outdoors, and write, write, write."

TALK IT OUT AND TAKE IT IN

What has helped me most in transitions is *people*. I have ended a relationship, am changing work and moving my house. Throughout this change I have been open with everyone I have met in discussing what is happening. I have found that the answers have just been pouring in, and I currently feel fully in the flow of my life and destiny. Although it could be perceived as a difficult time, I am finding it to be a period of great enlightenment.

You ask what bothers me the most, and I think it is the *uncertainty*, which at times can feel like a great excitement, but also like unwelcome anxiety! My insight into life changes is that it's not the actual situation, but how you respond to it which determines your emotions during the period of change, and what you will learn from it.

Brenda, grocery clerk

Neither Fight nor Force

AN ENGLISHWOMAN named Rachel left a high-paying job at an Internet publishing company, a nice apartment, and good friends in order to sail around the world, which had been a dream since childhood. "My main concern was giving up a safe and promising job to follow my heart. But I couldn't ignore my intuition, so I gave my boss notice. Since I made the decision to leave, everything has clicked. I have been staggered by the extent to which life seems to be trying to reassure me that I made the right decision. Synchronistic events of the past few weeks let me know that I'm on the right path, and also remind me to stay in touch with the life force.

At times I get so caught up in the physical concerns of life that I lose sight of the spiritual. I see now that life changes are inevitable and healthy. I don't try to fight change anymore, nor do I try to force it to happen either. The right thing will happen at the right time as long as you are looking for it. Only *you* know what's best for *you*. Even if the mainstream questions your decisions, that doesn't make them wrong; it just means that they're not what others would choose."

The Current Situation Has a Perfection

BE HERE now encapsulates the philosophy of being present, aware, and conscious in each moment of our lives. Being present is central to spiritual teachings all over the world. *Be here now* also carries the corollary *Accept what you cannot change.* Of course, that is not what we want to hear when we are eager to make life changes.

In collecting stories for this book, I often received responses from people who said that a conscious acceptance of a situation took them to new and positive places. While one must be aware when it's time to get out of situations where there is any physical, emotional, or psychological abuse, trusting the deeper purpose of our process connects us to what we are creating and where we need to take responsibility. For example, Bertil of Sweden wrote to share his journey. "Many years ago I came to the realization that I often tried to escape a situation in order to avoid looking at my own shortcomings and inadequacies. This made me feel imprisoned, so I tried another approach. I decided to choose to be fully present in the actual situation, taking full responsibility for my part in it. This led to a new 'space' for me, a space of freedom and several new options.

"A few years ago, I had been fully expecting a promotion to section leader, but I was passed over. I had worked years for this outcome. Over one long weekend, I tried to cope with my disappointment. I finally decided to accept the situation as it was. I told the new manager that I accepted the situation and wanted to offer him my full support, especially in those areas where I knew he had very little knowledge and experience. He was very much relieved and thanked me from the depths of his heart. Suddenly, several new options opened themselves within the organization for me to go further than I had ever thought I would."

GIVE AND RECEIVE THE BLESSINGS OF PRAYER

My biggest life transition was with my son and his battle with Crohn's disease. The battle led to nine months of feeding tubes, major weight loss, and ultimately surgery to remove a blockage. He was fourteen years old. There was nothing I could do.

Against my nature, I had to "let go and let God." All I could give my son was me, my time, my prayers, and my love. Prayer ended up being my support while I supported my son. I truly understood for the first time in my life what the power of prayer can do. It kept me sane when I was falling apart, and I believe it helped my son recover as quickly as he did. He is sixteen now and growing like a weed. How lucky I am!

Denise, mother

When our lives are unexpectedly uprooted without our conscious desire to change, it's easy and natural to assume that we're experiencing a detour or distraction from our true "purpose." Staying open to whatever experience emerges can be a very large task, perhaps best done on a minute-by-minute basis, paying attention to what is being asked of us.

A woman named Mary writes about caring for her grieving mother after Mary's father died. Her siblings either lived far away or chose not to get involved. "I was living out of state when my dad died and made the big decision to move back to be with my mom. I had never been close to my mom and at no time had ever expected to be her caregiver in her golden years. During a three-day drive through a snowstorm, I had plenty of time to pray and search my soul for answers. I knew, without a doubt, that my major objective was to 'take care of my mom,' but I didn't have a clue as to how to do that.

"It has been a year of growth for both of us. The secret I have learned is to totally immerse myself in the 'present moment' while I am with her. We talk on the phone every day and are together two to three nights a week. There are days when I don't think I have the emotional and spiritual strength to do it. It is truly such a growing experience to be fully living in the present moment that I now look forward to every second of it. It gives me an emotional high like I have never had before. I know without a doubt not only that I am helping someone I love but that my soul is benefiting from living in the present moment also."

Sometimes We Have to Turn Our Lives Around Three or Four Times Before Things Click

NO ONE has witnessed major transformative life changes more vividly than Robert, the founder and director of a homeless shelter. During his many years of working in the community, Robert has seen a variety of people from all kinds of backgrounds come to the shelter. "Certain people stand out for me over the years," he recalls. "I remember one shelter resident who had been a teacher and a poet and who had taught at Stanford. In his late forties he developed a personality disorder and began to say weird and off-the-wall things. He reverted to childhood manipulation patterns and turned people off. He let his hygiene go, and his behavior became very quirky. He made himself almost an outcast. Pretty soon he couldn't hold on to a job, and his health started to slip. He became homeless. He was at the shelter trying to save money and get his life together when he was diagnosed with a fast-moving cancer. I was with him when he died." Obviously, this memory touched Robert deeply. It was an honor for him, he says, to be with this man at the last moments of his life.

Robert recalls others who showed a fiercely independent streak. "There was another guy who used to own a famous nightclub. Because of losing a lot of money in a couple of divorces and some bad investments, he came to the shelter. Even in the shelter he was always looking for the next big thing to make a million. He got Parkinson's disease, but that didn't slow him down much. While he was at the shelter he went back to school and got his GED [high school equivalency diploma] at the age of sixty-two—when most guys wouldn't have thought they needed it. He acknowledged that the shelter helped him get his life together. Now he has his own place, and he publishes a sports newsletter. He is always doing something, even though his health and his age are problems. I love that about people, how you can never count them out till the very end.

"Another friend of mine is a guy who ran a shelter at one time. He had a drug history, got into recovery, helped open a shelter, and came to work with me. He had four kids and a whole life, and then went back on drugs and lost it all. He ended up in the same shelter he started."

Why and when do people make changes? I asked the man who had seen thousands of struggling people come and go.

"It's timing," Robert answered. "I haven't found the magic formula. Each person has to find the meaning in his or her life. Sometimes people have to turn their lives around three or four times before things click."

> We have the gift of life, and if we do not use it fully, we create an imbalance in the world, for others must support us with their energy.
>
> Tarthang Tulku, *Skillful Means*

Good Work Is Permanent

"I THINK I'll retire from the shelter next year," says Robert, "but I know I'll continue to do some kind of service work. Maybe I'll paint old people's houses if there's a need for their houses to be painted. I always love the feeling of brightening someone's day. Personal action gives you more of a feeling of purposefulness and fulfillment than just giving money.

"People are always wondering how they can get involved in helping others. You know, Mother Teresa just started out bathing one person who was lying in the gutter and dying. Fame and fortune are transitory. Good work is permanent. When I leave here, there will be a shelter where people can get their lives together. I didn't do this alone, but I stuck it out through all the politics, through the objections of all those people who didn't want it in their backyards. I feel good that I helped get this concrete thing accomplished. I hope God has something else in store for me. I don't have to cure world hunger. I'm content to do a lot of little things. My suggestion for people who want to make a change in themselves is, find a way to give to others. The sooner you find out about giving to others and not being so self-absorbed about your own destiny, the more happiness you will have."

Whenever you feel lost or disconnected from life, tired or discouraged, open this book at random. Which practice or principle might help expand your thinking or offer a little support for the road ahead? You can also write down your favorite ideas in the book one at a time on index cards. Each day you can draw one from the stack as an inspiration.

> *New year dawning clear*
> *Cheerful sparrows*
> *Chatter*
> *All day like people*
>
> Ransetsu

12

❧

Handle Fear

We can't know
what the divine intelligence
has in mind!

RUMI

What Do You Fear?

ON THE first day of college, I had to give an extemporaneous speech to determine whether I needed to take public speaking. With no warning a feeling of total panic descended upon me. I felt as if my ears had closed up and I was sealed inside myself. I will never forget how a sudden body heat fogged up my eyeglasses, and I could no longer even see the class in front of me.

Today I make my living speaking in public. I love being in front of an audience. If I had been told that day that my livelihood would depend on this skill, I think I might have jumped off the nearest bridge.

In my twenties I had a pronounced fear of flying. In the first few flights of my life, I was unable to stop thinking about the distance between my seat on the plane and the cold, hard ground below—or, even worse, the bottomless depths of the sea, where the plane would break apart and I would disappear forever. I irrationally believed that only my rigid vigilance to every strange sound or sudden movement was keeping the plane aloft. I thought if I didn't move around very much, nothing bad would happen.

Today I am a premier member of United Airlines's frequent flyer program, since my public lectures and seminar work require that I fly thousands of miles all over the world. I was back in the air a few days after September 11, 2001. I love to fly.

I am still working on various fears in other areas of my life, but since those early days when fear ran my life, I have learned that fear is not a good enough excuse for not moving ahead with whatever I want to do. Experience has shown me how to face my fears and desensitize myself by moving in the very direction in which they lie in wait.

Are you impatient about moving forward but fear keeps you from taking any steps? Are you thinking that you'll make a change in your life but it's not time yet? Have you been waiting for the right time for a *long* time? What do you think is the problem? Do you think your obstacle is (1) not enough clarity; (2) procrastination; (3) lack of money; (4) lack of needed skills; (5) resistance; (6) a particular "block"; or (7) just plain fear?

FEAR IS A TEST

If a soul only knew love and peace, it would gain no insight and never truly appreciate the value of these positive feelings. The test of reincarnation for a soul coming to Earth is the conquering of fear in a human body.

Michael Newton, *Journey of Souls*

We All Share Fears of Inadequacy and Unexpected Events

NO MATTER how far along we are in life, we all share some inner fears—of making the wrong decision, of looking stupid, of not being able to take care of ourselves, of rejection, failure, public speaking, death, and being mediocre. Studies show that fear of public speaking tops the list of our fears, outranking even death! Fears about certain events, such as not finding a mate, getting fired, getting divorced, or going bankrupt, are of course the surface level of our inner fears about ourselves. I think the fear of not finding one's purpose, or of feeling that one has reached only a mediocre level of one's potential, is very deep-seated, and shapes a good portion of our self-esteem.

THE TWO BIG QUESTIONS ABOUT LIFE CHANGES

THERE ARE two questions that people invariably ask in my workshops on life purpose and life changes. The first is, How do I find clarity about my life purpose? And the second is, How can I handle fear?

After some years of reflection, I can see how the two are related. The question about clarity, in my opinion, is really a cry for the security of a guaranteed outcome. "I won't move until I'm sure I'm going to get what I want." Waiting for absolute clarity may be a trap that keeps us from acting at all.

In order to illuminate the question about how to handle fear, let's examine some of its possible origins. First, many people hold the belief that events in life are random, that life is a very scary prospect, and that it's better not to "rock the boat." This point of view offers little support to the idea that there is something to be gained or learned from every experience. This view starts out with resistance to change.

Fear also arises from black or white thinking—an outcome has to be either good or bad. If it's bad, you've made a mistake (rather than gotten feedback and learned something).

Fear arises when we face an unknown. Will we succeed in a new venture? (Do we even have criteria for success so we'll know when it arrives?) Will we be sorry we took the leap? What if we can't handle what the new situation demands of us? A liberating thought for this aspect is: you almost always have a chance to make another choice.

Fear arises when we feel that we risk losing what we already have. Perhaps we feel that we will let someone down, or that we won't get the love and support for new decisions from the people we care about the most.

Fearful thinking can easily go to extremes: "I'll be a bag lady. My kids will starve." One woman I spoke with was trying to decide if she should leave a twenty-year job to start her own business. She asked, "What if I quit and can't take care of my daughter?" This is a good example of black or white thinking, which creates a *false conflict*. The conflict is not between "doing her own thing" and jeopardizing her daughter. Of course, her priority has to be her daughter's life. But that does not mean that she has to give up her dreams. The real issue is to start taking small steps to open up new possibilities, but also to maintain adequate means during the development of the new direction. For example, our situation may demand that we take a couple of interim part-time jobs before the new career creates adequate income. Fear often creates a false sense of urgency. Taking a longer view usually helps create confidence in being able to handle the unknown. So-called overnight successes commonly happen after years of conscious or unconscious preparation.

When we ask, "How do I handle my fear?" we may very well be using the idea of fear as a reason to procrastinate and stay within our comfort zone. After all, if you tell others that you are confused, that you have no clarity, that you have fears about the future, you will probably get a lot of consolation, advice, and confirmation that life is risky and you should be thankful for what you have. It's easy to stay in this kind of victim-of-circumstance mode and get lots of mileage out of talking about change, but never actually having to make any!

Giving in to generalized fear is an easy out for doing nothing. Generalized fear is a place where all your past mistakes, failures, and self-criticisms take root and thrive as good reasons for not moving on. You can choose to cultivate your garden of fear, or you can weed out some areas and plant new seeds for action. These seeds are affirmations such as: "Whatever happens, I'll handle it!" "I'm exploring a lot of exciting new ideas!"

If you want to handle your fear right now, let's get specific about exactly what your fear is saying.

COMMON FEARS THAT HOLD US BACK

Fears About Ability and Identity

I'M AFRAID . . .

I don't have enough clarity about what to do next in order to make a move.

Without clarity, I don't know where to start.

I'm not lucky like some people, who know what they want to do.

I'm too old to start over.

I don't have what it takes to be any more successful than I am now, so why rock the boat?

I'm not good at selling myself.

If I do make a move, what if it's no better than what I have?

Fears About Work and Career

I'M AFRAID . . .

I'll have to sell my soul to make a good living.

If I try to go into business for myself, I'll have to be more competitive and assertive than I'm comfortable being in order to be successful.

It will take too long to get started in my own business, and I don't have enough money saved.

I won't be able to find enough clients to make my business profitable.

I'll have to find clients all by myself.

If I do make a move, what if it doesn't work out?

Fears About Relationships

I'M AFRAID . . .

If I want to make a change, my spouse is not going to go for it.

If I do make a move, what if it doesn't work out?

I don't know what I would do if I lost my spouse.

I'm not attractive enough to be lovable.

I'm visibly aging.

I'm not willing to change my life very much for somebody else.
I'm not good in social situations.
If I put myself out there, I'll get rejected.
I'll always be alone.

Fears About Money

I'M AFRAID . . .

Going to school will cost more than I can afford.
My rent is going to double and I can't afford to buy.
I don't have enough money to make the changes I want to
  make.
I don't have enough saved for retirement.
My debt is out of control.
My debt is growing, but my charge card is my only way to meet
  certain necessary expenses.

Fears About Health

I'M AFRAID . . .

I don't have health insurance.
This pain might be cancer.
I might become disabled and not be able to work.
I don't have anything to fall back on.
My habits aren't very healthy.

The Ultimate Fear—
Not Being Able to Handle the Unknown

IN EACH of the preceding statements, the underlying ultimate fear
is that we won't be able to handle what the future is going to bring.
We don't trust ourselves to be able to learn, adapt to, and handle
whatever comes our way.

When we were kids we didn't look under our beds at night for
fear of seeing the glowing eyes of the monsters who might live
there. We were little and had no way to defend ourselves against

the powerful and frightening unknown that was—we were convinced—out to get us.

A friend of mine told me that his favorite quotation was from Albert Einstein, who once said that the only real question in life is whether or not the universe is friendly. One of the benefits of being in the flow of life purpose is that it feels as if the universe is friendly. We feel connected to something larger and more meaningful that expresses itself in daily living as well as in transcendent moments. When we are in fear mode, we are disconnected from that sense of larger movement and intelligence. We're not at all sure that the universe is friendly. We point out all the real and visible instances of suffering, pain, hunger, poverty, ignorance, violence, greed, and disharmony. Since we feel that there is not enough goodness to go around, we had better get our abundance before someone else gets it. We resist moving because it's too scary to think we might have to give up what we already have for something we don't yet see.

This kind of thinking keeps us feeling like victims and robs us of our power to be fully who we are. We see ourselves in a world of chaos, terror, and random pitfalls. We feel small, alone, helpless, confused, scared, and on the verge of humiliation and failure.

The Key to Handling Fear

HOW, THEN, do you get past the fear? *Train yourself to have the attitude that whatever happens, you'll handle it.*

The key to success is being willing to do whatever it takes to move forward, even with the possibility that the worst could happen. If you have the attitude that you will deal with whatever happens, you hold the secret of handling fear. Fear is not going to go away forever, so don't wait for the fear to disappear before you make a move forward. Just recognize that it is there, feel it, and go ahead and do something.

Your job is to start trusting yourself and your intuition, despite the outcome of your decision. Your job is to build your problem-solving skills, beef up your adaptability, fire your creativity, stay in contact with your network of friends and family, and open to the spiritual guidance and synchronicities that arise as you need them. You do all this through making the practices and principles we have talked about part of your daily life.

Recall how you've handled the unexpected in the past. You've already demonstrated your ability to adapt and survive, otherwise you wouldn't be alive and reading this chapter. Maybe you will want to write in your life changes journal about how you've handled past upsets. For example, how did you handle that betrayal when your best friend married your fiancé? What helped you that time your car stopped dead in traffic? What happened when you lost your wallet and passport in Morocco? What did you do when you didn't get the promotion? How did you handle getting ignominiously fired? What did you do the last time you got sick on a weekend and your doctor was out of town? You handled it.

CROSSING THE THRESHOLD

The biggest difference I saw between women with six-figure incomes and underearning women was that every high earner came to a point where she thought she couldn't do something, and she went ahead and did it anyway. That was the threshold they crossed to become higher earners. The underearners got to that threshold, but they came up with all the reasons they couldn't do something and so they didn't do anything. They couldn't envision themselves doing it.

The higher earners didn't think they could do it either, but they did it anyway. They didn't always succeed, but they always learned.

Barbara Stanny, author of *Secrets of Six-Figure Women*

Find the Limiting Belief

REVIEW AGAIN these fear statements and see what mistaken beliefs or limited thinking might be fueling some of the fear.

I'm afraid . . .

I don't have enough clarity about what to do next in order to
make a move.

Limited Thinking: I need a guarantee of results before I do anything.

*Unlimited Thinking: I go in the direction that has the most
energy for me.*

I'm afraid . . .

If I try to go into business for myself, I'll have to be more competitive and assertive than I'm comfortable being in order to
be successful.

Limited Thinking: I'm not good enough the way I am. I have to
know everything. I have to be perfect.

*Unlimited Thinking: I don't know how to do this, but I'll find
out. I'm always learning.*

I'm afraid . . .

If I do make a move, what if it's no better than what I have?

Limited Thinking: There's only one right answer.

*Unlimited Thinking: Every time I move forward, I learn some-
thing new for next time.*

I'm afraid . . .

If I put myself out there, I'll get rejected.

Limited Thinking: I'm easily crushed. I have to protect myself
against what people think of me.

Unlimited Thinking: You win some, you lose some.

I'm afraid . . .

I don't have enough money to make the changes I want to make.

Limited Thinking: I lack what I need. Money is the only answer to being able to move forward.

Unlimited Thinking: *Anything is possible.*

The Good News

ONCE WE have looked our fears in the face and are willing to handle whatever happens, our path becomes an adventure—*regardless of the outcome*. The good news is that it doesn't really matter in the long run which path we follow. Each option has its own unique opportunities and lessons by which we grow stronger, wiser, and more experienced and potentially successful.

The other good—and liberating—news is that it's not our job to control events. It's also not our job to mutate into perfect human beings to handle the next step into the unknown. What we can do is develop the attitude that says to the world, I can handle whatever comes, and I'm willing to go forward no matter what. Fear is a natural part of our decision-making system for discerning the best course. Both our fears and our life purpose direct us to pay attention to something. After we listen to what they have to say, we make a choice and let go of how the course plays out. We continue to act as impeccably as we know how. I have always been struck by Mother Teresa's principle that it is not a good idea to hoard things, since hoarding communicates to God that you don't really trust Her to provide when you need it.

Use Your Time Wisely

LET'S REVIEW the attitudes and practices for thriving in uncertain times. It's a good idea to have these reminders written down somewhere (index cards are portable) so that, when fears arise, you can direct your attention to something more useful. Write them out and put them on your refrigerator.

- Feel the fear but keep moving forward.
- Don't act urgently unless it's really an emergency.
- Maintain your sense of humor. This keeps you open and relaxed.
- Turn over the task of creating what you want to your subconscious mind.
- Ask life to give you answers you can clearly understand.
- Look for answers or confirmations of your intuition everywhere (phone calls, chance conversations, radio, books).
- Pay more attention to your gut feelings when making decisions.
- If you feel confused, slow down a little. Commit to taking one action that will answer a *small* part of your question.
- Go in the direction where you feel the best energy.
- Do things that will make you feel good about yourself after you've done them.
- Say no when you feel overwhelmed. Keep life simple.
- Set your goals, but let the universe handle the details.
- Act in a timely manner.

When you feel stuck:

- Try putting more heart into your present situation.
- Say to yourself, "I'm willing to handle whatever happens."
- Be willing to live with uncertainty for a while.
- Adopt the attitude that any event or development could be good, could be bad.
- Choose *one area or topic* about which to become more knowledgeable or skilled.
- Practice giving and receiving (volunteer somewhere, help a friend, or play with a child).
- Be willing to be dismembered in order to be put back together at a new level!

It's all an adventure, no matter what happens. Your security lies in your ability to perceive, to adapt, and to respond. An enhanced ability to see what's happening (perception and attention) and the ability to respond quickly and accurately are the principles by which all life-forms survive and evolve. In uncertain times (which is another way of saying that a *lot* of people are feeling anxious), be willing to make friends with uncertainty. The gift of uncertain times is that you are more likely to appreciate what you have and to cherish your relationships. Uncertain times actually strengthen and refine us!

When You Make a Decision

IF YOU feel any fears about your next step, follow these guidelines:

- *Feel the fear.* Get clear about what you fear you can't handle.
- *What's the worst that could happen?* Are you willing to handle that?
- *Keep an open mind.* Who knows if something is good or if it's bad?
- *Show up.* Listen to your intuition and do whatever you know you need to—make a phone call, apologize, get up earlier, take care of that promise, review your notes, get more information.
- *Stay positive and light.* Notice how you are talking about yourself and your plans.
- *Keep it simple.* Concentrate on what really matters.
- *Take time to do things that nurture you.* Play ball, go dancing, garden, walk, run, listen to music, watch the birds, spend time with your family.
- *Expect a miracle.* Ask for your next step to be taken care of in the easiest and most delightful way possible.
- *Take responsibility for your decisions.* Avoid assigning blame. If a decision doesn't work out the way you expected, do whatever is necessary as impeccably as you know how to do and move on.
- *Be curious.*
- *Make a fallback statement.* "If it doesn't work out, I'll . . ."

A woman wrote to me anonymously, offering a poignant glimpse of her life as she turned fifty. "Getting back to and nurturing my spirit was the only thing that got me through my last transition. I was divorced after a very unhappy six years. I moved to a new city—very alone—and started a new life. I scrutinized my behavior, my responsibility, and found that I had neglected and let go of *my* spirit. I began to read many books on spirituality.

DO LESS

Simplify your life today by doing less than usual. Do you feel lazy or unworthy when you don't accomplish a lot? Remember you're not just what you do.

Penney Peirce, *The Present Moment*

"I awoke on my fiftieth birthday knowing that I want to live the next fifty years in a different way. I quit a good job where I felt burned out, simplified my life (sold many of my possessions and paid off bills). I began my journey to the next fifty years by loading my important things into my vehicle and began driving. I visited friends, camped, read, and just experienced. I had a catastrophe midway across the United States that set me back for a time, but even it was a valuable experience. My vehicle with everything but my laptop and a third of my clothes, which were in my friend's house, was stolen. I am currently on the West Coast 'regrouping' and will continue my drive, I hope, early fall or late summer. I have come to see that all things lead to God. There is no one right way to do anything. I appreciate all that life is and am committed to taking care of myself and others along the way."

What is it that you appreciate about your life? What nurtures you? Keep looking for things that make you happy, and avoid feeding thoughts of what you don't want.

To get through the darkest period
of the night,
Act as if it is already morning.

The Talmud

13

Move Forward

The biggest temptation is . . . to settle for too little.

THOMAS MERTON

Take Care of Business, Let the Universe Handle the Details

I FIND it of great comfort to know that I don't have to make miracles happen. That's God's job. My job is to stay happy, ask for what I want, and do the footwork that develops the opportunities offered.

We all experience synchronistic flow if we pay attention. A woman named Marge was feeling strongly that she wanted to retire. She told her boss she was planning on leaving soon. The next day a brochure from the Sofia Center at Holy Names College in Oakland, California, arrived in her mailbox. She enrolled, and the program of spiritual studies is exactly what she wanted.

Another example of being open to the flow comes from a woman in Australia who e-mailed me. She writes, "I had a strong intuition to open a shop that people would just 'feel' to come to. I wanted to operate it by donation. First, I went through two nights of fear, thinking, How on earth am I going to pay the rent? My husband asked me, 'What's your contingency plan?' and I said, 'I don't have one!'

"The day before I opened the shop, I met a man who felt as I did. I asked him to come along to the shop and 'feel' it and he would know if it was for him. It was, and he said not to worry, if we don't make the rent, he would top it up.

"Many people came even though there was no sign on the shop. So much happened, mostly good. I learned many of my own life lessons (like how I was needy and dependent, so I attracted other people who needed and depended!). I closed this shop after three months simply because the lessons had been learned."

Another woman, Betty, wrote in an e-mail that she believes a higher good is working things out for the betterment of our lives, even though it may not look that way at first. She lost her job of seventeen years and had to learn computer technology quickly in order to take another job at half her previous salary. Everything she had thought stable came tumbling down. In addition to her job change, she had to sell her house, move in with her parents, and reduce her belongings to what she could fit into two small rooms.

CREATE WEALTH BY SHARING WEALTH

If the whole idea of the hidden potential and imprints creating our very reality is true, then there can be no greater way of creating wealth than sharing it indiscriminately.

Geshe Michael Roach, *The Diamond Cutter*

For two years Betty struggled with juggling finances and living with parents whose rigid and conservative views contrast with her own lifestyle and beliefs. Soon after she moved in with them, her dad had a heart attack and underwent double bypass surgery. Betty and her mother were both seriously ill with arthritis. During this time she had to move her office four times and had four major surgeries within five months.

"Throughout all of it, I steadily maintained that my highest good was manifesting," writes Betty. "I believed my parents' higher good was manifesting as well. Unexpectedly my dad made the decision to move to a house needing less maintenance. Even though this was another huge change, the new area is far better than the old house location. It's open, uplifting, and well-designed. I love the new view, miles of nature, treetops, lakes, and the little piece of garden I have all to myself in the back. When I let my life open itself to me, and let the universe provide, it always turns out for my benefit. I tell people to hold on to the idea that a higher good is working out, no matter what the physical reality looks or feels like. Become excited with the anticipation. Expect the good, the exciting, the unanticipated marvels that the universe and its caretakers can provide for us!"

WHAT'S THE RUSH?

The biggest pitfall as you make your way through life is impatience. Remember that being impatient is simply a way of punishing yourself. It creates stress, dissatisfaction, and fear. Whenever your Chatterbox is making you feel impatient, ask it, "What's the rush?" It's all happening perfectly. Don't worry. When I am ready to move forward I will. In the meantime, I am taking it all in and I am learning.

Susan Jeffers, *Feel the Fear and Do It Anyway*

Carrie writes about the unexpected support she received two years ago. After years of suffering the debilitating pain of fibromyalgia, she woke up one morning and decided to get a job. "I turned on the radio and heard my favorite inspirational talk show host. Within minutes the program ran a commercial for her enrichment center, in which she was advertising for the position of a part-time receptionist. I called the number, and the girl who answered didn't even know they were hiring. She told me to come in in the morning, and the next day I got the job.

"Part of my salary was given to me as discounts on alternative therapies. Within months I was off painkillers, which allowed me to feel my pain [and explore its causes]. I confronted my issues and discovered who I am and why I hurt. Two years later I feel great. I work full-time now and am the client service counselor."

Carries's story shows how our unconscious wisdom—which knows things that we don't know we know—can prompt us to turn on the radio at the right time, or take some other action that leads us unknowingly to a solution we could never have found with our logical thinking. After hearing dozens of these synchronistic stories, I now believe that if we have a date with destiny, the universe is going to make sure we are impelled to show up. If we miss it the first time, we may have other chances.

THE OBVIOUS PROBLEM MAY NOT BE THE PROBLEM AT ALL

Sometimes a client's work on an action step [in the financial plan] needs to be delayed because of financial limitations. In these cases I encourage the client to think of ways of meeting a particular need that cost little or no money. More often, however, clients discover that their needs are unmet not because of *monetary* restraints but because of the *emotional* bind they are in. This can be liberating to the clients.

Karen McCall, financial counselor

Return to the Vision

A REAL estate agent named Thomas admits that, although he has been very successful at it, he chose a career in real estate because it offered an interesting way to make a good living. The excitement of his early years in the field, however, has been gone for a long time. Reaching midlife, Thomas finds his priorities and motivations shifting. Like those of most of us, his life changes began with a feeling of restlessness. Restlessness turned into an attitude of searching for something that felt like it had his name on it. The excitement of the search and the vision of how life could be different both created a growing willingness to release some of the security of the present in order to follow the emerging path. "My present life change started with a vague idea that I wanted to be a minister," Thomas says. "Even though I would quickly dismiss the idea every time it came into my mind, it wouldn't go away.

"When I think about being able to bring a message of hope and love to people through teaching, speaking, and writing, I get a very special feeling in my heart," he writes. "Once I was willing to admit that I was in the wrong career, I started focusing on making a change. Fear definitely came into play. However, I also believe that 'Where God guides, God provides.' When I start to worry about money, I reconnect with the vision that created the desire for the new path. Just thinking about it usually brings tears.

"I feel like I am in 'the void' right now. I applied for a ministerial program but was not selected. I can reapply [next year], but in the meantime I have to find another way to connect with my vision. My wife and I are preparing to move to the Kansas City area, where the ministerial program is, and I am also looking into the executive recruiting field as an intermediary place for me as my path unfolds further. I see the recruiting field as a way for me to help people find their right path in life."

Thomas's creativity in holding on to his ministerial vision, and his flexibility in exploring a related field, are good techniques for working with fear and obstacles and moving ahead. Instead of inferring that his decision to become a minister was flawed because he was not selected for the program this year, he is staying attuned to his original vision of wanting to work with others on deep life issues. This gives the universe the liberty to manifest the vision as elegantly as possible. Perhaps becoming a minister is only one possible path amid many for inspiring others.

FIND A WAY TO TOLERATE UNCERTAINTY

If it is true that some people's brains cause them to feel a strong yet inappropriate need for certainty, confronting that problem involves disrupting those demanding thoughts. It involves confronting them consistently and directly every day to produce the change we want. This is where your new attitude comes in. You must find ways to accept risk and tolerate uncertainty.

R. Reid Wilson, *Don't Panic*

When You Feel Anxious Reset Your Thinking

WHEN YOU feel anxious about something you plan to do, reconnect with a past success. Remember who you are and what you have achieved. Remember the strength that you developed through hard times. If you can do that, you can do anything!

VISUALIZE A SPECIAL MOMENT OF GLORY FROM THE PAST

REACH BACK in your memory to a special time when you felt really great. You felt happy, relaxed, energized. You felt in tune with yourself and the world. Take a moment to jot down specific words that describe *exactly how you felt*. The words that describe your feelings may still be key values. If so, use them when you want to write an affirmation. A friend of mine who is house hunting in a tight real estate market keeps remembering other apartments and houses she found in the past. She thinks of herself as a person who always has good luck finding a great, affordable place to live.

Make your visualizations fun. Feel that fat new paycheck in your hand. Feel the big bonus check underneath the paycheck. Notice that underneath the bonus check is a letter from the head of the company congratulating you on how creative and thorough you have been at work. Keep going on your visualizations!

THE PERFECT HOUSE IS WAITING

THE COMPUTER specialist Aparna writes, "My husband and I looked for a new home for over a year and didn't find anything we liked, except for one model home, which we just loved. We loved the city it was in, the house was in the perfect location surrounded by nature, and the place had good schools. It was well lit and spacious, but it was too expensive for us.

"At one point, an idea was born in my mind that our perfect house was waiting for us, wherever it was, built or unbuilt. It was waiting for us as much as we were waiting to find it. I shared this idea with my husband, and we just completely believed in it.

"A couple of months later, synchronistically, we were visiting the neighborhood where the house was and decided to look at the model home we liked so much, just because it made us feel good to be in it. This time the price had been lowered and was no longer out of our range. We got the house, and I continue to love it immensely."

LET IT BE EASY

So I left CarParts.com on Thursday and had a job offer the next day from LowerMyBills.com. The company obviously cared about the personal well-being of their employees. The job offer seemed too easy. One of the women at CarParts reminded me that I don't have to fight for everything. If it appears to be good, go for it . . . and I did. It's been great ever since. Even if it doesn't work out, it will take me to the next level.

Linda

Another time Aparna was looking to change her job, which she resented because of the long commute. She applied the principles of feng shui (the Chinese spiritual art of space design) to strengthen and clear the energy in her office. She also decided to stop resenting anything about her job. She began to affirm that she was getting a job within ten minutes' driving time from her home, even though this idea seemed rather far-fetched, since there were only two corporations that supported her line of work within that distance. She further affirmed the kind of people with whom she wanted to work. "Within a month," Aparna said, "I had a job two miles from home. It had all the characteristics I affirmed for. Now I am on another search for a job that will make me feel more in line with my life purpose!"

Feelings are powerful attractors. Don't set a goal unless it makes you feel open, excited, and possibly a little scared. The goal should feel *almost* too good to be true and make you tingle with anticipation.

Carole writes from Australia, "You know when your heart wants you to do more than what your head tells you! I took a trip to the United Kingdom at Christmas in 1997 just because I knew I had to go. An inexpensive one-way flight came up, and I had only fifty pounds to take with me. I arrived and got temporary work straight-away. I stayed a few months, going through all of the learning that God had for me as well. The best thing? Spending my first Christ-mas in eight years with my family in the United Kingdom. I had a feeling then it would be the last time I would be with both my mum and dad together. It was, and I am so glad I trusted my intuition. I believe that if you recognize and acknowledge your energy vibra-tion and intuition, it will take you exactly where you need to go."

A TO Z

Traveling this journey involves pain. There is no jumping from A to Z in this process. You have to go through the alphabetical cal-endar of growth. It's exhilarating and at times it feels crazy, and you may well ask yourself, "Why am I doing this?"

Paedar Dalton, psychotherapist

Be Willing to Get Smart

BARBARA STANNY, author of *Prince Charming Isn't Coming: How Women Get Smart About Money* and *Secrets of Six-Figure Women,* comes from a wealthy family and was married to a stockbroker who gambled away a huge portion of her assets during their marriage. One day she received a bill from the Internal Revenue Service and a bill from the state of California totaling over one million dollars for the taxes her husband had never paid. Stanny says she panicked. When her family refused to help her out, she went into a total breakdown of self-confidence. "My brain would fog over," she recalls. "In those early years, I truly believed I needed a man or somebody else to help me handle my money. I would take a class, but I was so sure that I couldn't learn anything that I literally couldn't see. I couldn't take in the information. There were times, during my separation and divorce, when I really thought I was going to die. And I was furious with God.

"At the moment that I decided to really commit to taking charge of my money—whatever that might mean—my life truly began to change. Around this time, I was hired as a journalist to interview thirty women who had money. Half of them had earned their fortune, half had inherited it. What I learned from them changed my life.

"Each woman told me how she went from stupid to smart. It dawned on me that no one is born with this financial knowledge!

"Since I've learned how to manage my money, my relationship to myself and others has completed changed. I can see that it's not the amount of money you have that makes you feel secure as much as it is the feeling that you have knowledge that gives you the ability to take care of yourself. It's the most empowering process I know of. It's even made me closer to my parents.

"In the past my mother always let my father handle the money. That was pretty normal for their generation. But since she read my book, she has started an investment group with a bunch of her friends. With the women of this generation—those who have no real idea of their financial condition—there is always an unspoken fear of what will happen when they lose their husbands. They assume they will just transfer their dependence on their husbands to another authority, like a financial planner.

"The fascinating thing I found was that so many financial advisers and stockbrokers who make their living helping others often make a shambles of their *own* finances. I've found that it's not the facts of investing that are so difficult, because it's really not that hard. The difficulty comes from our fear of our power and individuating and growing up and taking care of ourselves. Women will say, 'Oh, I don't have enough time.' Or 'It's too complicated. Finances are boring.' These are just excuses for the fear of growing up and taking responsibility, or of going against family taboos about money."

WHEN YOU ARE ANXIOUS, TURN YOUR ATTENTION OUTSIDE YOURSELF

I think you can appreciate just how much time and attention you devote to dreaded anticipation. There are so many valuable things to be doing with your attention.

When you are anxious, turn your attention outside yourself.

Become connected to life, and allow that rich healing contact to influence your feelings. Stop trying to figure yourself out! Be anxious and *simultaneously* become interested in your surroundings.

R. Reid Wilson, *Don't Panic*

During her research on women with money, Stanny began to see that once women attained security and comfort, they were using their money to make a difference—in their lives, in the lives of those they loved, and in the world around them. "I really see that when enough women get smart about money, we're going to change this world and change the planet. Women's philanthropy is different. The way we run our businesses is different. I think it tends to be more humane and nurturing. We use our money as a reflection of who we are—that could be staying in luxury hotels, buying designer clothes, supporting a battered women's shelter, or contributing to a woman's political campaign. That's what heals us and heals the planet."

Be Willing to Experience the Discomfort of Change

WHEN YOU begin to take charge of any part of your life that you have been avoiding for a long time—such as your financial situation or your health—it's very likely you will go through a dark, overwhelming, or scary period while you change your approach. Stanny remembers, "When I started to really learn about my finances, it was not comfortable. I would feel stupid, scared, and inadequate—all the things about myself I didn't like. It wasn't fun.

"I had to deal with the secondary issue of these fears, which was that for years I said I wanted to be smart but deep down I felt if I was smart and independent no one would love me. Staying stupid was self-protection. There would be times in those early years when I was struggling to become knowledgeable that I would be in the fetal position on the floor! That kind of fear and trepidation is part of the process of expanding our world. The willingness to go through that dark night is part of the transition. It takes courage to shift gears, to go to the next level of being."

Go Where You Fear

STANNY ONCE had a reporter ask her if she had a motto, and she answered, "Yes. Go where you fear." She believes that wherever you're afraid, that is your next step. If you don't know where your next step is, ask yourself, Where is my fear? "For me," she said, "being in charge of my money was a very spiritual experience. I see handling money as one of the most divine activities we have to create what we want in our lives.

"The most important questions to ask yourself are: What do I want? What do I want my money to do? What do I want to use my money for? This is just as important as knowing the difference between stocks and bonds. It doesn't take a lot of time or money to accumulate wealth. It's not that complicated. You're never too old to start, you just have to make a decision to start."

When you start getting clarity about any issue, there is bound to be a gap between what you have and what you want, or a gap between the order and system that you desire and the chaos you face. For example, with money, you may be tempted to go back to familiar spending habits and back into fogginess in order to lessen the tension. The key is to allow yourself to stay with the questions and tension, and to create new behaviors and new habits in spite of the tension. This is true for all kinds of life changes that require new habits, such as going back to school, taking training, or volunteering or interning.

Stanny suggests the best way to start changing your thinking is to take small, tangible steps. "Read a page a day on something to do with finances. Save two dollars a day. Do this for three months, and you will become a different person financially. Your life will change dramatically. Ask people if they have tips about handling money or investments. Take your kids to the financial planner and get the family involved. I've found the power of simple gratitude amazing. When I was in terror, I would write 'thank you' on each check when

I paid bills. I found something to be grateful for every day. It really is transformational."

SIT WITH FEELINGS; DON'T RUN

It's taken a long time to get deep enough into myself to know what I'm about, and to know what I should do. Of course, there is discovering what you need to do and then doing it, and those can be months and months apart. . . . Being able to sit with your feelings and not run away is really difficult.

Victoria, sex educator

Work Through Personal Issues

WHENEVER WE want to make changes, especially in career or jobs, our minds automatically prefer to proceed in a linear way. When we can't see how to get to our goal, or even define what our goal might be, we feel discouraged. The unknown looks like a big, blank, scary place. Our first reaction may be that we don't have what it takes to change our lives. Our fears dominate our thinking.

Often whatever issues are still unresolved from the past will pop up in the form of self-doubts, feelings of victimhood, or resentment. Even though we think we need to work logically to move in the direction of finding a new career (looking in the newspaper or going to career counseling), we may find that cleaning up old negative *feelings, about anything,* will actually create positive movement in unforeseen directions. When we feel good about ourselves, we don't see the monsters under the bed so frequently. Fears have a way of simply dissolving because they are not attached to suppressed energy.

Susan, a nurse who lives in Wisconsin, has a deep and passionate interest in many areas, one of which is research in social anthropology. She writes, "When I went through a divorce, I was filled with hate and resentment, and life took a continuously increasing downturn. A major turning point happened when a member of a support group suggested I start to regard my former husband and father of our children as a 'business partner.'

"Peace of mind resulted. I then extended this thought pattern by visualizing him and his wife as happy and fulfilled. The internal change on my part seemed to initiate healing all of us and our extended families.

"My problem now is that what I do in the field of anthropology, which I love, is voluntary. It doesn't seem to fit into the real world. I am fifty-five and live joyfully and fully yet have a low income, no retirement or access to medical coverage, no savings. In the past two years I have been in and out of jobs whose policies clearly define the 'old world' and stifle freedom and creativity. I have a rusty old car and a small house in an affluent neighborhood. I don't know how to change my thinking to change the situation without selling my soul to the world of the old status quo."

Susan's statement reveals her belief that the only way to change the situation is to sell her soul. She and I discussed this idea by e-mail. A few days later she wrote back to say that she had decided to continue as a part-time home health nurse, because she really enjoys the work and it gives her a good deal of freedom as well as hands-on creativity.

A few months later Susan had created a very full life: "Since we last talked, I realized my basic needs have always been there when needed. My former husband just sold me his 1992 Oldsmobile in nearly perfect condition, just in the nick of time. I have thus thrown financial concerns to the wind and now work full-time on a stipend for the American Peace Corps (Americorps) at 'The Neighbors' Place' as donations coordinator/family liaison. I assist socially and economically disadvantaged persons, mostly Hmong, Black, and Hispanic, to have better chances at life.

"I may use my future educational grant from Americorps to become certified as a therapist in that field. Classes are generally held in beautiful places around the globe, and my son's job with an airline provides nearly cost-free parent passes! Occasionally, I have time to devote to my ancient sociocultural passion, but it seems necessary to curtail most of that cutting-edge work until the Americorps assignment is completed. In one sense, my life has become chaotic, but it seems to be pulling all kinds of dormant internal factors forth. . . . I think that one can successfully wrestle fun out of anything if one maintains a simple life peppered with elegance and a flurry of interestingly diverse people from all walks of life."

Susan's inner work allowed her to shift her attitude from one of fear and resentment to one of exploration, trust, and goodwill. She continues to hold the vision of her deep passion for anthropology and allows the universe to help with the details of bringing her ever closer to this interest. Essentially she shifted her focus from what wasn't working to what *is* working.

DO ALL THAT YOU CAN, BUT NEVER HURRY

Do all that you can do in a perfect manner every day, but do it without haste, worry, or fear. Go as fast as you can, but never hurry.

Remember that in the moment you begin to hurry you cease to be a creator and become a competitor. You drop back upon the old plane again.

Whenever you find yourself hurrying, call a halt. Fix your attention on the mental image of the thing you want and begin to give thanks that you are getting it.

Wallace D. Wattles, *The Science of Getting Rich*

Take Responsibility

SOMETIMES OUR lives become so out of balance that we can no longer cope. Depression settles over us with a frightening finality. Kathy, a psychotherapist, relates the story of one of her clients, whom we shall call Sandi. At the time Kathy met her, Sandi was forty-nine. She was a twice-divorced single mother with two children. Sandi came to therapy because of acute depression. She had been on Prozac but did not want to continue with drug treatment. For several weeks in therapy she mainly talked and cried. At that time she was a director of human resources. She admitted that she had two big fears—a great fear of failure and an even greater fear of the debt she had accumulated.

In therapy it became obvious that the debt had built up from buying beautiful designer clothes, decorating her house beyond her budget, and eating out or picking up fast food for her boys most of the time. Both her sons had learning problems and were having difficulties at school. In the past, Sandi said, when she got deep into debt, her parents would help her out, but they had developed health problems and could no longer help her.

Sandi's turning point came when she saw that all her life she had tried to win her mother's approval, but her mother in fact had never approved of anything she did. As a result, Sandi had spent her whole life trying to look better than everyone else and had to have a house and career that outshone everyone's. This inauthentic and competitive lifestyle was making her depressed. She used shopping as a way to numb herself, and paying with credit cards created a huge debt. The debt kept her focused on an external problem that was not the real issue. The cycle of bingeing on shopping and feeling remorseful kept her trapped. Being in debt validated her worst fear, that she was not going to be taken care of because she was unlovable.

What was life changing for Sandi was coming to the realization that all she needed to do was just be who she really is. She finally understood that she could never do enough to get her mother's approval, and that she didn't need approval to be who she is.

YOUR OWN FRESH, WILD WAY

All the good stories are out there waiting to be told in a fresh, wild way.

. . . What you have to offer is your own sensibility, maybe your own sense of humor or insider pathos or meaning.

Anne Lamott, *Bird by Bird*

In the beginning, Sandi was terrified to go to financial counseling by herself, so Kathy drove her to her first session. With financial counseling Sandi was able to work out a spending plan to avoid bankruptcy, and she began to set up and maintain a realistic budget. As part of her new decision to live within her means, for example, she started cooking meals at home. At first her children did not like the changes, but within a short time they settled down, and the whole family began to feel better. After six months of eating at home and not eating fast food, the children's ability to concentrate increased and they began to do better in school. Sandi was able to pay off some of her debt with the money she got from selling three closetfuls of designer clothes to a secondhand shop. She now buys clothes on sale at regular stores and wears them more than once.

Start Somewhere

AS WE make deliberate changes that improve certain areas of our lives, we are able to grow deeper, and to take on habits and practices that would not have been possible earlier. For example, as Sandi's healing progressed, she added new tools for self-development. She learned to meditate, began reading spiritual books, and listened to tapes to stay centered on achieving her new goals. She began to see the lessons in her conflict. Her mother liked the positive changes in her daughter and even began to give her encouragement and support. They grew closer, and now have a very good relationship for the first time.

Sandi began to trust herself more, which led to making better decisions. For example, she let go of the administrative pressures of her old job and took a less stressful position. She plans to go back to school to earn a counseling degree. In Kathy's final note on Sandi's healing, she says, "Sandi has so much more energy now that she doesn't have to impress anyone in any way."

When our lives seem overwhelming and we feel helpless, we start by recognizing that we are no longer coping. With the support of a good friend or professional counselor, we begin to examine the fears that led us to make some of our choices. The change we want always comes one step at a time. Life unfolds as we take responsibility for our choices. Even though we think we'll find an external answer to counteract our fear, there is no global "fix." Rather there is a gradual peeling away of the layers of denial, hurt feelings, low self-esteem, and fear of being unlovable. The only way to the other side is through the fear. Each day we begin again.

By having an attitude that there is no one right way to do things, we free ourselves to do something different. We can trust that when a path seems to have positive energy, that's the best path for now. At the very least we will learn something we didn't know before we went in that direction.

NO FAILURE, NO BLAME

I try to teach the lesson that people don't fail. People make choices that either work out or don't work out. Those that do not work out are our lessons. I say, learn the lesson and move on.

I don't like to use the words *guilt* or *blame*. With these words out of the way, people quickly open up to a new way of thinking.

Kathy, psychotherapist

Avoid Either/Or Thinking

ONE OF the biggest contributors to fear is believing that there is only one right path—either *this one* or *that one*. We tend to see our life choices as either/or situations. For example, "If I quit my job, I won't have financial security." "If I marry, I'll lose my independence." "What if I move to England and it doesn't work out?"

In truth, there are almost always many more options and outcomes than we had imagined. Too often we look at the future through the eyes of the past, or through the eyes of conventional—and limited—thinking. Changing our attitude to curiosity about the opportunities that will come *no matter which path we choose* is the most liberating action we can take in handling fear.

Jackie from Ohio writes: "I am searching for a new direction. Both children are out of the house, and I have completely lost interest in my twenty-year career at a college. It's very frustrating to be in a 'waiting period.'

"Sometimes I feel I need to know where I am supposed to go before it materializes, and other times I feel that if it is supposed to happen it will happen. I feel trapped between these two beliefs. I wonder if this is what has kept me trapped—this contradiction of two beliefs."

Jackie's comment about being trapped between two beliefs is a common way we create a static situation to prevent taking risks. We could personify her statement "I feel I need to know where I am supposed to go before it materializes" as one voice within her— let's say the voice of the Planner. Her other statement, "I feel that if it is supposed to happen it will happen," might be the voice of the Fatalist. Jackie is right in wondering if these two conflicting perspectives have kept her trapped. Intuitively she can feel the double bind that paralyzes her: waiting for absolute clarity on the one hand and the passive desire to see what will materialize on the other. How do we reconcile this type of thinking in order to move ahead to create changes in our lives?

DEFINE THE CONFLICTING PERSPECTIVES YOU HAVE ABOUT YOUR SITUATION

THE FIRST step is to define the conflicting points of view (there could be several) within your psyche. For example, Anita, a business consultant about to turn sixty years old, wrote to me of her deep desire to marry. She wanted to know why she had not yet found a life partner. Anita wrote that she had been single for fifteen years after her second marriage ended. Since then she had dated off and on, but no real partner had come along. She wrote that she felt that she was attractive, open-minded, and fit. Her income is good, and she travels extensively in her work. She owns a home in a community-minded neighborhood, which she loves.

In working with a therapist, Anita identified four "voices" in her inner psychic "household," each with a different agenda about "finding a man."

Her therapist asked her to close her eyes and see which voice wanted to speak first. The first voice was the part of herself who had "bought the house and secured a good living situation" for Anita. Anita called her the Homebody. The Homebody did not want to leave her nest and security; therefore, the Homebody cast a suspicious eye on any man who might come into Anita's life and take her out of the neighborhood to "unknown" destinations.

Anita's second inner voice was the Teenager, who seemed to be cast as the one in charge of "dating" and the social scene. This teenage Anita was tired of her role of being provocative and pretty, and saw herself as both flirtatious and a shy wallflower—an uncomfortable inner double bind. This duality indicated that she was conflicted in her "job" of finding a life partner. *Double bind* is a psychological term for being between a rock and a hard place. Double binds paralyze our capacity to move forward for fear of making a mistake, being abandoned, or even physically or emotionally dying. In a double bind you feel as if you can't win or resolve the contradiction.

The ego-based or conscious Anita, who is dynamic and busy with her work, wanted the Teenager to "hurry up and find the man" so she could keep working! The Teenager was becoming more and more resentful, and therefore either Anita was attracting inappropriate men—too young or unavailable—or she found herself saying things that put her dates off and they never called again.

Finally, the fourth figure—the Grandmother—emerged (Anita's son and his wife had just had twins, and Anita was reaching her sixth decade—a major benchmark). Anita wrote that the Grandmother spoke quietly and emanated a peaceful, calm solidity that spoke of an emerging integration within her as she shifted into the archetype of the elder, wise woman, stage of life.

Anita explained that, with her therapist's help, she could identify these conflicting issues of aging, security, and desires for new adventures, romance, and intimacy, which were being worked out on the inner planes. The key, she said, was making these differing needs *conscious*.

Anita wrote at the end of the e-mail, "I've just gotten engaged to a man who is also turning sixty this year! We plan to live part of the time at my house and part of the time abroad. I am astounded at how easy this seems to me now, and how impossible such an event seemed a year ago."

TAKE ACTION WHEN YOU FEEL GOOD ABOUT SOMETHING

HOW WILL the next step become clear? It will feel good! You will feel excited about doing it. Expect to feel a little scared in the beginning of the change, but don't let that stop you.

Recall that the Law of Attraction says we attract opportunities that match our state of being and feeling. Once we keep our focus daily on things that please us (making improvements in our surroundings, weeding the garden, the brilliance of winter light, kitchen smells, funny friends, our kids playing, or whatever else strikes us as marvelous and nurturing), we can relax knowing that the Law of Attraction is resonating to this inner happiness.

Then, when we have an epiphany such as Anita's realization that her inner figures had to feel safe before they would allow a man to show up, we can begin to take action on what is presented to us by the universe.

Felicia is a fifty-two-year-old prizewinning interior designer living in Southern California. She is married to Raymond, a stockbroker who works extremely long hours. He gets up every day at 4:30 A.M., and by the time he comes home, has a workout, and eats dinner, it's time to go to bed at 8:30 P.M. Raymond and Felicia agreed that they would downsize their lifestyle, and Raymond agreed to move to some property they owned in Boulder. They engaged an architect to build a smaller home. Because she was frequently in Boulder, Felicia began to collaborate with the architect on some other homes in the area. When the stock market took a downturn, Raymond panicked. The move and career shift now seemed ill-timed and frightening. Without discussing it with Felicia, Raymond refinanced their home to pay business debts and did nothing to extricate himself from his business ties. In addition, their expensive home has failed to sell. Suddenly, Felicia's momentum on Plan A has come to a halt. "When I think about staying in Southern California," she writes, "I feel absolutely no energy. My life here just seems finished, and in my mind, I've already made the move to Colorado. I don't know when Raymond will be ready to move. He's in fear mode. I have to make a choice about what I want to do. Do I stay here just to keep up appearances that our marriage is still working, or do I go where I feel I need to to grow for my own development?"

These kinds of dilemmas are not uncommon as two people work through different phases of the individuation process. "I can stay trapped by Raymond's fear, but that doesn't feel right to me, nor does it really feel supportive of him either. I'm not sure where our marriage is headed, but I'm feeling that I need to go ahead and make the move and see how that changes us together. I have to trust that the positive energy in Colorado is where I need to learn my next lessons."

WHAT IS THE PURPOSE OF LIFE?

That depends on which level of observation you are on. On the level of an atom, the answer would be to become part of a molecule! If you ask a molecule, the molecule would say, "To become part of the cell."

Each time we become flesh, we become incarnated. In mystical Judaism, we believe in reincarnation. It's called *gilgul*. We believe each time we incarnate, we move a step forward. Coming down one time prepares me for the task I have to do the next time. Whatever I conclude in this lifetime, if I come back again, I can take up from where I left off—not with the same memory, mind you, but with the same traces and vibrations and merit and clarity and God-connection that I had. If I learned a lot this time around, I get to teach the next time around! If I did wrong this time, I may get a chance to fix some of the wrong I did.

Rabbi Zalman Schachter-Shalomi, in *Tying Rocks to Clouds*

Lean into Resistance

WHEN WE hit a wall in external situations or within ourselves, we want to run away or break through. When we are thwarted, stymied, and stumped, we want to resolve the tension by taking action, usually to get away from something.

What action can we take in the face of resistance? Obviously there is no one answer to this question. However, one of the best attitudes when you're stuck is just to accept that it's what's happening right now. It's where you are, and there's a reason for it. We can accept *not with resignation but with an attitude of curiosity.* Accepting where we are brings us back into the present moment, where we *no longer blame anyone,* including ourselves. Being open to the present moment gives us the viewpoint of an explorer. Resistance is a tool of fear. Perhaps it gives us time to get to know our fear and find out what our fear is saying or wanting us to do. Resistance can be used as a time for rethinking what is important to us.

We often desire change because we think we are bored and have exhausted the present situation. By becoming more alert to our boredom and open to the unfolding *now,* we are inevitably moved forward. We need not deny our feelings or fight them. We can lean toward the feelings as if listening to a whispering friend. What is whispering to us in this situation?

If you are experiencing resistance to making a life change, how would you answer these questions:

- What is whispering to you?
- What are you afraid of?
- What is over for you?
- What still has energy for you?
- What is emerging?
- What is faintly stirring on the distant horizon?

MAKE FEAR AN ALLY—FIND OUT WHAT YOU NEED TO FEEL SAFE

WE WILL never completely rid ourselves of fear, but we can learn to accept that fear is a normal component of change. We can sort out what we are afraid of, and look at what our options are. We can keep the attitude that we will be able to handle whatever comes up as we move forward. Each day is a chance to start fresh. We can take the view that whatever comes up, *we can handle it*.

An e-mail from a woman named Ursula is a good example of how bodily feelings and sensations guide us to what is inappropriate and appropriate. Ursula writes, "The fear feelings told me that while the decision to move on was correct, time was required to travel through all the fear-based obstacles and doubts, so [I should] stay put for now. But my body also told me that one day, when a sufficient amount of the 'objecting' energy had been shifted, embraced, and released, I would just wake up, feel the power, and say . . . *Now!* That's how it was, too. I think we often push too hard against resistance to change, create pain and hardship for ourselves, instead of waiting for all the parts of us to shift, bit by bit."

Ursula continues, "Several years ago my body told me it was time for my higher love. I called for him. Much to my surprise, my ex-husband turned up. Gosh, I asked my body, is this him? Yes, it said. You're ready for each other now. Ego mind kicked up a real stink. Again it's a matter of listening to those feelings and allowing time for yourself to die to the objections, which are an illusion anyway, albeit convincing! After a two-and-a-half-year separation, my husband and I did reconcile. We learned that relationship depends on, and only flourishes with, never-ending change. We also learned that nothing is certain and that forever doesn't exist. It's day by day. We are very, very happy.

"Today I was fascinated by how different parts of me shifted, and at different speeds, integrating and assimilating bit by bit.

"I am a competition tennis player and have developed my own pretty good serve. My technique is poor, but it's accurate and fast. My tennis coach wanted me to change my serve, recognizing how limited it was. While my spiritual mind (searching for higher ground) desired the change, my logical ego mind said, 'If it ain't broke, why fix it?' It took ages for my body to 'get it,' and at first I totally lost the strength and speed of my serve. My body was annoyed, confused, and irritated. It kept throwing up resistance. *Go back,* it said. At a recent tennis tournament I watched excellent players serving the perfect serve repeatedly for four days.

"Today I noticed that my body had adopted the new style. It somehow decided to drop its attachment to the old 'technique,' and it was agreeing to the new. It was allowing it to be integrated. I was amazed to observe how it had let go of its habitual attachment to the old familiar way. I could feel the flow, the grace of this new style. My body rejoiced as well, and gradually I played with different ways of making small improvements. I can feel this technique has fewer limits built into it, and I'll go further with it.

"I'm fascinated that although my 'thought' process sought a new way, my body was fearful of letting go of familiar territory and guar-anteed results. Emotions kicked in to support my body's insecurity.

This won't work. Abandon this madness. Watching the servers was like absorbing the 'feel' of the new way. It was like a repeated mantra or affirmation. Eventually I must have become the new movement. Now I'm playing with more alternatives.

"It occurs to me that our cellular structure is habitually attached to 'old ways.' We don't often seem to be able to surpass its resistance, even with the most powerful thought forms. I wonder, what is it we have to shift when we invite in change? In what order does it happen? Which parts lead, which follow, which resist, and which encourage the change? Observing my 'serve' transition was amazing, like a schizophrenic observing the different parts of self moving from Point A to Point B, some arguing for a retreat, others wanting to give up, others forging forward. It took a lot of patience and compassionate allowance for me to let the parts come together at the end, in their own time. Now my body hardly recognizes the old style. I can't even do it. It's like a memory lost in the universe, done with."

> So you see the imagination needs moodling—
> long, inefficient, happy idling, dawdling, and puttering.
>
> Brenda Ueland, *If You Want to Write*

14

❧

Become Prosperous

In order to see yourself do well in business and prosper
financially, plant imprints for this in your subconscious by
maintaining a generous state of mind.

GESHE MICHAEL ROACH,
The Diamond Cutter

Take Charge of Your Money

A YOUNG, single Internet executive in Portland, Oregon, earning
$110,000 a year was baffled that, even with a sizable income, he felt
as though he lived hand to mouth and had nothing to show for his
efforts. He lived in an expensive apartment. The living room furniture consisted of a lone desk and chair. His home had few other fur-
nishings besides a bed, upon which he slept in a sleeping bag
because he owned no linens. Despite his high earning power, he
had no savings, and his credit card debt was up to $45,000—a result
of divorce from an expensive but short-lived marriage and charging
items such as vacations, clothes, and stereo and computer equipment in the five years since he'd left college. He wanted to get married again, but the woman he was dating was anxious about
marrying someone with so much debt.

Surviving in uncertain times all too often means that we have to
deal with money. Even in the best of times, for many of us, money is
definitely in the Big Unknown category. Maybe we believe that lack
of money is stopping us from doing what we would like to do, or we

can't imagine how we could create more money, or we have habits that don't allow us to keep the money we do earn and feel a sense of accomplishment. If we're thinking about starting our own business, we may be paralyzed by the idea of giving up a paycheck. If we're looking forward to retirement but are worried that there's not enough saved to stop working, we may not feel much freedom about developing new interests or a second or third career. In order to move forward, what do we need to know about handling our money?

According to financial counselors, stories of unbalanced finances are becoming more and more frequent. A recent article in *Forbes* magazine cited several examples of people whose careening lifestyle choices led to financial ruin. One such case was a forty-five-year-old East Coast doctor earning $300,000 a year and living in a $750,000 house. His children attended private schools and went to expensive summer camps. Despite his high income, the family's credit card debt eventually forced them to file for bankruptcy.

How does this happen? What drives us to make the choices that keep us financially chained instead of liberated?

When thousands of people at the highest income levels are struggling to make ends meet or save money, it becomes obvious that the idea that all financial problems can be solved simply by having more money is an illusion. Perhaps the answer lies in the deeper issues of beliefs about ourselves and our abilities, as well as the emotional states that drive behavior.

According to recent government statistics, as many as 40 percent of the households in this country spend more than they earn. Well over a *million* households a year file for bankruptcy, and that number continues to climb. The truth is, no matter how much money we make, if we spend more than we earn, eventually we'll be broke. With easy credit and unlimited material temptations, debt can become a crippling burden very quickly. The imbalance created by feeding monthly finance charges on credit cards can seem like an overwhelming and unsolvable problem.

If debt is steadily creeping upward every year, we may feel helpless to change our situation and justify our helplessness by thinking that we are not good with money. We may go through several bouts of debt consolidation or refinancing, mainly to "rob Peter to pay Paul." When we obsess constantly about cash flow, or put on a show of keeping up with our friends when we can't really afford it, or argue constantly with our mates about spending, we tend to look to outside resources to change the situation. Guilt, low self-esteem, secrecy, frustration, and bounced checks, as well as a feeling of time deprivation, are all red flags that our *lives* need to change. How can we change our money problems in order to bring new feelings of peace of mind, fullness, order, and generosity? We have to change in two ways: Change our thinking and change our behavior.

In this section you will find simple but effective practices that, *if you do them,* will lead you to financial well-being regardless of whether you are earning $25,000 a year or $250,000 a year. All the good advice in the world, however, will be useless unless you believe that change is possible. Good advice is fruitless if it remains an idea rather than being practiced. But changing lifelong habits takes time.

INCREASE

- The intelligent substance which is all, and in all, and which lives in all and lives in you, is a consciously living substance.
- The desire for riches is simply the capacity for larger life seeking fulfillment. That which makes you want more money is the same as that which makes the plant grow; it is life seeking fuller expression.
- The universe desires you to have everything you want to have.
- Nature is friendly to your plans.
- It is essential that your purpose should harmonize with the purpose that is in all.
- You must want real life, not mere pleasure or sensual gratification.
- Life is the performance . . . of every function—physical, mental, and spiritual—without excess in any.
- You must get rid of the thought of competition. You are to create, not to compete for what is already created.

Wallace D. Wattles, *The Science of Getting Rich*

Review Old Messages

ONE OF the financial counselors I interviewed for this section is Susan Bross, who has a practice in Mill Valley, California. Her views are consistent with those of a growing number of professionals who specialize in helping people make lasting changes in their finances through understanding the *emotional* underpinnings of financial problems, as well as changing dysfunctional money patterns.

Bross remembers one of her clients, who was earning $90,000 a year and was $60,000 in debt. By reviewing his childhood history with money, he realized that his parents had taken and spent his savings account on more than one occasion. For him putting money in savings was equated with helplessness and loss—why save? His ability to save money began only after he brought this early fact to consciousness. Five years later he has created a net worth of $250,000 by addressing this old belief and changing his behavior.

Changing how you see yourself and your capabilities begins with reviewing all the messages about money that you received from childhood, such as "Money is the root of all evil." "Rich people make money by exploiting others." "Buy now, pay later." "Everybody's in debt." "You can't change human nature." "Enjoy it while you can." "Don't rock the boat." "There's never enough to go around."

Replace Fear with Clarity

FEARFUL THINKING steals power from us and sabotages our ability to start making changes that, over time, will be significant. In a helpless frame of mind, we tend to push away the fear with rationalizations: "I'm too far behind." "I don't make enough money to save anything." "I can barely pay the rent, let alone think about the future." "Dealing with money is too complicated." "I don't understand about investments." "I'm so far behind that buying this won't make any difference."

Changing our financial condition requires us to be mindful about our attitudes and our behavior. For example, if we decide to cut our expenses radically in order to pay off a credit card balance, we have made only a *reactive* move. We have not examined the *reasons* the debt grew so large. We are still acting from the old thinking that created the problem.

THE RICHES THAT ARE IN FORMLESS SUBSTANCE

Never look at the visible supply. Look always at the limitless riches in formless substance, and *know* that they are coming to you as fast as you can receive and use them. Nobody, by cornering the visible supply, can prevent you from getting what is yours.

Wallace D. Wattles, *The Science of Getting Rich*

Develop the Four Capacities

IN ORDER to change your negative financial life to a positive one, you need four capacities:

1. Willingness to ask for help and desire to make necessary changes
2. Clarity about how much you earn, spend, owe, save, and need in order to live a balanced life that brings joy and satisfaction
3. Positive beliefs that support your resourcefulness
4. Consistent, sustainable action over time.

Be Willing to Make Changes

WHEN LIFE changes, it's often seen as an upsetting shift that we blame on circumstances beyond our control. When life doesn't change, we similarly look for something to blame—often ourselves. "I don't have enough money." "I must be doing something wrong." "I don't like my job or career, but I don't know what else to pursue." An old teacher of mine used to say that if you don't have the new thing in your life, you must not be 100 percent willing to have it yet.

Do you really want to make the effort to find a new career? Or is it easier to talk about how you feel about your current situation and get sympathy from others? How many times do you hear yourself saying in answer to a friend's helpful advice, "Yes, but . . ."?

Take a moment to feel how motivated you are to make a change. Sometimes it's helpful to write down all the reasons our money is not where we want it to be. This exercise helps us gain clarity about our *beliefs* about money. I knew one man who managed to stay in graduate school for several years, living on part-time student employment. He said he couldn't imagine having more than $1,500 a month income because he wouldn't know how to handle a lot of money. Needless to say, his attitude will most likely prevent him from increasing his income beyond his perceived comfort level.

By contrast, a woman told me that she and her husband managed to buy a house despite having absolutely no money for a down payment at the time they made the decision to buy. They and their extended family of seven people were looking for a place to rent but kept being turned down by landlords because the family was too large. Her husband, finally reaching his limit of frustration, told her, "We are going to buy a house." She was shocked at his statement because, at that time, they had no money saved up. They even had to borrow the $25 it cost to get a credit check. However, their strong intention to buy a house began to take effect. First, delayed payments owed to their day-care business suddenly appeared. Second, the family made adjustments in their spending. Third, they received a loan from a family member. At the end of three months she and her husband had accumulated a $10,000 down payment. They found a real estate agent willing to work with them and located a property they could afford. Today they own their own home.

Get Clear About Income, Expenses, and True Needs

SUSAN BROSS suggests that people get an overview of their financial picture as the first step to clarity. She works with clients to develop a realistic monthly spending plan that addresses important needs and wants while keeping a list of unmet wants and needs that can be addressed in the future. She helps them discover where they might feel a sense of deprivation, the roots of which may go back to their early family history. Low self-esteem and having been emotionally or physically abandoned as a child are patterns that may cause impulsive spending, which ultimately sabotages financial well-being. How many times do we go out and buy something when we feel depressed, angry, or emotionally empty?

Bross encourages her clients to brainstorm on ways to meet needs that aren't just through money. For example, expensive meals out might be traded for entertainment at home, like spending time on hobbies or playing with the kids—things that don't necessarily cost money yet bring true personal satisfaction.

If there's not enough income to go around, the plan needs to be carefully whittled down *in each area across the board* to match income and other resources so that no one area is left out. The monthly plan also includes amounts set aside for future periodic expenses, like new tires for the car or vacations, to prevent these expenses from ending up on a credit card.

The next step is to keep track daily of what is spent. Record keeping—even if it means just jotting down the cost of your café latte on a piece of paper in your wallet—helps on many levels. First, tracking expenses allows us to feel more in control of our money, rather than the other way around. People feel better when they feel they have some control over their lives. Second, jotting down expenses helps keep us more *conscious* about spending. Being conscious helps to express the *intention to have more money.* Third, having a *realistic plan* usually makes us feel less anxious. Feeling more relaxed creates a flow of creativity and optimism.

With increased clarity about spending patterns and motivating feelings, each month's expenses become easier to plan. Realistic decisions can then be made about looking for higher-paying work, perhaps, or letting go of expenses that drain money without giving any real value in return. So many times I have heard participants in my workshop express their desire for clarity before taking a new career step. I always advise that clarity about the next step is often impossible to have. We simply do not know what the future will bring or whether our plans will work out. However, the one place that clarity is achievable—and essential—is in our finances.

Develop Positive Beliefs About Real Security

ONE REASON it may be hard or scary to make a life change is carrying a huge load of debt on credit cards. Fear about how to handle this debt during a transition may keep people in jobs they have outgrown or come to hate.

One of the hardest things for heavily indebted people to accept, says Bross, is giving up use of their credit cards, an absolutely necessary step in regaining balance. Credit cards are viewed by most people—especially those carrying large debt loads—as signs of security and status. Financial counselors address this false belief by helping clients redirect their reliance on credit cards so that they can find a sense of self-worth and security in *themselves* as they take charge of their money lives and find creative ways to fill their needs and wants without the use of credit.

With a commitment not to use credit cards *for anything,* three things occur. First, the debt cycle is arrested, so that making small payments will begin effectively to reduce the principal. Second, using cash to pay for something causes one to think more seriously about whether the item is really necessary and reduces impulse buying. Third, by taking charge of your money in this balanced way, your self-esteem naturally grows stronger. Success in one area breeds an expectation for success in other areas. Life changes that formerly felt overwhelming, suddenly seem easier when you have found a deeper sense of security within yourself.

Take Consistent, Sustainable Action

AS WE have seen, the key to making long-term change in one's financial life depends on three things:

1. Making a decision not to increase consumer debt for any reason.

2. Ensuring that all important living needs are covered during the month.

3. Making a written spending plan monthly and tracking cash flow (so that you can make adjustments if necessary mid-

month and compare the plan with actual spending at month's end). A big benefit of actually writing the plan down *on paper* is that this discipline allows us to release the constant juggling act in our minds. Having a plan allows us to relax and feel open. This mental state encourages more creative flow and allows us to receive unexpected benefits from universal intelligence.

Financial counselors remind us also that, if our spending plan is very tight, it may be necessary to call creditors and negotiate longer terms or smaller payments. Making smaller payments—with no new charges—will actually allow us to be more responsible in meeting our obligations. Following through with reliable payments goes a long way to establishing a good working relationship with creditors—even big companies.

The main point of all this considered planning is to ensure your basic living expenses and not set yourself up with unrealistic goals, which will, in the long run, undermine your debt-clearing program. "The truth is that none of our resolve to get those debts paid down will work for very long if we are living unbalanced lives," says Bross. "The key is to get your life balanced first, and then take care of the debt over time. The key to doing that is to promise yourself *that debt is no longer an option.* You have to eliminate debt as a solution to financial problems so you can develop your creative muscle with other solutions. Then, instead of sending huge amounts of money in payments to the cards, make smaller or minimum payments and begin to set money aside for things that you would ordinarily charge on a card." When credit card purchases have stopped and small payments are being made, the card debt will eventually get paid off. The new habit of putting money aside for things that would have been charged before—clothes, car repairs, tires, dental work, furniture—begins to eliminate the thoughtless impulsivity from which we often make our purchases and prevents future credit card use.

The second point is that we are now carefully choosing to allocate our money for savings, vacations, hobbies, or other self-nurturing activities that keep us from feeling deprived. We are retraining ourselves to know that we can meet our own needs and wants on a consistent basis *without credit.* When charging is no longer an option, we have the opportunity to consider whether we really need this item, whether we could buy it secondhand, whether we can make it ourselves or acquire it in a more creative way. This behavior marks a major step in attaining and maintaining financial health. We have moved from surviving to thriving.

ANYONE CAN CHANGE

Even though these ideas may sound easy, it's not necessarily a simple thing to stop using credit and put money aside. It takes discipline and a hard, clear perspective and commitment to really wanting to change your life to get this going.

I have seen enough change in people to know that *anyone* can change. But the people I work with often don't believe that initially because they feel they've already been working hard and they haven't been able to make progress.

Susan Bross, financial counselor

If you have not made the changes in your life that you want because you don't believe you have enough money, Bross emphasizes the importance of looking for positive role models so you can see that financial well-being is possible. In addition, you may want to get a professional counselor. Ultimately, of course, you have to make your own decisions, but you don't have to figure out how to do everything all alone. Looking and asking for help to make changes is a sign of maturity. Making a change starts with believing that you *can* change. Bross says, "You have to believe you can change, otherwise it will just seem like certain special people have it together but not you."

Select a Benchmark So You'll Know When You've Arrived

ACCORDING TO Bross, people in transition often have identified the direction they want to go but not the destination. She asks,

"How will you know when you've arrived? What monthly income do you want? How many employees do you want if you're in business?" Lack of definition, she believes, is what keeps people in chaos. Success is sabotaged without discernible milestones.

Fear about the future and about our ability to be successful keeps us thinking that we aren't making enough money, or that we're not doing enough to get ahead. Having a clear goal can help us know when we have enough. Bross suggests that people start with a "photograph" of where they are right now. How much is in your savings account? What is your monthly income? What is the amount of your debt? It's equally important to write down your financial dreams. New car? When? House? When? Travel? Where and when? How many trips a year? Would you go to school if you had the money? What charitable causes would you like to support?

Bross has seen that when her clients set specific goals, such as cutting debt in half by this time next year, or increasing income by 10 percent this month, unexpected solutions increase significantly.

Recognize Invisibility and Denial

DO YOU feel that you have been working very hard but have virtually no savings or sense of security? Besides chronic debting, two other ways we may keep ourselves from accruing tangible results from all our hard work are (1) keeping ourselves "invisible" by not acknowledging our profit or success; and (2) denying any surplus by not accumulating savings.

Becoming invisible, according to Susan Bross, is a defense mechanism we can develop in childhood. She explains, "Becoming invisible, hiding out, minimizing success or fear, being quiet, not speaking up for themselves—which are all forms of disappearing from abuse and pain—allow children to avoid punishment, verbal abuse, and other negative consequences. As adults they can continue to be invisible by sabotaging their success and money through creating struggle, chaos, debt, and other draining financial habits."

To counter this defense mechanism, Bross helps clients recognize the area in their financial lives where they need to "show up." For example, do they need to face their delinquent IRS taxes and pay them? Do they need to reduce debt? Do they need to fulfill financial commitments like child support or debts to friends and family? Do they need to acknowledge their wants and satisfy them? "In that process of showing up," Bross says, "I find that they become so enthusiastic and feel so much better about themselves that they get the momentum going to carry themselves to full financial maturity."

BUILDING SECURITY

- Start a retirement program early. I didn't start until forty, and I regret that.
- Trust your gut. If you get a weird feeling about a client, it's a big red flag.
- Refuse to work with terrible clients just because of the money.
- Find a business mentor to talk over problems or ideas.

Arielle Ford, literary agent

Reframe Your Problem

OUR FINANCIAL problems seem insurmountable because we keep projecting the same fears and insecurities on every situation. We usually need help in seeing our patterns and allowing new solutions to arise. For example, one of Susan Bross's clients typifies the pattern of the classic underearner. Underearners need to expand their thinking rather than constrict their relationship with money.

Bross's client had decided to work part-time while exploring a career transition. However, instead of using her free time to find a new career, she spent most of it worrying about her finances. Servicing her debt with the minimum payment left her with no disposable income every month. As a result of her constant worrying and letting the debt rule her life, her outlook was becoming increasingly hopeless. Her response to her burdens was to spend as little as possible on everything and to "get smaller and smaller" in how she lived. She believed her only way out of the dilemma was to need less and to earn more money. She had already virtually eliminated her personal expenses and, with her fearful outlook, could imagine earning more only if she spent more hours at the dreary work she was already doing. The idea of working even more hours was untenable given her exhausted and contracted state of mind.

The first step Bross worked on was to get her client to extend her thinking beyond simply spending less. Since underearners' thinking is based on limitations, the healing takes place as they begin to expand their thinking about options and increase their sense of self-worth.

Bross recalls a significant turning point when the woman began asking for additional work and was offered an unexpected, interesting project. "It is often my experience that when people start to do the footwork toward a positive solution, little gifts are synchronistically offered to them in the form of an easier pathway or more available income, as though to ease them along the way as they strive toward their goal," says Bross. "I remember another woman who was struggling with her monthly income and had no possibility for doing additional work. She received 'unexpected' checks *four* times during the year. Because of her vagueness about money, she had completely forgotten they were due her.

"I have watched clients move from being greatly in debt with no assets to owning a home, purchasing a car, and having no problem with debt in the course of three to five years," Bross says with a smile. "I've seen struggling entrepreneurs who were essentially running an 'expensive hobby' evolve into having viable, ongoing, and profitable businesses within a year or so. I've watched clients who haven't been able to maintain a balanced checkbook start a savings account in a relatively short time and then clear up past debts with the IRS. I have never found a client who, when focusing positive energy toward her or his money life, hasn't been able to make *significant* change in the first year," she concludes.

ENOUGH

Enough is a fearless place. A trusting place. . . . It's appreciating and fully enjoying what money brings into your life and yet never purchasing anything that isn't needed and wanted.

So what's all that stuff beyond enough? Clutter, that's what! Clutter is anything that is excess—*for you*. It's whatever you have that doesn't serve you, yet takes up space in your world. Enough is a wide and stable plateau. It is a place of alertness, creativity, and freedom. From this place, being suffocated under a mountain of clutter that must be stored, cleaned, moved, gotten rid of, and paid for on time is a fate worse than dearth.[*sic*]

Joe Dominguez and Vicki Robin, *Your Money or Your Life*

Switch Roles to Create New Patterns

FOR COUPLES struggling to make changes in their financial life, the situation may feel even more overwhelming. There is much work to be done to coordinate two different approaches to spending and saving. When arguments become heated or partners engage in passive-aggressive behavior that creates tension, guilt, resentment, and anger, the emotional climate is not very conducive to healing! Examples of passive-aggressive behavior are giving someone the silent treatment, making major purchases without consulting the other person, or concealing purchases by paying cash or keeping the new items hidden. Passive-aggressive comments usually take a sarcastic form that wounds, but doesn't create a good space for real dialogue: "Another pair of shoes?" "You bought books?" "Whatever." "Don't you ever look at our bills?" "I can't believe you."

I asked Bross what she recommends for couples. One married couple, whom we will call the Browns, seemed to symbolize the inner work that must be done by two people to identify goals and values, practice clear communication, and achieve family well-being.

Mr. Brown owned his own business, but the business was struggling. He really wanted to take a more creative direction, but he didn't feel he could do that because of the couple's high consumer debt. Mrs. Brown was beginning to lose confidence in his ability to handle their finances, and this fear was exacerbated when she became pregnant and had their child. She felt their money was out of their control at a time when her security needs had increased.

Bross did not focus on getting Mr. Brown to become more

responsible or even change any habits. Instead, she suggested that Mrs. Brown take over the finances, which would not only help increase her knowledge and get her more involved but eliminate some of the pressure Mr. Brown was feeling. Bross provided ongoing support as Mrs. Brown began to take charge of the recording and reconciling the monthly spending plan the couple made as a team. Instead of making Mr. Brown "wrong" for his past handling of the finances, Bross helped the couple focus on strengthening Mrs. Brown's knowledge so that they could proceed on a fresh footing. In learning this new skill, Mrs. Brown didn't mind asking the basic questions that her husband hadn't felt comfortable asking. It was clear that he had a fear of asking for help and risking looking incompetent. The most common reason clients don't ask for help, in Bross's experience, is the fear of having their worst fears about themselves confirmed. With both partners involved in creating a solid footing, the Browns came up with solutions that created a whole new foundation for the business. Within months new gains were made. The business started to become successful, and Mr. Brown was able to develop new creative avenues. Mrs. Brown gained not only increased financial competency and self-esteem but also peace of mind and a feeling of security.

Once the Browns were able to clarify their vagueness about their money and take positive and consistent new actions, they started to pay off their debt. Within three years they were completely out of debt, and the creative arm of the business is now making $10,000 a month thanks to Mr. Brown's improved focus.

YES

In terms of assessing our own attitude to risk, the question we should ask ourselves is not: Should I take a risk and invest in the market? The answer to that is an emphatic yes. The critical question is this: How much risk can I take? The answer: enough to stay ahead of inflation but still sleep at night.

Barbara Stanny, *Prince Charming Isn't Coming*

Bross emphasizes the importance of couples working together and sharing the *factual data* of their situations. Otherwise, she says, there are misconceptions and shared resentments about where the money is going and who is spending it.

The Browns' money situation came to a head as each partner began to individuate more fully. Having a child increased Mrs. Brown's need for safety and well-being and prompted her to pay attention to the warning signs of debt and continuous struggle. The solution was for her to grow past her previous beliefs that she was not good with money. For her to step into the financial picture, she had to walk through her own fears and self-doubts. Mr. Brown had to be willing to recognize what was not working and allow another solution to emerge, which ultimately freed him to go where the energy was most positive—deeper into the creative arm of the business.

Become a Millionaire

DAVID BACH, thirty-three, is an author, lecturer, and partner in the Bach Group. Since 1993 he's been on a crusade to teach women how to empower themselves financially. The principles of his books *Smart Women Finish Rich,* a *New York Times* bestseller, and *Smart Couples Finish Rich,* were featured on PBS television.

"I'm teaching people how to look at their values, and how those values affect their financial decisions," says Bach with enthusiasm. "I've seen people change their lives in a moment. There are only three or four financial decisions that people need to make that will affect their whole lives." I asked Bach to outline the most important points of his message:

1. *Pay yourself first.* The problem is that most people have heard this advice, but they don't know what it means. The simple answer is that the average person needs to be saving about 12 percent of his or her income before taxes. That means if you make $30,000 a year, you should be saving $3,600 each year. The only way to do this is to put it away every time you get a paycheck. Don't wait till the end of year. This money should go into a pretax retirement account, such as a 401 plan, an IRA, or a SEP IRA. When the money is invested, it needs to be invested

for *growth,* that is, in a stock-based mutual fund. If people did just this much, which, by the way, comes out to about ten dollars a day, and did this for thirty to thirty-five years, they would have *over a million dollars.* The problem is that today the average American has a savings rate of less than *1 percent* of income. This isn't even a savings rate; it's a spending rate. People come to me and want to know what stocks to buy. I tell them, You don't need to worry about that until you are paying yourself first with 12 percent of your paycheck.

2. *Pay down your home early.* After you have put your 12 percent into savings every month, start to pay down your home early. If at all possible, pay an extra 10 percent each month on your mortgage. For example, if your mortgage is $1000, pay $1,100. If you do that, you'll pay your home off ten years early, and you'll be mortgage-free in mid to later life.

3. *Spend less than you earn.* Cut up credit cards, and use only a debit (secured) card.

"If you do just these three things, you will be very wealthy in your later years," contends Bach. "One of the biggest problems is that people live in financial denial. I hear people say, 'Well, I don't care about money. It's too complicated.' Most people's strategy is not to have one. I know people with MBAs, who aren't saving 10 percent of their income. I have friends who make $300,000 a year and don't own their homes, who have no retirement, and who spend every cent they make. There are people who make $50,000 and, by saving, become multimillionaires. My grandmother was one of those people. She started saving when she was in her thirties. At that time she was making ten dollars a week. She saved one dollar a week and invested that money in the stock market. She learned about the market by trial and error and by taking classes. She had become a self-made millionaire long before she passed away in her eighties."

SELF-MADE MILLIONAIRE

I believe that whatever you do for others comes back to you a hundredfold. For example, I've worked hard for my money, but it has always come to me.

My uncle set an example for me when I was very young about buying property as an investment. I buy a house every year, and currently own twenty-five houses all over California. I'm a self-made millionaire. I bought my first house when I was twenty-five with fifteen hundred dollars, which was just enough for the closing costs. I borrowed all the rest of the money, including the realtor's commission, for a down payment. In the sixties I had a partner, and we would think up schemes to make money. For instance, one summer we bought steel drums during the drought and sold them to people who were conserving their water. We made about a hundred dollars each, and we did this every week until we had enough money for the next down payment on a house.

Robert, San Rafael, California

Find Role Models and Mentors

FROM HIS early experience with his grandmother, Bach emphasizes the importance of receiving mentoring. When he was seven years old she introduced him to the idea of buying stock. They were eating lunch at McDonald's, and she said, "You know, David, you could make money from this lunch." He thought she was referring to getting a job cooking burgers, and he told her he was too young to work. "She laughed and said, 'No, you won't make money working here, but you could buy stocks in this company,'" and she began to instruct him in the process. He started by reading stock prices in the newspaper to keep up with the shares she bought for him in McDonald's. By continuing to learn and invest, Bach became a self-made millionaire by the time he was thirty.

"I always say people overestimate what they can accomplish in one year, and they underestimate what they can accomplish in ten to twenty years."

It's never too late and the problem never so large that you cannot begin to make the changes that will put joy and fulfillment back into your life. Your learning process alone will begin to open up creativity, new friendships, and an infinite array of synchronicities. Find a financial mentor and then become one. Share what you know with a young person.

SMALL ACTS MAY HAVE BIG REWARDS

You cannot foresee the results of even the most trivial act. You do not know the workings of all the forces that have been set moving in your behalf. Much may be depending on your doing some simple act, and it may be the very thing which is to open the door of opportunity to very great possibilities.

You can never know all the combinations which supreme intelligence is making for you in the world of things and of human affairs. Your neglect or failure to do some small thing may cause a long delay in getting what you want.

Wallace D. Wattles, *The Science of Getting Rich*

Take Action

NO MATTER what kind of life change you desire, money will constitute part of that change. Money is one of the areas in your life over which you *can* exercise control.

Here are tips for handling various problems, such as chronic debting or underearning. While these tips seem simple, they are not always easy to follow on your own. Although many people would rather talk about their sex lives than about their checkbooks, you might consider finding an open-minded friend who also wants to learn new ways of handling money. You can make it a project to learn together.

If you are thinking of moving, going back to school, ending a marriage, starting a new business, or writing the next great thriller—and you don't know where to begin—start with putting into action any one of the financial ideas in this section that intuitively increases your optimism and sense of well-being when you read about it. When you put your life on a sounder, more conscious financial foundation, you will be surprised at how things automatically start to change in other areas.

However, if the idea of following any of these tips makes you cringe, and you don't feel you have a clue about how to get started, you probably need to find a professional financial adviser. If you go to a counselor, be sure to find out his or her views on changing behavior around money. Discuss the items on this checklist, and see if these are ideas the counselor also uses. Not all financial counselors are trained to work on emotional healing in conjunction with finances, and not many psychotherapists are trained to deal with financial problems. As in choosing any professional help, use your intuition; if someone doesn't feel like the right person, look elsewhere. Once you set an intention to improve your relationship to money, you will be amazed at how rapidly, and unexpectedly, positive changes happen.

Checklist for Financial Action

Chronic Debting

- List
  1. Who you owe
  2. How much you owe
  3. Your interest rates per credit card
  4. The total amount you pay in finance charges each month
  5. Your total minimum payment due for all cards

- *Stop using credit cards.* As long as credit is an option, it will be the only option you will use. Not using a credit card allows you to apply your creative juices to *other options.*

- *Figure out the triggers that make you spend money when you don't have it.* What happens to you just before you find yourself in the mall, pulling out a credit card?

- *Decide on a doable debt repayment plan.* If you are paying down three credit cards, pay off one of them. Take the money you were using to pay that one each month and apply it to the other two.

Don't stop until you're at a zero balance. That way, all the debts get paid off and you'll cut years off your overall debt repayment schedule.

- *Don't pay all your money to reduce your debt.* If your plan is too stringent, it won't be sustainable for long.

Money Vagueness

If you bounce more than two or three checks a year, you probably lack awareness about your bank balance, your income in relation to spending, and periodic expenses that could take you by surprise but shouldn't (property taxes, quarterly tax payments, annual insurance policies, and so on).

- *Keep track of your spending for at least three months.* Keep a notebook in your purse or wallet for recording daily cash expenditures. Keep a check register even if you have on-line banking. (This encourages a more hands-on relationship with your bank balance.) Double-check each credit card charge on your monthly statement. It will add to your clarity to know exactly what kinds of things you buy on credit.

- *Commit to being proactive.* Attention and planning increase your sense of competence. When you feel good, you are automatically more creative.

- *Set a **specific** goal against which to measure your progress.* For example, "I want to pay off my smallest credit card balance by the end of the year." Or "I am going to fully fund my Roth IRA for the current tax year." Break that goal down into small steps each month to reach that goal.

Underearning

If you are an underearner, you are not earning what you are worth. You either undercharge for your product or services or accept employment that doesn't match your abilities. You might not feel you deserve to make money or have fulfilling work. Change involves healing your confidence, raising your expectations, and enlarging your vision.

- *Focus on **expanding** rather than **contracting**.* The theme song for underearners is "I am not good enough" or "I'm not worth it." This belief translates directly into one's financial life. Identify your fears and push your envelope. If you don't face your fears, you will continue to stay small. Underearning is also related to how you deal with what you do earn—keeping yourself small or invisible. For instance, do you regularly bail out friends or family? Do you maintain a heavy debt load? Do you feel uncomfortable knowing that you earn more money than your friends, your parents, or your spouse? Do you feel uncomfortable saving money and spend it as soon as possible?

- *If you are working in a job below your capabilities, ask yourself what you are avoiding.*

- *If you are an entrepreneur, be clear about your ratio of expenses to income.* A common dysfunctional behavior is to put all the profits back into the business, leaving ourselves feeling deprived in our personal lives. Is your business really growing on a sound basis, or are you building a business at the expense of building a life?

- *Check habits of overworking.* Exhaustion can lead to rationalization of binge purchases; for instance, "I've been working so hard, I deserve to eat out tonight." It's much healthier and easier to work smarter rather than harder.

- *Look for a message of struggle in your early family.* If your parents struggled to make ends meet, it may not feel right for you now to make a comfortable living. To earn others' love, we sometimes act small or helpless.

- *Track your daily actions.* Every evening before bed review the day and write down the three best things you did and the three worst things. Don't make a judgment about yourself or feel guilty. When you *track*—be very present in your life—you will automatically change. When you *change*, your reality will change.

Here are some tips to remember from the experts as you take steps to make changes in your financial life.

Keys to Abundant Living and Financial Harmony

Take Charge of Your Money

- Set a goal for making more money.
- Save money every month.
- Measure where you are now:
    Monthly income
    Total debt
    Total monthly finance charges
    Amount of savings
- Track your spending for one month.
- Compare, assess, and adjust for the next month.
- Make a new spending plan each month.
- Save for periodic expenses like tires or insurance.
- Include something fun (a movie, massage, dinner out) each month.
- Pay cash. If you tend to buy on impulse, leave your credit card at home when you shop.
- Find a mentor and be accountable to him or her.

Stop Rationalizing Unnecessary Purchases

It is very easy for a compulsive shopper to rationalize or justify any purchase as something he "needs." If a person is unable to recognize rationalization and justification when they arise, he is setting himself up for yet another round of compulsive spending, *because we can never get enough of what we don't need.*

Karen McCall, financial counselor

Increase Your Self-Mastery

- Examine your beliefs about money:
    I have to work long hours.
    Money comes only from an hourly wage.
    There's only so much to go around.
    Rich people have sold out.
    Investing is too hard to figure out.
- Educate yourself about how you can make your money grow. Don't wait for some large amount to appear.
- Do something you don't think you can do.

Barbara Stanny, author of *Prince Charming Isn't Coming*

Increase Your Money

- Know what you want to do with your money.
- Express gratitude for what you already have.
- Take small steps to educate yourself about investing.
- Be consistent with new habits.
- Put money in an envelope every day just for the fun of seeing how quickly it accumulates.
- Count the money you've put aside in one month. Use it to invest in a mutual fund.
- Give away small amounts of money regularly.
- Avoid references to lack. Instead of saying, "I can't afford that," say, "Maybe I'll do that another time."
- Write thank you on each check you make out.
- Imagine how you would spend a million dollars. Who could you help?

Work Toward Wealth and Well-being

- Start investing now. Be consistent.
- Pay yourself first.
- Save 12 percent of your income before taxes (about $10 per day) every month.
- Put the money in an IRA, Roth IRA, or SEP IRA.
- Invest for growth.
- Pay an extra 10 percent on your mortgage every month, and pay your house off early.
- Spend less than you earn.
- Cut up your credit cards, or use only debit or secured credit cards.

David Bach, author of *Smart Women Finish Rich*

Never let go of integrity, generosity, and love, for these, coupled with energy, will lift you into the truly prosperous state.

James Allen, *The Path to Prosperity*

15

Embrace the Transitions
of Mystery

Love, Loss, and Death

> We are not only going to communicate with each other verbally, but at a different level, we shall commune with one another, which seems much more important than mere verbal communication.
>
> J. KRISHNAMURTI,
> *Talks with Students*

Changes Occur *and* Love Is an Eternal Connection

HOW CAN we more consciously handle radical life changes that happen to us? Divorce, death of a loved one, and illness, for example, are significant rites of passage that not only have the power to tear us apart but also can teach us.

Loss is inextricably linked to love. However, when we lose someone who occupies an important place in our lives, the loss may also bring a shutting down of certain possibilities and dreams of our own. Death and divorce leave huge holes in our lives. They can strip away people who carry our memories and history and are parts of our identities. Paradoxically, loss may also bring us deeper into our authenticity and closer to the spiritual connection we didn't even know we were seeking.

These deep states of emotional piercing are part of the shaping of our destinies. Before being born in this life, our spiritual selves yearned for touch, sight, sound, smell, taste, and creative freedom.

Before birth we were part of All That Is, whole and as yet untouched by the physical and emotional pain created by dualities—such as good and bad, strong and weak, joy and sorrow. That wholeness changed with our first breath of air, when we suffered our first loss—of our safe, warm, and perfect harbor. Thus began our independent journey of new experiences.

Life Is a Mystery School

MYSTERY SCHOOLS in the ancient world believed that life on the Earth is a mirror of life in the spiritual world—As above, so below. The students of these various Ways throughout the ages look for truth and meaning in everyday occurrences. They believe that the journey of life is the path by which we are tested and by which we gain spiritual enlightenment. They speak of the essential forces or archetypes that live in the human soul and remain accessible to us in myth as well as ordinary and extraordinary life experiences. Many of us have gone through extraordinary circumstances that take us to deep levels of grief, wonder, and love. What can we learn from those who have gone through the soul-altering fires of deep loss?

Powerful stories are powerful medicine, from which each of us draws lessons needed for our personal healing and support. All the stories in this section are meant to be offerings of support, perhaps stored in the imagination as inspirations for another time.

I met the artist Dinah Cross James through a friend and later traveled to India with her and a group of nineteen people to meet Tibetan healers and teachers. Dinah is a fine painter and in earlier years was a fashion illustrator and an illustrator for Sunset Books and *Reader's Digest.* Through painting she has been able to understand and integrate even the most hellish and most sublime of her life experiences.

"My daughter, Tali, was born in 1971," Dinah began. "I remember in her early teen years my work had a strong element of the natural world—rib cages of deer, bones of dinosaurs, erupting volcanoes, all of which came out of trips we took to Africa and to Mt. St. Helens when it was erupting.

"Tali was a crazy teenager, climbing out of windows at night. I wanted to express the anxiety I felt as her mother, and I started a series of Raggedy Ann paintings. [Raggedy Ann and her brother Raggedy Andy were popular dolls in the early nineteen hundreds. They have round faces with red yarn hair and red-and-white striped stockings.] There were all kinds of Raggedy Anns flying through dark skies and red skies, with smoke blowing in the background. When Tali was in college at Berkeley she fell in love, and I wanted to express her freedom and her beauty. She lived at home that summer, and I painted her then as a bird.

"At the end of Labor Day weekend, I was working on a painting of a dead zebra with a raven coming down. It was disturbing to me. My husband and I were leaving to celebrate our twenty-fifth anniversary. Tali took us to the airport on the day of our anniversary. We never saw her again. Four days later she was killed in a fraternity fire. She and her boyfriend, Doug, both died trying to save a third student in the fire. It had never occurred to me that those early pictures of Raggedy Ann were pictures of flight and fire.

"When I got back to the studio after her death, my palette, which had been so somber and foreboding, completely switched to light colors, like peach, yellow, white, turquoise, and gold. Images of birds began to fill my canvases and paper. After her death, my paintings took on lightness and luminosity. All my friends were surprised that this shift toward the light would have taken place *after* her death. Until she died, I never realized what I had really been painting in the bone imagery, in the volcano, and in the Raggedy Ann series. In retrospect, it was clearly about loss, grief, separation, and soul energy."

CHOICES

Souls who become involved in these tragedies are not caught in the wrong place at the wrong time with a capricious God looking the other way. Every soul has a motive for the events in which it chooses to participate.

Michael Newton, *Journey of Souls*

How often is a coming loss indicated, giving us a chance to prepare, even in an unconscious way, for devastating suffering? Does the soul live on? How can we know? These questions are naturally triggered as we struggle to make sense of our grief and pain, and to understand the value of another's often too-short life.

Dinah believes now that the soul does live on. She says, "Two days after the fire, we found a little alarm clock of Tali's, but the battery was dead. I thought it would be a wonderful thing to have next to my bed. The clock had stopped at 6:30, and I thought someday I would get it fixed. I began to carry it with me when I traveled.

"Six months later I was visiting with Doug's mom for the first time, and we were going over some letters from the kids. The alarm clock went off even though the battery was completely dead. After that it would go off on all sorts of occasions, such as whenever we were with any of Tali's friends, or at significant times between my husband and myself. For example, the second year after she died, my husband and I decided to go to Squaw Valley to ski for Christmas Eve, and the alarm went off in the car five times. After the fifth time I opened the base of the clock and the big hand started to move. The clock would go off on my birthday, on Christmas, and on the Fourth of July."

Dinah's marriage ended not long after their daughter's death, and through that difficult period the alarm clock continued to go off. "As unbelievable as it is," says Dinah, "the clock worked for seven years on a dead battery. The hands went around and everything."

Throughout these trials of loss, grief, and abandonment, Dinah continued to express her emotions through painting. "I have read a lot about grief," she said, "and I agree with writers like Ram Dass and James Van Praagh that creative activities such as gardening, cooking, helping others, painting, playing music, and journaling really help when you are in a lot of pain. Drawing the fire and Tali's transition through the fire, and drawing my feelings about my divorce—no matter how painful the imagery—has been a big part of my healing. It was forceful, ugly imagery, but I feel working it through on paper is better than becoming diseased. I have not had a cold or flu for nine years, by the way. That's another indicator that there is a strong energy around me. I've gotten rid of a lot of toxins in the body by finding ways to express emotions. Otherwise, I might have ended up sick.

"Talking to the one you've lost and reaching out to the person is also a form of prayer. I try to be aware when something synchronistic happens, or of any subtle energies that I sense. For example, I may be thinking of Tali as a bird, and all of a sudden a hummingbird flies up into my view. Those things have meaning for me."

BY THE CITY GATE

A year ago today by
this very gate your face and
the peach blossoms mirrored each
other. I do not know where
your beautiful face has gone.
There are only peach blossoms
flying in the Spring wind.

Ts'ui Hao

Love and Ladybugs

DEBORAH, THE waitress we met in Chapter 10, has had her share of loss and change, even though her work life has been stable for many years. In her view the death of her husband helped her to develop a deeper appreciation of all life, as well as spiritual values of faith, trust, love, and service.

Deborah's husband, Billy, died of an aneurysm at age forty-four. He left this world while sitting in his favorite chair with his cats and listening to music. She remembers that his last words to her on the phone that evening were "I'll talk to you in the morning. I love you so much." "He was a very special man, and even though he's gone, I still feel a connection to him." Deborah believes strongly that Billy's spirit visits her in different ways—sometimes as a feeling or even in the appearance of insects. "I think when people pass away they tend to come to you in a way that only you will understand," she said. "Once when Billy was alive, he and I were out walking in the woods. We saw some bushes with clusters of ladybugs all over them. It was a really special moment for us. Two days after Billy passed away, a ladybug came to my door and stayed three days in the same spot. I just felt so sure that he was trying to communicate with me. Another time about two months later I was in the high desert with my twin sister. A ladybug flew into the car on the passenger side. My sister said, 'Ladybugs don't live here. This ladybug could be Billy's spirit.'

"Years ago I lost one of my favorite earrings, and Billy and I looked all over for it. Last year on my birthday, after he had passed away, I woke up and wanted to do something fun and positive for myself. I needed an extension cord to work outside on my art. I knew there was a cord behind this little shrine I had for Billy. When I carried the extension cord to the backyard, I found the earring on it. I felt like it was a birthday present from him."

PATCHES

I collected the pieces of the story as I would the patches of a patchwork quilt—not knowing what pattern would emerge. Often, the patches refused to behave. They seemed to have a spirit all their own.

For the next three years I whined, kicked and screamed, and persisted. Sticking with something for a long period of time, the day in and day out of doing of it, the living with it, was teaching me humility and patience I hadn't known before.

Sue Bender, *Plain and Simple*

Healing from the Suicide of a Loved One

"SUICIDE LEAVES some of the most devastating aftereffects to deal with," says the therapist Selma Lewis. "Because no matter what people have done to help the person who committed suicide, they judge it as not enough. They constantly go over and over in their minds, 'If only I had done this or that.' There is tremendous self-blame. It is also very hard to be angry at the person who committed suicide, because he or she is dead. Most people get depressed because they can't feel their appropriate anger, so they blame themselves instead. Being angry at the person is actually more mentally healthy than blaming themselves. In time, we hope, people will move into forgiveness for both themselves and the suicide."

In many families, Lewis says, it's very difficult to talk about the person who died or the issues, such as the mental history or the events that led to the suicide. This lack of communication and exchange of feelings and general coming together retards or prevents healing. "There may be secrets that have never been told," Lewis says, "as well as shame, blame, anger, and resentment. The separation between family members is its own sadness.

"The results of suicide reverberate through the years. This ultimate act teaches a hopelessness about living and facing life situations. Unfortunately, statistics show that the children or close family members of suicides may be more prone to commit suicide themselves. Like other aspects of family violence and abuse, suicide creates a negative imprint and template for how to live in the world. The cycles of violence tend to get repeated if they are not confronted and healed."

TEACH YOUR SONS TO CRY

LISA, SIXTY-ONE, is a research project manager whose twenty-year-old son, Dan, committed suicide. A few years after her son's suicide, she says she feels a more spiritual strength and greater personal authenticity, which she believes are results of her suffering. "Dan had fallen in love with a girl who was a teenager at the time, and two years later she got pregnant," Lisa says. "I talked with him on the phone briefly one afternoon. A day later I came home from shopping and my husband said, 'Dan shot and killed himself last night.' Everything changed in that moment. For one thing, the brutal way my husband announced Dan's death—in that instant—revealed to me just how bad my marriage really was. I looked out the window in shock and disbelief, and my first thought was I'm divorcing [my husband] just as soon as I get a place of my own.

"We found out that Dan's girlfriend had been out on a date with someone else when she came home and found him. He had shot himself and was already dead when she called the police. He had written a note to me telling me that he couldn't bear the loss of his closest love, and that he was going to find some peace. I found out later that his girlfriend had aborted his child and he had become desolate. He had told everyone in his immediate environment that he was going to kill himself and had been saying it for a week. Nobody took it seriously. Nobody called us.

"I was on the plane flying home after his funeral when I heard him say to me as plain as day, 'I love you, Mom.' It was very reassuring. I heard it twice. Now I knew I could go on. When I'm really upset, all I need to do is go for a walk and ask to see a butterfly. I'll look up at the sky, and I always see one—the classic symbol of immortality—even in January in Maine. It's happened so many times. I've had so many unusual synchronicities since his death."

Lisa has gone through the pain of loss, the fire of guilt, and the acceptance of life as it has been given. Speaking now with the wisdom of the return from the void, in the integration period when our lives show us the lessons received, she says, "Dan's death has cemented my belief in an afterlife. It took me about three years, though, before I could cry, I was so closed up. My advice to mothers is Teach your sons to cry. Also, if someone is depressed, make sure he gets help or medication. Ask your children how they feel. If your children's life plan is to die early, they will die. You can't stop that. Love them. Be generous.

"Having a child die makes you stop and hope to God it never happens to your worst enemy. But it made me stronger. I'm less of a perfectionist, and my relationships are better now. Also, I suggest to people that they think long and hard about living with a punitive mate or someone who is really negative. Ask yourself, How is that affecting our children? Don't put up with abuse in a relationship."

> Where there is sorrow, there is holy ground.
>
> Oscar Wilde

Intervention and the Power of Grace

AFTER THE suicide of her husband of twenty-two years, Daria went through a very dark and confused period. Just before their twenty-second anniversary, she had asked him to move out. Now she reflects that he had been in a deeply depressed passage that overwhelmed him before he could see his way to the other side. She describes the period after his death as one of feeling like a failure, and feeling that God had let her and her family down. She felt guilty, angry, and alone. "Even before his death, things were chaotic in our family," she recalls. "One daughter became pregnant out of wedlock, and one daughter was raped." The search for answers led Daria to make a big change in her spiritual ties, and she converted from being an evangelical Protestant to being a Roman Catholic. "I was reading all kinds of mystical literature like Teresa of Avila and *The Cloud of Unknowing*. After J's death, every light went out," she says.

Some months after the suicide, Daria left her nine-room home on the Atlantic Ocean to live in a four-hundred-square-foot apartment in Berkeley, California, so she could embark on a course of studies at the Graduate Theological Union. "I needed to get away from my old environment. I wasn't coping," she says. "Our family therapist said the children would heal from J's suicide only if I went on with my life. It was a big thing to leave the girls, who were living on their own by then, and go out to California. I just wanted to stay in a closet and lock the door."

PRAYER HEALS

The more people prayed about their deceased spouses, the healthier they were. Prayer, in fact, worked the same way as talking to friends about the death. Prayer is a form of disclosure or confiding.

James W. Pennebaker, *Opening Up*

After spending one year in the spiritual studies program, Daria returned to the East Coast to study for a master's in pastoral counseling and spent three years working as a chaplain. Recently she was appointed a director of the program. Her girls have gone on with their lives, graduated from college, married, and given her a grandson.

THE GOD IN PEOPLE

DURING THE year in Berkeley, Daria attended classes with a man who had been a priest for twenty years and had left the priesthood. When he came East to teach he called her. After avoiding his calls for a while, she started going out with him, and they married in 1998. "I'm in heaven. He's a great grandparent and stepfather to my girls. Even though I couldn't find God for a long time, God put such wonderful people in my life.

"Sometimes when there is a remaking of us, we have to depend on an intervention other than our own resources. I had no power, no faith for a long time. I had no positive thinking that would work. I was powerless, but there was an intervention. God used the kindness of people and circumstances that would get me into the right place. Money came in from kind friends. I can't take much credit for the changes that happened in my life during this period."

Daria now works with abused children, from infants to twenty-one-year-olds, in a social work department. She feels that her own "depth of darkness" has allowed her to relate deeply to these children. "I can see God enter into their lives. They have little hope, but in our program they can step out of their terror for a moment and have a little love.

"I have these five-year-olds who have been badly abused. We play hide-and-seek, and it's a very healing game for them. I play the part of the Good Shepherd who has lost her sheep, and I am so sad. 'Where are my sheep?' I will say. 'Where is my little Susie with those beautiful green eyes? Where is she?' And they say, 'Here we are.' And we do it over and over again, finding the little sheep. Last week I did it thirteen times. Calling out their names and finding my little sheep. They are so happy to be found.

"We were giving out little gifts, and there was one little boy who looks like a Biafran child. He is so guarded, and he was in such terrible angst that he wouldn't get his gift. I said to him, 'What if Jesus came in here today, what do you think he would say? He would look right into your eyes, and he'd say, 'I was once eight years old.' The boy reached out and grabbed my arm and said, 'Thank you. When will I see you again?' What could be better than that?"

Loss as an Open Door

WE SPEND a lot of time thinking about how to keep what we have and how to get more of whatever it is that we hunger for. Often that hunger has no name until we lose something precious to us. Losses frequently awaken us to what has true value.

A few years ago Alison was a successful market analyst in fashion. She lived with her husband in wealthy Westchester, New York. In her e-mail to me she described a life centered on material accomplishment and accumulation: "My husband and I and our friends and neighbors were all mostly interested in our careers, homes, and cars." Neither she nor any of the people she knew were spiritually oriented.

In 1989, at the age of thirty-nine, Alison found out she had breast cancer. At that point, she says, she had no belief in God. Her parents were Holocaust survivors, and while they were religious she didn't feel their religious observances had much depth or integrity, so she rebelled. She viewed religion as more about following the rules because of what people would think than about a truly meaningful spiritual connection.

During her first two bouts with cancer, she was so terrified she didn't even realize how much she was in denial. Her answer to being sick, she said, was to get back to work as quickly as possible and keep moving on. Her husband's response to her disease was to insist that she get the best doctor and technological care possible, but he offered little other support. He laughed at the idea of the mind-body connection, about which she was beginning to read. Neither of them discussed the impact of the disease on their lives. It wasn't until Alison saw her husband talking to a man on the commuter train whose wife had died of cancer that she realized how terrified she herself was.

Within months the relationship between Alison and her husband, which had not been good for some time, broke down and they divorced. She realized that she could no longer live with such high levels of negativity. Her values were beginning to shift as her terror about the disease forced her to go deeper within. However, even at this point she said she was still focused on keeping her cancer secret, putting on a strong front, and pushing to climb the ladder of success at all costs.

ARE YOU RECYCLING?

When you don't stop to determine whether you need to *evolve, release,* or *complete* a relationship, the relationship can start to deplete precious spiritual and emotional energy from you. Healthy relationships *recycle* and replenish spiritual energy while unhealthy relationships consume and deplete your spiritual energy.

Debrena Jackson Gandy, *All the Joy You Can Stand*

After her third bout with cancer, Alison had to have her breast removed. "I lost my job the same day I was diagnosed for the third time. On some level, I realized that the job loss was a gift because my work environment was so dysfunctional.

"I was still determined to keep my condition a secret, and I went to all my medical appointments by myself. I told only my closest girlfriend what was happening. I was ashamed that I was going to have a part of my body removed. At one point a doctor wanted to perform a double mastectomy, and I was completely mortified. Somehow, thank God, I listened to my intuition, because this didn't feel right to me. I fired him and got a new doctor, and my reconstruction process proceeded well. I got back on my feet quickly because I had to find a new job. I still allowed only my mother and my girlfriend to visit me.

"A year after I was divorced," Alison says, "I was single, and I didn't think anyone would want me. There was no one to talk to about this. Most women in support groups were married or young."

She immediately started a new job in the specialty market of bras and underwear, and was still climbing the ladder of success. "The moment I came back from that surgery, my interest in clothes and color and design was over. I worked in that company for another four years but didn't enjoy one second of it."

Alison's turning point came six months after her surgery, when she met her soon-to-be second husband serendipitously at a friend's party. It was a snowy night, and neither had really wanted to go to the party. "Steve is definitely not my type, but when we started talking, that was it. He was happy. He wasn't striving. He was spiritually connected. It showed me how dissatisfied I was. I was commuting three hours a day, was not fulfilled in my work, and was working with dishonest people. I started to see it as the end of a chapter."

Alison's story has a happy ending. After another job layoff, she left the retail field for good. Since then she has been developing a personal coaching practice, after realizing that all her previous work was always basically coaching and advising. "I love helping people grow, and I love working at home in wonderful surroundings. Now I'm writing a book about the connection between breast cancer and issues of relationship and intimacy."

Alison's journey was one of enforced and accelerated individuation. Through the losses of her health, her first marriage, and her interest in her retail career, she had to create a whole new life. In the process she also found a more authentic self. With a more awakened and expanded perspective, Alison has regained a zest for life and a sense of meaning.

THE MYSTERY REENCOUNTERED

Again we encounter the unknowable—for, try as we might, we can never fully plumb the depths of the unconscious and understand its role in prayer and healing. This *mysterium* is simply ineradicable; try as we might, we shall not be able to abolish it.

Acknowledging this mystery leads not to a forlorn but to a glorious conclusion—for the unknown is the approach to the sacred, the spiritual, the unnameable, the *numinous*. To honor this dimension is to be healed. As Jung described, "The approach to the numinous is the real therapy and inasmuch as you attain to the numinous experiences you are released from the curse of pathology. Even the very disease takes on a numinous character."

Larry Dossey, *Healing Words*

The Teachings of Grief

A WOMAN named Wendy shared her experience of the transcendence that grief often delivers in her e-mail note. "My only brother died from cancer, and we had just gone to his hospital room, where he had only moments before passed away. I was wondering what to expect when I got in there, because I also had broken my foot and was in a cast, using a wheelchair. I rolled into his room and felt such peace, like I had just come inside heaven's door. So much love and peace, it was awesome! Even though I had prayed for him to heal from the pain and suffering, when he died I realized that God had a better plan for him. I read *The Celestine Prophecy* by James Redfield, and that book has changed me. I have a better outlook on life and God, and I feel more energized than before—like a new person!"

A note from Shawn also reminds us of the incredible gifts that may come through grief: "My only sister died of breast cancer last year after a seven-year battle. What helped me most during the last three years of her life was a deep inner knowledge that I was doing everything I could to bring joy to her life. I spent time with her, took her to her treatments, arranged gatherings with her friends. In the end, I knew her spirit would always be with me. She was the one person who was with me through every hill and valley of my life.

"Once I accepted that she truly was losing her life energy, I asked my higher source repeatedly what I was supposed to be doing for her. I got regular, clear messages about small, joy-filled things that I could do to bring happiness to her experience.

"Right after she died, I woke up with a distinct 'message' that told me, 'No matter what happens, everything is going to be all right.' I'm certain it was my beloved sister helping me. I had thought that when she died, I would be devastated and riddled with grief. Instead, those of us who love her, and who were with her during her transition, have found a deep peace and are somewhat surprised at how well we are doing."

Emotional Dramas Disappear

LOSING A loved one has long-term effects on the personal life of the one who is left. Once the old mind-set and expectations have evolved through the crucible of deep change, new opportunities are offered. Shawn says, "The life situations that used to send me off into emotional drama no longer affect me in the same way. Old relationships that had been difficult for years have been healed. After three months of working in a higher-level job with higher pay, I have come to realize that I am not in the right field. For ten years I have struggled to feel good about my administrative jobs in corporate America. At age fifty-one, I have finally had an epiphany that I would be a wonderful elementary school teacher! This came to me from a casual remark from the [coffee bar] *barista* I see every night after work. When she said to me, 'You look like a second-grade teacher,' it was as though I had been given a gift! My heart and soul said, *Yes!* That's what I want to do next.

"For ten years I have 'hung in' with my job because everyone else kept telling me that I work for such a great company, with such great benefits. It bothers me a little that I feel like I had to get permission to pursue my goal, but all things happen in the right time! I don't want to fret about the past. I can honestly say that I have found a sense of comfort since I received—and believe—the message 'No matter what happens, everything is going to be all right.'"

Give Yourself Time to Grieve

TIME HEALS; this we know. But in our culture, although we may not speak about it overtly, we sometimes expect people to come back to work and be whole relatively soon after the funeral. We don't really realize or allow for the depth of the grieving process and the amount of time it may take. Everybody's timing is different. According to the therapist Selma Lewis, many patients—particularly men—who have lost loved ones tell her they are disappointed in themselves because they are still in the grieving process after a few months have passed. They think they have a character flaw or are "wimpy" because they have not bounced back emotionally. She assures them that there is no fixed time when grieving ends, although stages of letting go gradually allow the body and spirit to heal and move on. The grieving process—different for each person—appears to offer unique blessings and insights along the way.

Nothing Happens Without God's Knowledge

I MET Joerdis Fisher one night in a hotel restaurant in Cleveland, Ohio. I was speaking at a conference the next day. It was after nine o'clock, and the large dining room was empty of other diners. The waitress seated Joerdis and her friend right next to my table, and it seems we were fated to meet. Within minutes we had introduced ourselves, and the story of her son, Ian, unfolded as we ate. She showed me photographs of him taken the week before he died.

Joerdis and her husband, an internal medicine specialist, live in Lima, Ohio, and are the parents of two sons. She has been an elementary school teacher in the inner city, a full-time mom, and a professional volunteer, president of Junior League and PTA and the Medical Auxiliary of doctors' wives. She has worked diligently in the community as president of the board of the cerebral palsy clinic and in various other groups, including a hospice program. Two years ago her son, Ian, died when his house caught fire. Since that time her life has completely changed, and her understanding of death has been forever altered.

"Ian was unusual from birth," she explained. "He started talking at six months, and by nine months he was speaking in sentences. I remember distinctly a day I was changing him when he was six months old, and my husband, Eric, came into the room. Ian looked up at him and said, 'Hi, Dad.' My pediatrician explained that some children have early verbal skills, and some have early motor skills.

"By the time he went off baby food at nine months, he never ate meat. When he was about a year old, he asked me where his food came from. Before he would eat anything he would ask us where it came from, and he was a vegetarian until he met his [future] wife.

"Even when he was little, Ian heard voices at night. Both boys would hear the same spirit voices. Like in the movie *The Sixth Sense,* they told me, 'You know, Mom, there are people talking in our room.'

"When Ian was eight years old and in third grade, he made me drive to another town fifteen miles away, where there was a recycling station. He insisted that it was so important for the earth to recycle. This was in the Midwest, before most people had even thought about recycling. At about the age of twelve, he read an article about how cattle in other countries are raised for the fast-food industry and [people in the] villages were starving. After that we weren't allowed to eat fast-food hamburgers anymore.

LIFE CHANGES INVENTORY
FOLLOWING EXCEPTIONAL EXPERIENCES

Studies on people who have had near-death experiences or out-of-body experiences show significant shifts in nine value clusters:

1. Increase in appreciation for life
2. Greater self-acceptance
3. Greater concern for others
4. Decrease in concern for *impressing* others
5. Decrease in materialism
6. Increase in concern for social/planetary issues
7. Increase in quest for meaning
8. Increase in spirituality
9. Move toward less sectarianism and more universalism in religious observance

Kenneth Ring, *The Omega Project*

"From the time he was small, Ian could see auras. I remember him coming home from high school one afternoon. He'd stopped at the gas station, and what he saw disturbed him so badly he came home and threw up. He told me he saw a young man get out of his car, and the cloud (aura) that covered him was so thick and so dark that he almost couldn't see him. Later we found out that this guy had murdered his aunt and uncle the week before Ian had noticed him at the gas station!

ENERGY FIELDS

I had heard of energy fields around people, which I dismissed as occultic until my wife went into labor with our daughter. I started at one point to put my arms around her in a protective, supportive way, and found, to my surprise, a moving field of energy about a foot out from her body, as vibrant and palpable as though material.

One morning in meditation I experienced a "sphere of energy" resonating out of myself in vibratory waves extending about a foot, arcing over and back into me. I perceived that this energy was my own consciousness "broadcast" out and coming back as my physical reception of what was being sent.

The screen of the world out-there was the screen of my own mind, and was out-there by virtue of this ongoing dynamic.

My meditation teacher once said that our life force extends out about one foot from us and therein lies our universe.

Joseph Chilton Pearce, *Evolution's End*

"Ian was always bringing home people who had nowhere else to go. We never knew who would be sleeping on our sofa. He was always there for the underdog. When he moved to Colorado, I remember I was in Vail with him, watching a documentary on runaway teenagers. I had met some of those kids at Ian's apartment. He told me that he knew some of the kids, and he explained that he often took in the overflow when the shelter became full. He always had a unique philosophical understanding of things.

"After he passed over, one of my metaphysical friends was at the house and looking at his artwork from the time he was little. She was amazed how much of his artwork dealt with the chakras, Hindu and theosophical symbols, and other Eastern mystical religious symbols. We didn't know what these symbols were when he was little.

"In retrospect I see how Ian prepared for his death. From a young age he had said to me, 'Mom, I know I'm not going to live past twenty-five, and I know I'm going to die in a fire.' During the six weeks before he passed over, he contacted friends he hadn't talked to in seven years. At Thanksgiving he told his wife's aunt that he was hurrying to get his house remodeled so that if anything happened to him, his wife, Katie, and their daughter, Kaya, would have a nice place to live. He made peace with my father-in-law, with whom he had always had a tumultuous relationship. The Sunday before he died, I wanted to take pictures of the whole family for a Christmas card. The boys wanted to wait until the next Sunday, but I said, No, let's take them now, and if they don't turn out I'll take them again. Ian changed into a T-shirt he had just bought. It was black, with flames all across the chest and two spirits walking a soul through the flames. Katie told me how excited he was when he found that T-shirt. To me that was his way of saying, Hey, guys, look, this is what's about to happen, and it's going to be okay.

"That weekend my husband and I took our granddaughter, Kaya, to the mountains near Vail. On the second or third night in the mountains I had an amazing dream. In the dream my friend Maryann was dressed in a white pantsuit, and she said, 'There are three things I want you to meditate on today: (1) Death is never an accident. (2) There are no coincidences. (3) Only love is real.' That was the first peaceful night's sleep I had had since we arrived. I told my husband about the dream in the morning, and I meditated on those three things and thought about them all through the day.

"That night the phone call came that there had been an explosion and that we needed to call the emergency room at the University of Denver. I began to have a sense of why I had been prepared. We called and were told that Katie and Ian's house had caught fire, and that she had escaped, but Ian had not. The doctor said that as soon as Katie could accept that Ian was gone, they were going to disconnect the life support. As soon as I heard that, a peace enveloped me and I knew that Ian was fine.

"At the hospital, I felt like I was walking in a cloud of peace. I was fully aware and did not go into shock. No one suggested I take a sedative. One of the ER nurses was very upset because she had a son the same age as Ian. I felt I needed to comfort *her*.

"When we got back to the hotel room, my other son, Scott, was there, and he said, 'Mom, I think our reading was in preparation for this.' He and I had read Dr. Brian Weiss's books on reincarnation.

"I think it was the following night that I felt someone come into bed behind me and give me a big hug. At first, I thought it was Scott who had come in from his room. But I turned around and there was no one there. I could smell a burning-house smell. It wasn't at all unpleasant. It was like smelling gardenias, it smelled so wonderful to me. That's when Ian began his continual contact with us. He let us know that he was there. For example, lights would turn off and on by themselves. One time my husband and I were staying in a hotel and we had two television sets on at once. They were both on the same channel, but the one in the bedroom was showing an old movie that the cable show did not have. These unexplainable occurrences still keep happening."

One of Joerdis's initial contacts with Ian happened during meditation. She said she felt his presence and heard him ask if she wanted to experience what it was like for him when he passed over. She said yes. She says she felt herself whooshed through a greenish tunnel, with no sense of time or space, just a vast outpouring of love. She said he asked her playfully—in just the same frisky way he would have done in life—if she'd like to do it again, and she had the experience a second time.

NO FEAR OF DEATH

[A subject in a research experiment said], "My near-death experience just changed my whole life a flip-flop. . . . I used to worry about life and living it and trying to get ahead, trying to make life easier by working harder to make more money to make life easier. I don't do that no more. . . . I just live from day to day . . . but I'm going to live what I've got left, and I'm going to enjoy it. I know where I'm headed to, so that I don't have to worry about dying any more."

Anonymous report, in *The After Death Experience*

Ian's spiritual contacts take place with all members of the family, including his young daughter. "Kaya sees and hears him a lot," said Joerdis. "On the way to her third birthday party, she told me, 'Mimi, Daddy says he has a surprise for me for my birthday.' My daughter-in-law had just picked up the cake at the bakery. She had ordered a Winnie-the-Pooh cake, but instead they made a Scooby-Doo cake.

The lady in charge of the bakery was apologetic because the order form clearly stated Winnie-the-Pooh, but Katie assured her that it was fine, because Ian and Kaya's favorite cartoon was Scooby Doo. When Kaya saw the cake, she started laughing. 'See, I told you, just like Daddy said!' "

THE LIST FLIPPED OVER COMPLETELY

Before my [cardiac] arrest, I had my priorities mixed up. I learned that life was to be lived one day at a time. I've learned that the candle of life can go out at any time, and I have too much to do before it goes out. . . . Life is now, not yesterday, not tomorrow, but right now. And right now, this minute, I'm in love with life. I know now that we take nothing out of this life except what is in our hearts.

Near-death experiencer, in *The Omega Project*

Spiritual Contact Expands Our Reality

TELEPORTATION OF objects has also been a mode of contact between Ian and his friends and family. One year after Ian died, Joerdis had a ceremony for all the people she knew who wanted to honor their deceased loved ones. "I asked each of my friends who was coming to bring a large rock to put in a fire circle in our yard. My friend Jim forgot his rock, but friends of his, Nancy and Dan, had found a rock on an antique chest of drawers in their storage bin, and they gave this rock to Jim.

"After the ceremony, Dan dropped Jim off at his house, fifteen miles away. As they were walking up Jim's steps, they both tripped over the same rock that Jim had left in the fire circle at my house! Jim called me and asked me to look around the fire to see if his rock was still in the circle. I went out and it wasn't there. Unbelievably, it had teleported back to his house. Dan was there to verify that it was the identical rock. That same night, the clock in our kitchen stopped at the same time Ian had passed over. Our computer turned on by itself, showing a screen saver that my husband had removed three days before, which just happened to be Ian's favorite ski run at Whistler, British Columbia.

"Since then we've had other objects disappear and reappear. I had put our passports in a locked drawer, but when I went to get them, they had disappeared. I called a psychic friend who sometimes helps me find things. She had a strong image of Ian, and he told her that he wanted me to find an old, angry letter he had written to me and his dad when he was young. He wanted me to burn the letter and then he would bring back the passports. He told me in which drawer I would find the letter, which I did. Even though it was an angry letter, I wanted to keep it because it was part of him. He didn't want me to keep it, but with the help of my friend, we finally agreed that if I cut off the bottom, where he says how much he loves us, that would be okay. Three days later the passports reappeared on top of my husband's shaving equipment, which he uses every day. They were covered with beige dust."

Joerdis and her family have been changed greatly by the death and spiritual contact of their son Ian. She says, "Ian's death has taught me to approach life from love instead of fear. It has taught me that absolutely everything we do has God's hand in it. We are all on our own individual spiritual evolutions. Wherever we are is just fine. I can now look at a situation without judgment and just observe. I know that I don't have all the information about what someone else is going through, and I'm not supposed to. I don't listen to the news anymore or read the newspaper. I don't want the negativity in my life right now."

WORKOUTS FOR THE SOUL

By surviving different challenges our soul identity is strengthened. . . . My subjects say the real lessons of life are learned by recognizing and coming to terms with being human. Even as victims, we are beneficiaries because it is how we stand up to failure and duress which really marks our progress in life. Sometimes one of the most important lessons is to learn to just let go of the past.

Michael Newton, *Journey of Souls*

We Keep Evolving and Changing in the Spiritual Plane

PHYSICAL DEATH is our last physical life change, and a rebirth into our next plane of existence in the discarnate phase of our ongoing soul life.

The ideas of life after death and the eternal existence of the soul—which is both eternal and ever-changing—have been explored in many books and teachings on reincarnation. From the hundreds of thousands of people like Joerdis and her family, who have personally experienced contact with deceased loved ones, it seems our missions and life lessons continue to expand or intensify through death, not disappear.

According to Joerdis, her son is still working in the spiritual realm to help others, much as he did as a teenager, taking in the homeless and working with street addicts. She remembers having a reading with the spiritual medium James Van Praagh (author of *Healing Grief*). She says, "After the reading that night, the spirits of Ian and Glenn—my friend Joanie's brother, who died in a car accident a week after Ian passed away—came to me. We learned that Glenn had had a heart attack as he was driving. He let us know that during the accident he had worked very hard to get the car safely off the road. He also reminded his sister about 'the scream.' It turns out that when Joanie learned at the hospital that he was not going to live, she screamed a loud scream. Glenn said that his sister's scream was to him the most perfect expression of love. It went straight into his heart and severed the silver cord, enabling his spirit to be free. Ian's spirit told us that Joanie's scream was what had called him to Glenn's spirit so that he could come to his aid and help him pass over.

"Since Ian's death, I continue to be amazed at how many people tell me that they are still being touched by his spirit through dreams and visitations. It seems as if he is still guiding and helping many souls from the spiritual dimension in almost the same manner as he did when he was alive. For example, he recently reunited a woman with her two adopted daughters by putting the idea in her mind to attend a line dancing class at which her daughter was the instructor, which she did not know. The other daughter, who had never attended the class, synchronistically showed up the same night, and the three women were reunited."

INTUITION AND LIFE CHANGES

I believe we all know, at the deepest level of intuition, that the human world is changing. The shift has been slow and gradual, but the polling data accumulated over the last decade is unmistakable. We are becoming more spiritual. A Gallup poll from November 1999 contains an amazing finding: Between 1994 and 1998, the number of people reporting that spiritual growth was a very important part of their lives increased from 59 to 84 percent, and all indications suggest that this trend is continuing.

How will our world change as the twenty-first century unfolds? I believe that our highest intuition provides the answer. As we become more intuitive, more sensitive to our own best path of accomplishment, human progress will speed up in relative terms and we will move more quickly toward the spiritual ideal at every level.

Here's how it will happen. First, increasingly people will move synchronistically toward their best domain of inspired work and creativity; in other words, toward that area of human life in which synchronicity is leading them to make a contribution.

James Redfield, in *Imagine*

Epilogue

WE HAVE been on quite a journey together in this book. I know *my* life has changed in many ways since I decided to write it and started collecting stories of life changes.

It is my wish that the many voices in this book will go with you as encouraging companions as you move through the gateways of your destiny. Whenever you need to remember who you really are, open the book and see what message comes through on the page. Trust that your life is changing in the most fulfilling way, and that you are part of the greater life changes on this planet. Speak up when the moment demands it. Don't be afraid to make a mistake. Be willing to go away and come back again. Be willing to venture upon a quest, and also be willing to stay at home. Stay with your bewilderment, and let your trust in divine guidance grow. Laugh as much as you can, and bring your attention into the present moment.

Your desire to know and to love will find an opening. When life changes or you wish it would, trust that synchronicity, intuition, logic, and feeling will direct your journey.

> *I don't know whether the union I want will come*
> *through my effort, or my giving up effort,*
> *or from something completely separate*
> *from anything I do or don't do.*
>
> Rumi

Notes

1. EMBRACE THE CYCLES OF CHANGE

9 Joseph Campbell, Power of Myth video series, vol. 1: The Hero's Journey, Mystic Fire, 1991.

13 Laura Dern, in *Talk,* October 2000.

18 Larry Leigon, personal interview.

2. TRUST THAT CHANGE IS PURPOSEFUL

19 Jack Kornfield, *A Path with Heart: A Guide Through the Perils and Promises of Spiritual Life* (New York: Bantam, 1993), p. 167.

20 Joseph, Campbell, Power of Myth video series.

23 Ibid.

29 Marvin J. Cetron and Owen Davies, "Trends Now Changing the World," *Futurist,* March–April 2001, pp. 27–42.

31 Lindsay Gibson, *Who You Were Meant to Be: A Guide to Finding or Recovering Your Life's Purpose* (Far Hills, N.J.: New Horizons Press, 2000), p. 38.

33 William Bridges, *Transitions: Making Sense of Life's Changes* (New York: Addison-Wesley, 1980), p. 35.

3. FIND THE SPIRIT OF ADVENTURE

37 John McQuiston, *Always We Begin Again: The Benedictine Way of Living* (Harrisburg, Pa.: Morehouse, 1995), p. 17.

39 Renay Jackson, *Oaktown Devil* (Oakland, Calif.: LaDay Publishing, 1999).

41 Epictetus, *The Art of Living: The Classic Manual on Virtue, Happiness, and Effectiveness,* edited by Sharon Lebell (San Francisco: HarperSanFrancisco, 1995), p. 18.

50 Joseph Campbell with Bill Moyers, *The Power of Myth* (New York: Doubleday, 1988), p. 214.

4. FOLLOW POSITIVE ENERGY

51   Alain de Botton, *The Consolations of Philosophy* (New York: Pantheon, 2000), p. 211.

55   James Hillman, *The Soul's Code: In Search of Character and Calling* (New York: Random House, 1996), p. 205.

58   Ira Progoff, *Jung, Synchronicity, and Human Destiny* (New York: Julian Press, 1973), p. 109.

68   Thaddeus Golas, *The Lazy Man's Guide to Enlightenment* (Toronto: Bantam, 1980).

5. HOLD THE VISION

69   *The Essential Rumi,* translated by Coleman Barks with John Moyne et al. (San Francisco: HarperSanFrancisco, 1995), p. 146.

70   Shiki, in *Haiku Harvest,* Japanese Haiku Series 4, translated by Peter Beilenson and Harry Behn (Mt. Vernon, N.Y.: Peter Pauper Press, 1962), n.p.

72   Pema Chödrön, *When Things Fall Apart: Heart Advice for Difficult Times* (Boston: Shambhala, 1997), p. 61.

85   Richard Carlson, *Don't Sweat the Small Stuff . . . and It's All Small Stuff* (New York: Hyperion, 1997), p. 20.

87   Wallace D. Wattles, *The Science of Getting Rich,* 1910, downloaded from www.scienceofgettingrich.net (Olympia, Wash.: Certain Way Productions), p. 49.

89   Robert Fritz, *The Path of Least Resistance: Principles for Creating What You Want to Create* (Salem, Mass.: Stillpoint, 1994), pp. 74–75.

89   Unity School of Christianity, press release for first World Day of Prayer, 1994.

90   James Redfield, *The Secret of Shambhala: In Search of the Eleventh Insight* (New York: Warner, 1999).

91   Osho, *The Path of Yoga: Commentaries on the Yoga Sutras of Patanjali* (Pune, India: Rebel Publishing House, 1976), p. 137.

93   Sue Bender, *Plain and Simple: A Woman's Journey to the Amish* (New York: HarperCollins, 1989), p. 142.

94   Tarthang Tulku, *Skillful Means* (Berkeley: Dharma Publishing, 1978), p. 29.

96   David Samuel, *Practical Mysticism: Business Success and Balanced Living Through Ancient and Modern Spiritual Teachings* (Denver: Bakshi, 2000), p. 98.

6. WATCH FOR ANSWERS

99   Anne Lamott, *Bird by Bird* (New York: Doubleday, Anchor, 1994), p. 147.

101   So-In, in *Haiku Harvest,* Japanese Haiku Series 4, translated by Peter Beilenson and Harry Behn (Mt. Vernon, N.Y.: Peter Pauper Press, 1962), n.p.

102 Jacob Needleman, *Time and the Soul* (New York: Doubleday, Currency, 1998), p. 91.

103 Charlene Belitz and Meg Lundstrom, *The Power of Flow: Practical Ways to Transform Your Life with Meaningful Coincidence* (New York: Three Rivers Press, 1998), p. 175.

105 James Hillman, *The Soul's Code: In Search of Character and Calling* (New York: Random House, 1996), pp. 101–103.

107 Bill O'Hanlon, *Do One Thing Different: And Other Uncommonly Sensible Solutions of Life's Persistent Problems* (New York: Morrow, 1999), p. 164.

110 Thich Nhat Hanh, *The Heart of the Buddha's Teaching: Tranforming Suffering into Peace, Joy, and Liberation* (Berkeley: Parallax, 1998), p. 133.

111 Joseph Campbell with Bill Moyers, *The Power of Myth* (New York: Doubleday, 1988), n.p.

7. TRUST THE PROCESS

112 Wallace D. Wattles, *The Science of Getting Rich,* 1910, downloaded from www.scienceofgettingrich.net (Olympia, Wash.: Certain Way Productions), p. 40.

115 Pema Chödrön, *When Things Fall Apart: Heart Advice for Difficult Times* (Boston: Shambhala, 1997), p. 9.

115 Osho, *The Path of Yoga: Commentaries on the Yoga Sutras of Patanjali* (Pune, India: Rebel Publishing House, 1976), p. 6.

116 Ibid., p. 5.

117 Jane Katra and Russell Targ, *The Heart of the Mind: How to Experience God Without Belief* (Novato, Calif.: New World Library, 1999), pp. 112–113.

118 Saigyo, in *The Penguin Book of Japanese Verse,* translated by Geoffrey Bownas and Anthony Thwaite (Harmondsworth, United Kingdom: Penguin, 1967), p. 101.

121 Wayne W. Dyer, *Manifest Your Destiny: The Nine Spiritual Principles for Getting Everything You Want* (New York: HarperCollins, 1997), p. 154.

8. LET YOURSELF EVOLVE

131 Kenneth Verity, *Awareness Beyond Mind* (Shaftesbury, Dorset, Great Britain: Element Books, 1996), p. 86.

138 Eckhart Tolle, *The Power of Now: A Guide to Spiritual Enlightenment* (Novato, Calif.: New World Library, 1999), p. 98.

139 Penney Peirce, *The Present Moment: A Daybook of Clarity and Intuition* (Chicago, Ill.: Contemporary Books, 2000), p. 52.

142 Gail Sheehy, *Understanding Men's Passages* (New York: Ballantine, 1999), p. 104.

145 David Samuel, *Practical Mysticism: Business Success and Balanced Living Through Ancient and Modern Spiritual Teachings* (Denver: Bakshi, 2000), pp. 60–61.

146 David Samuel, personal interview.

148 Hyrum W. Smith, *What Matters Most: The Power of Living Your Values* (New York: Simon & Schuster, 2000), p. 108.

151 Paul H. Ray and Sherry Ruth Anderson, *The Cultural Creatives: How 50 Million People Are Changing the World* (New York: Harmony, 2000), pp. 174–175.

9. DEVELOP MASTERY

155 Sidney Bechet, in Frank Barron, Alfonso Montuori, and Anthea Barron, eds., *Creators on Creating: Awakening and Cultivating the Imaginative Mind* (New York: Putnam, Tarcher, 1997), p. 140.

157 Nancy K. Schlossberg, *Overwhelmed: Coping with Life's Ups and Downs* (Lanham, Md.: Lexington Books, 1989), p. 47.

161 Gail Sheehy, *Understanding Men's Passages* (New York: Ballantine, 1999), p. 107.

165 Natalie Goldberg, *Long Quiet Highway* (New York: Bantam, 1993), p. 182.

168 Eckhart Tolle, *The Power of Now: A Guide to Spiritual Enlightenment* (Novato, Calif.: New World Library, 1999), p. 161.

10. BE OPEN AND PRESENT

169 Charlotte Joko Beck, in *Radiant Mind: Essential Buddhist Teachings and Texts,* edited by Jean Smith (New York: Riverhead Books, 1999), p. 287.

170 Pema Chödrön, *When Things Fall Apart: Heart Advice for Difficult Times* (Boston: Shambhala, 1997), p. 46.

173 Penney Peirce, *The Present Moment: A Daybook of Clarity and Intuition* (Chicago, Ill.: Contemporary Books, 2000), p. 238.

174 J. G. Bennett, in *Creators on Creating,* edited by Frank Barron, Alfonso Montuori, and Anthea Barron (New York: Putnam, Tarcher, 1997), p. 74.

180 Carol Orsborn, *The Art of Resilience: One Hundred Paths to Wisdom and Strength in an Uncertain World* (New York: Three Rivers Press, 1997), p. 153.

182 Nancy Rosanoff, *The Complete Idiot's Guide to Making Money Through Intuition* (New York: Alpha Books, 1999), p. 288.

184 Rick Jarow, *Creating the Work You Love: Courage, Commitment, and Career* (Rochester, Vt.: Destiny Books, 1995), p. 71.

188 James A. Ogilvy, *Living Without a Goal: Finding the Freedom to Live a Creative and Innovative Life* (New York: Doubleday, 1995), p. 107.

190 Charlotte Joko Beck, in *Radiant Mind,* p. 233.

11. GIVE AND RECEIVE SUPPORT

191   Ram Dass, *Journey of Awakening: A Meditator's Guidebook* (New York: Bantam, 1990), p. 201.

192   Nancy Rosanoff, *The Complete Idiot's Guide to Making Money Through Intuition* (New York: Alpha Books, 1999), p. 203.

194   Federico Fellini, in *Creators on Creating,* edited by Frank Barron, Alfonso Montuori, and Anthea Barron (New York: Putnam, Tarcher, 1997), p. 33.

199   Tarthang Tulku, *Skillful Means* (Berkeley: Dharma Publishing, 1978), p. 121.

200   Ransetsu, in *Haiku Harvest,* Japanese Haiku Series 4, translated by Peter Beilenson and Harry Behn (Mt. Vernon, N.Y.: Peter Pauper Press, 1962), p. 12.

12. HANDLE FEAR

201   *The Essential Rumi,* translated by Coleman Barks with John Moyne, et al. (San Francisco: HarperSanFrancisco, 1995), p. 84.

202   Michael Newton, *Journey of Souls* (St. Paul, Minn.: Llewellyn Publications, 1997), p. 69.

208   Barbara Stanny, personal interview.

213   Penney Peirce, *The Present Moment: A Daybook of Clarity and Intuition* (Chicago, Ill.: Contemporary Books, 2000), p. 215.

13. MOVE FORWARD

215   Michael Roach, *The Diamond Cutter: The Buddha on Strategies for Managing Your Business and Your Life* (New York: Doubleday, 2000), p. 217.

216   Susan Jeffers, *Feel the Fear and Do It Anyway* (New York: Fawcett Columbine, 1987), p. 213.

217   Karen McCall, personal interview.

218   R. Reid Wilson, *Don't Panic: Taking Control of Anxiety Attacks* (New York: Harper Perennial, 1996), p. 188.

222   Ibid., p. 185.

227   Wallace D. Wattles, *The Science of Getting Rich,* 1910, downloaded from www.scienceofgettingrich.net (Olympia, Wash.: Certain Way Productions), p. 40.

228   Anne Lamott, *Bird by Bird* (New York: Doubleday, Anchor, 1995), p. 181.

234   Zalman Schachter-Shalomi, in William Elliott, *Tying Rocks to Clouds: Meetings and Conversations with Wise and Spiritual People,* (New York: Doubleday, Image, 1995), p. 180.

237   Brenda Ueland, *If You Want to Write: A Book About Art, Independence, and Spirit* (St. Paul, Minn.: Graywolf Press, 1987), p. 32.

14. BECOME PROSPEROUS

238 Michael Roach, *The Diamond Cutter: The Buddha on Strategies for Managing Your Business and Your Life* (New York: Doubleday, 2000), p. 84.

239 Stephanie Fitch, "Busted," *Forbes,* (October 2000).

240 Wallace D. Wattles, *The Science of Getting Rich,* 1910, downloaded from www.scienceofgettingrich.net (Olympia, Wash.: Certain Way Productions), pp. 11–12, 13.

242 Ibid., p. 13.

247 Susan Bross, personal interview.

250 Joe Dominguez and Vicki Robin, *Your Money or Your Life* (New York: Penguin, 1992), p. 25.

252 Barbara Stanny, personal interview.

253 David Bach, personal interview.

256 Wattles, *Science of Getting Rich,* p. 35.

262 James Allen, *The Path to Prosperity,* in *The Wisdom of James Allen: Five Books in One* (San Diego: Laurel Creek Press, 2001), p. 143.

15. EMBRACE THE TRANSITIONS OF MYSTERY

263 Jiddu Krishnamurti, *Talks with Students* (Boston: Shambhala, 1970), p. 90.

265 Michael Newton, *Journey of Souls* (St. Paul, Minn.: Llewellyn Publications, 1997), p. 220.

267 Ts'ui Hao, in *Love and the Turning Year: One Hundred More Poems from the Chinese,* translated by Kenneth Rexroth (Toronto: McClelland and Stewart, 1970), p. 63.

268 Sue Bender, *Plain and Simple: A Woman's Journey to the Amish* (San Francisco: HarperSanFrancisco, 1989), p. 121.

270 Oscar Wilde, in Angeles Arrien, *The Nine Muses: A Mythological Path to Creativity* (New York: Putnam, Tarcher, 2000), p. 99.

271 James W. Pennebaker, *Opening Up: The Healing Power of Expressing Emotions* (New York: Guilford Press, 1990), p. 24.

274 Debrena Jackson Gandy, *All the Joy You Can Stand: 101 Sacred Power Principles for Making Joy Real in Your Life* (New York: Crown, 2000), p. 138.

275 Larry Dossey, *Healing Words: The Power of Prayer and the Practice of Medicine* (San Francisco: HarperSan Francisco, 1993), pp. 80–81.

279 Kenneth Ring, *The Omega Project: Near-Death Experiences, UFO Encounters, and Mind at Large* (New York: Morrow, 1992), p. 174.

280 Joseph Chilton Pearce, *Evolution's End: Claiming the Potential of Our Intelligence* (San Francisco: HarperSan Francisco, 1992), pp. 87–88.

282 Ian Wilson, *The After Death Experience: The Physics of the Non-Physical* (New York: Morrow, 1987), p. 199.

283 Ring, *Omega Project,* p. 177.

284 Michael Newton, *Journey of Souls* (St. Paul, Minn.: Llewellyn Publications, 1997), p. 230.

285 James Redfield, in Marianne Williamson, *Imagine: What America Could Be in the Twenty-first Century* (Emmaus, Pa.: Rodale, rodalebooks.com, 2000), p. 285.

287 *The Essential Rumi,* translated by Coleman Barks with John Moyne et al. (San Francisco: HarperSanFrancisco, 1995), pp. 206–208.

Index

Quill

Books by Carol Adrienne:

WHEN LIFE CHANGES OR YOU WISH IT WOULD
A Guide to Finding Your Next Step Despite Fear, Obstacles, or Confusion
ISBN 0-06-093456-5 (paperback)

Change can be exhilarating and terrifying—often both at once. Carol Adrienne discusses key aspects of making changes, from trusting that change has a purpose to finding your spirit of adventure; from watching for clues to accepting yourself while building your strengths.

THE PURPOSE OF YOUR LIFE
Finding Your Place In the World Using Synchronicity,
Intuition, and Uncommon Sense
ISBN 0-688-16625-3 (paperback)

Everyone really has a purpose in life; the question is: How do you learn to go with the flow and let your true nature guide you? Here, Carol Adrienne helps readers uncover the unsuspected, untapped power of synchronicity and intuition that will bring success, satisfaction, and serenity.

FIND YOUR PURPOSE, CHANGE YOUR LIFE
Getting to the Heart of Your Life's Mission
ISBN 0-688-17802-2 (paperback)

After years spent traveling the country helping people find and fulfill their life's mission, Carol Adrienne shares key principles for aligning with your soul's purpose and doing what you love.

Want to receive notice of author events and new books by Carol Adrienne?
Sign up for Carol Adrienne's AuthorTracker at www.AuthorTracker.com

Available wherever books are sold, or call 1-800-331-3761 to order.